The Psychology of Tragic Drama

*Ideas and Forms
in English Literature*

Edited by John Lawlor

Professor of English, University of Keele

The English Georgic
John Chalker

Number Symbolism
Christopher Butler

Ideas of Greatness
Eugene M. Waith

Voices of Melancholy
Bridget Gellert Lyons

The Grand Design of God
C. A. Patrides

The Ascendancy of Taste
Joan Pittock

The Psychology of
Tragic Drama

Patrick Roberts

Department of English, University College, London

Routledge & Kegan Paul

London and Boston

First published in 1975
by Routledge & Kegan Paul Ltd
Broadway House, 68–74 Carter Lane,
London EC4V 5EL and
9 Park Street,
Boston, Mass. 02108, USA
Set in Monotype Baskerville
and printed in Great Britain by
The Camelot Press Ltd, Southampton
ISBN 0 7100 8034 4

General Editor's Introduction

This series aims to explore two main aspects of literary tradition in English. First, the role of particular literary forms, with due emphasis on the distinctive sorts of application they receive at English hands; second, the nature and function of influential ideas, varying from large general conceptions evident over long periods to those concepts which are peculiar to a given age.

Each book attempts an account of the form or idea, and treats in detail particular authors and works rather than offering a general survey. The aim throughout is evaluative and critical rather than descriptive and merely historical.

J. L.

to Judith

Contents

Contents

Acknowledgments

My thanks are due to the General Editor of the series, Professor John Lawlor, for his patience and generous encouragement. I should also like to express my thanks to Dr Albert Mason, to whom I owe such understanding as I may possess of psychoanalytical ideas; to Mrs Betty Bradbury, who typed the manuscript and without whose devoted assistance this work would not yet have reached completion; and to my wife, whose clarity of mind and critical acumen have proved invaluable on many occasions.

I am indebted to Faber & Faber Ltd and Harcourt, Brace Jovanovich Inc. for permission to quote extracts from *Collected Plays, Collected Poems 1909–1962, Poetry and Drama*, and *Selected Essays*, by T. S. Eliot; to the Executors of the Eugene O'Neill Estate, Jonathan Cape Ltd and Yale University Press for extracts from *Mourning Becomes Electra* by Eugene O'Neill; to Calder & Boyars Ltd and Grove Press, Inc. for extracts from *The Lesson, The Chairs, Amédée*, and *The Killer*, by Eugene Ionesco; to Calder & Boyars Ltd and Atheneum Publishers for extracts from *The Persecution and Assassination of Marat as performed by the Inmates of the Asylum of Charenton under the Direction of the Marquis de Sade* by Peter Weiss; and to Eyre Methuen Ltd and Harold Pinter for extracts from *A Slight Ache and Other Plays, The Birthday Party and Other Plays, The Caretaker*, and *The Homecoming*.

Introduction

'The Freudian psychology', writes Lionel Trilling in his essay 'Freud and Literature',[1]

> is the only systematic account of the human mind which, in point of subtlety and complexity, of interest and tragic power, deserves to stand beside the chaotic mass of psychological insights which literature has accumulated through the centuries . . . the human nature of the Freudian psychology is exactly the stuff upon which the poet has always exercised his art.

It is upon this kinship of literature and psychoanalysis, despite the difference of method and purpose, that the justification and rationale of a psychoanalytical approach to literary criticism must rest. The kinship was early recognized; the period at which the writings of Freud first became at all generally known in England – 1910 to 1916 – was a time of extraordinary ferment in the arts, and, as the comments of contemporaries show, they played their part in the creation of that ferment, source of what is still the most productive period in modern literature, the period of Joyce and Eliot, Lawrence and Virginia Woolf. 'The arrival of the new psychology', wrote G. M. Young, 'had much of the excitement that attended the arrival of the new learning at the Renaissance.'[2] The theories of Freud could not have had this effect on writers and artists, it is reasonable to assume, had there not been some affinity between them and creative activity; one of the most remarkable statements of this affinity was made by the novelist J. D. Beresford, who wrote in 1920 that 'of all the theories of the nature of man ever put forward by a reputable scientist that of Sigmund Freud is the most attractive and adaptable for purposes of fiction.'[3] A little later Freud himself, at the celebrations of his seventieth birthday in 1926, disclaimed the title given him by one speaker 'the discoverer of the unconscious', remarking, 'The poets and philosophers before me discovered the unconscious. What I discovered was the scientific method by which the unconscious can be studied.'[4] Freud is indeed one of those men, as the widespread use and misuse of his name and his views show, who do more than make certain revolutionary discoveries about man's place in the world; like Copernicus and Darwin, he changed the tenor of human thought, altering permanently our way of looking at ourselves. Such men of genius inevitably have a profound influence, direct or indirect, on literature and the arts.

This kinship of literature and psychoanalysis can be considered under various heads. First, both stress the concrete and particular rather than the abstract and general: the material they share is human nature as it is embodied in the situation of particular individuals, felt and experienced in all its uniqueness. Though psychoanalytical theory must of course find its formulation in abstract and general terms and look for a general application of its tenets, this emphasis on the concrete and experiential is central to its ideas and to its therapeutic work; this is why it is notoriously hard to understand what psychoanalysis is about without some clinical experience. The presence of the living human being, and the acceptance of him in all his subjective complexity, parallels a similar process in literature and makes psychoanalysis anti-mechanistic; it sets its face against the narrow mensurative orthodoxy that even in studies like psychology, whose subject is the human personality, rejects all evidence that is not based on measurement and numbers. Its findings, though supported by scientific evidence, are not claimed to be provable in this sense, but the inference that this means there is no evidence that they are valid or no possibility of their beneficial application is rightly rejected as absurd; there are important areas of experience – areas involving the whole man and his responses – which are not susceptible to the statistical and materially verifiable techniques which the exact or natural scientist must often employ. (The belief that human nature and its problems can be dealt with in this manner is of course very attractive; by such oversimplifications of experience we make it easily classifiable and manipulable, and thus evade the responsibility of dealing with the human being in all his complexity.) It would hardly be disputed that aesthetic and literary experience belongs in this area; literary judgments, concerned as they are with evaluating our experience of literature, are clearly at a further remove from the methods of physical science than is psychoanalysis. But although the activity of making literary judgments is thus of a different order from that of psychoanalytical interpretation, it remains true that these literary judgments – the conviction, say, that *Hamlet* is superior to *Dear Octopus* – have in common with psychoanalytical findings that they are based on evidence but not susceptible of proof. It is interesting to notice in passing that, just as there has been an attempt to discredit psychoanalysis by submitting it to inapplicable criteria drawn from the exact sciences, so it has been the purpose, conscious or otherwise, of some critics in our time to endow literary judgments with the status and respectability of scientific truth by the use of a tone whose blend of the dogmatic and the impersonal suggests that a finality of judgment has been, and ought always to be, arrived at. In each case, the prestige of the exact sciences is to blame – a regrettable result of their cultural dominance.

Second, it is of the nature of literature to impose something of a pattern on its raw material, to provide it by every sort of device of selection and emphasis with a shape and meaning complete in itself and seemingly very different from our experiences of life. Although practical and conventional factors play their part here, especially in the drama, where both the acceptable length of a play and the expectations of the audience at any given period tend to lay down certain patterns in advance, it is clear that to shape and order its material in this way is a fundamental expressive need of literature in any form and at any time. Now, this basic predisposition of literature is often criticized, directly or by implication, as productive of excessive artifice or excessive exaggeration, dependent on the point of view of the critic and the nature of the work under discussion: *Othello* is criticized – by a Rymer or a Shaw – as excessively sensational, sacrificing truth to nature for theatrical effect; Henry James is regarded (by E. M. Forster) as achieving his effect of 'triumphant pattern' at the cost of a sacrifice of 'most of human life', which has to disappear before he can 'do us a novel'; Hardy is judged to have ignored the probable and even the possible in order to impose on his characters a pattern representing his own bleak view of life. A

3

paradoxical emphasis of Shakespearean criticism in our time has been to insist on the plays' artifice, their departure from truth to life, but to see this as a merit; as a critical position it represents a reaction from earlier attitudes, prevalent in the eighteenth and nineteenth centuries, which equated the artificial with what was unreal and therefore unsatisfactory. On this view the tragedies are 'airy edifices' in which we are to look for vivid dramatic and emotional effects and the presentation of situation rather than character by means of the poetry which 'leads one to accept and delight in the improbable things said or done. To treat the play-world as though it were the real world must often result in serious misrepresentation . . . . Shakespeare's characters are not psychologically treated in any modern sense.'[5] We are not to expect to make psychological sense of the apparent contradictions and implausibilities of the action – thus, in *Othello*, Iago's malevolence, and his invisibility, are to be explained in terms of the prevalence and dramatic effectiveness of the current convention of believed slander; there is no point in searching for further significance. Often in traditional literature the pattern may take the form of the apparent intervention by forces outside man in the destiny of the characters: the personalized gods and devils of mythology, and the giants, witches and magic properties of fairy story, find their more sophisticated parallel in the oracle and fate of tragedy, where sometimes the characters enact with apparent rigidity a mysterious destiny laid down for them from the beginning – the *Oedipus* is the most notorious example, but throughout Greek tragedy Fate (in Yeats's words) is the protagonist. Though much less marked and schematic, destiny and the supernatural play their part in Elizabethan tragedy also, from the star-crossed lovers of *Romeo and Juliet* to such manifestations of the non-human world as the Ghost in *Hamlet* or the Witches in *Macbeth*.

Two of the basic principles of psychoanalysis are, first, that there is an important element of pattern and continuity in the mental and emotional life of the individual, and second, that the explanation of this pattern is to be sought in the satisfaction of unconscious needs and goals. (J. A. C. Brown remarks that psychic determinism and the role of the unconscious are postulates that 'have been accepted in one form or other by all the analytic schools and probably by most of those psychologists . . . who concern themselves with the study of personality'.[6]) Actions,

whether trivial or important, are normally found to be symptomatic and therefore meaningful in terms of the whole character-
structure of the individual; we choose our activities, and the
nature of our human relationships, in order to satisfy certain
needs and attain certain goals to which our psychic energy is
directed. The principle applies equally to unimportant events,
which might be regarded as without any significance – acts of
forgetting, slips of the tongue and other mistakes in speech or
writing – and to obviously important events, such as the choice of
a career or a marriage-partner. Moreover, what has the appearance of coincidence may be governed by hidden choice. If we go
on to ask the explanation of the individual's choice, this must be
looked for in the unconscious, which is found to play a crucial
role in mental life. 'Freud pictured [the unconscious]', writes
J. A. C. Brown, 'as a dynamic force rather than as a mere waste-
paper basket of ideas and memories which had fallen below
the threshold of awareness because they were relatively unimportant. . . .'[7] Its contents – primitive instinctual urges that
provide all the psychic energy of the individual – are kept out of
consciousness by the mechanism of repression 'not because they
lack significance but because they may be so significant as to
constitute what is felt as a threat to the ego'.[8] Thus in concealed
and displaced forms they have a decisive effect on action and
character; in Groddeck's phrase, 'we are lived by our unconscious'.[9]
It follows that we are often ignorant of our own real motives and
governed by forces we cannot understand or even identify: the
explanations we offer ourselves and others for our actions are
often rationalizations of buried irrational impulses. A parent may
argue that he permits his children maximum freedom from
control because he genuinely believes that this is the best way for
them to develop their personalities; but he may in fact be motivated by an unconscious wish to indulge the dominant child in
himself, whom he is thus able to gratify indirectly in his own
children. Again, a man may present his lack of ambition and
unwillingness to compete effectively with professional colleagues
as a superiority to the rat-race and an indifference to material
power and gain; the truth may be that he cannot compete because
his original aggressive feelings towards rivals – probably the
original family siblings – were unbearably strong and therefore
had to be repressed altogether rather than find outlet in the

socially acceptable form of competition. In both these cases, the man's acknowledged motives may be genuine enough to a greater or less degree; it is often forgotten that rationalizations, to be effective, need to possess some plausibility. 'It may be a damned ghost that we have seen'; there are many grounds on which we may feel unable to accept Hamlet's reasons for such prolonged inactivity, not least the variety of reasons that he propounds to himself, but this is not to say that they do not attain some degree of plausibility, in his own eyes or ours. A Don Juan may be motivated by fear of impotence, or repressed homosexuality; but he would be unlikely to practise a successful deception on himself if he did not, in fact, succeed in seducing a number of women.

It must also not be forgotten that the repressed unconscious motives, though they play a dominant role, act in a displaced and hidden manner; they may often represent the neurotic element in an otherwise normal and justifiable course of action; like Iago's malevolence, they are invisible (except to the privileged spectator, who has been given the essential missing clues), although under stress they will begin to give unmistakable signs of their presence. Thus, what may be called the incestuous content of Hamlet's feelings for his mother, normally repressed, begins to emerge in various ways during the course of the play – in the intense depression, expressed in the first soliloquy, at her second marriage; in the way in which, when his pent-up feelings finally find a release in the closet scene, he dwells with the relish of disgust – characteristic evidence of strong sexual feeling – on her sexuality; most of all, as Freud pointed out in 1900, in his inability to take vengeance on Claudius, the man who has taken his father's place with his mother – 'the man who shows him in realization the repressed wishes of his own childhood'.[10] The postulate of unconscious motivation thus means that what is manifest and visible on the surface is in constant tension with what is hidden and latent in the depths: 'our unknown selves in life are sometimes more potent than our known',[11] a principle, as J. I. M. Stewart argues, of significant application in Shakespearean studies and therefore in dramatic studies as a whole. We must not, he submits, 'neglect . . . those terrifying, surprising but authentic shadows of our unknown selves which the penetrating rays of the poetic drama cast upon the boards before us'.[12]

Freud's comment on *Hamlet* may serve as illustration of his remark already quoted, that 'the poets and philosophers before me discovered the unconscious'. The discovery by psychoanalytic investigation of the vital dynamic role of the unconscious confirmed a truth intuitively perceived by imaginative writers since before the time of Christ; that this contention is well-founded I shall attempt to show in the studies that follow. Trilling, in 'Freud and Literature', argues that what the Freudian system has provided of especial value for literary criticism has been precisely this:[13]

> the licence and the injunction to read the work . . . with
> a lively sense of its latent and ambiguous meanings as
> if it were, as indeed it is, a being no less alive and
> contradictory than the man who created it.

An enacted awareness of the fruitful tension between the hidden and the seen, action and motive, the doer and the deed, gives to some of the best literature of pre-Freudian times that rich ambivalence and multiplicity of meaning that Freud found to be a basic constituent of the psyche itself.

In my final chapter I attempt to consider the effect, in terms of profit and loss, of the contemporary creative writer's conscious awareness of Freudian theory; the critic who seeks to apply psychoanalytical insights to the study of literature or the writer who seeks to embody them in his work, must clearly be on his guard against appearing simply to provide a key to a door previously locked, or to cast light on a hitherto dark place, assuming unconsciously a posture of superior awareness in relation to his more 'primitive' subject. Freud's own modesty in face of the arts, despite his ambivalence about their value, points the way to a different kind of relationship.[14] For the moment, it is sufficient to recall that awareness of this ambivalence and of the significance of the buried life of course pre-dates Freud's researches and is extensively found in the literature and criticism of Romanticism in the eighteenth and nineteenth centuries, from Blake and Coleridge at the beginning to Dostoevsky, with his remarkable insights into the fascination of the repellent and the love that is closely meshed with hate, at the end. Freud cites an early instance of this understanding of all that is hidden and repressed from Diderot's 'Rameau's Nephew' (1762):[15]

> If the little savage [i.e. the child] were left to himself, if he retained his foolishness and united the irrationality of the child in its cradle with the violent passions of a man of thirty, he would wring his father's neck and sleep with his mother.

Even an orthodox Romantic critic of Shakespeare, A. C. Bradley, whose admirable insights into character seldom herald Freudian theory at all directly, remarks of Macbeth[16] that here

> Shakespeare has concentrated our attention on the obscurer reaches of man's being, on phenomena which make it seem that he is in the power of secret forces lurking below, and independent of his consciousness and will.

However, Freud's systematic exploration of the dynamic role of the unconscious brought a far fuller and more detailed understanding of the matter than had been possible before; he brought confirmation of the method of presentation, and insight into the meaning, of such seemingly implausible and unmotivated acts as that of Oedipus, a man held rightly in high esteem who had destroyed his own parents, an act which though unintentional is not presented by Sophocles as accidental; of Hamlet, who is shown by Shakespeare as dedicating all his great energies to avenging his father but casting away successive opportunities for its effective performance; of Macbeth, a previously honourable and courageous soldier who commits a murder in the highest degree dishonourable and cowardly. Plots that appeared exaggerated or artificial, actions that seemed inconsistent or inexplicable, characters whose 'deeds do not belong to the doer nor the doer to the deed',[17] may now be found to make sense in terms of a deeper consistency and a more complex and penetrating understanding: Freud revolutionized our whole concept of the normal, for it is generally accepted by psychiatrists today that the difference between the normal and the neurotic is one of degree, not of kind.

If the postulate of the unconscious mind and its dominant role can afford us fresh insights into character, so too the other postulate with which the first is closely linked, that of psychic determinism, can serve to reveal as meaningful and coherent the thematic structure of works of literature and the whole relationship of action and character. The pattern we are so often conscious of in the working out of drama or fiction, and which may seem imposed on the characters either by the influence of external fate or by the author's manipulation, may find its warrant and justification in the surprising degree of continuity and consistency in the psychic life of the individual, including the author. Here two further basic concepts of psychoanalysis must be mentioned, the importance of fantasy, and the developmental theory of personality, by which the traditional notion of the child as father to the man is given a new meaning. The role of fantasy is important when considering the question of the structure and pattern of drama, for that which in fable or fiction may seem extravagant, absurd, or artificial if judged by standards of observable truth to life may be found to express substantial psychological truth in the light of psychoanalytical investigations into the nature of mental processes. Once again, Freud was to some degree anticipated by the writers and artists of the Romantic period, with their intense interest in dreams – 'Our dreams', said Gerard de Nerval, 'are a second life' – and their realization of a kinship between the dreaming and the poetic mind, both working pictorially and figuratively, without logic but not without intention or meaning. However, Freud and his successors wrought a transformation in establishing that such characteristics belong not just to the dreaming mind but to the mind itself. I remarked earlier that in Freud's view the unconscious contains as its content those instinctual urges that provide the psychic energy of the individual. These urges are experienced as fantasy, the nature of which is most easily seen in the content of dreams but which is in fact omnipresent, as shown by analysis of free association, and indeed revealed by many symptomatic actions – from the infant's thumb-sucking to the adult's cigarette smoking. Melanie Klein, one of the most important of Freud's successors, writes:[18]

> There is no impulse, no instinctual urge or response which is not experienced as unconscious fantasy. . . . Fantasy represents the particular content of the urges or feelings (for example, wishes, fears, anxieties, triumphs, love or sorrow), dominating the mind at the moment. Unconscious fantasies are . . . an activity of the mind that

occurs on deep unconscious levels and accompanies every impulse. . . .

There are two important consequences of this finding. First, in the words of Lionel Trilling, '. . . of all mental systems, [it] is the one which makes poetry indigenous to the very constitution of the mind';[19] and he adds, 'What is most important of all, Freud, by the whole tendency of his psychology, establishes the *naturalness* of artistic thought.'[20] The kinship is between poetry and the mind itself, not the dreaming mind only. The primitive mind, responsible not only for dreams but for the myth which is at the source of so much tragic drama, is no longer felt to be a crude relic of the past which civilized man has outgrown; it is the underlying mind, whose constant activity is only not seen for what it is because of the disguises it wears. It follows – this is the second consequence – that the non-realistic elements that form the staple of myth and fairy tale and play an important part in tragedy, from wars in heaven to intervention by oracle, fate and supernatural forces, are of the greatest psychological significance, being pictorial representations of universal fantasies: in Freud's own postulation, myths are 'thinly disguised representations of certain fundamental unconscious fantasies common to all mankind'.[21]

Tales, common to many mythologies, of rebellion against the father, of parricide and of incest with the mother, and of the dismembering of and cannibalistic attacks on the children, may be found to derive, like vast shadows thrown on to a screen, from the earliest fantasies of the infant. What may seem impossibly violent, crude and exaggerated, sheer melodrama, by the standards of truth to life, in the accounts of Saturn devouring his children, of Pentheus torn to pieces by his mother, of the cycle of cannibalism, matricide and madness in the history of the house of Atreus, finds a disturbing confirmation in the unconscious fantasies of the inner life. The same principle applies to many features of later stories, where cultural development has brought about greater surface realism, and where consequently such features – Iago's invisible malevolence, Hamlet's delay, Macbeth's sudden plunge into evil – are in danger of being dismissed as mere conventional story-telling devices. J. I. M. Stewart comments on the principle in discussing Elizabethan story-telling conventions:[22]

This invisible . . . villain is indeed an immemorial

stand-by in romance, but conceivably he earned his place there not as something stagy, delightfully and horrifically unreal; he earned his place there because he expresses a psychological truth.

The malevolent hostility of Iago to Othello and Desdemona, and his almost magical though not total success, far from being a conventional stage-device, expresses an acute awareness in Shakespeare of complex forces at work in the human psyche, forces having to do with the effect of fantasies of envy and persecution on the structure and development of our relationship with others. What looks like melodrama (in the current derogatory sense of that word) turns out to be something very different: whatever distinguishes melodrama from tragedy – and the distinction is not easy, for as Eric Bentley remarks, 'Melodrama is the Naturalism of the Dream Life'[23] – it is not the element of the seemingly exaggerated and improbable; this, the staple of melodrama, is frequently present in tragedy also.

At a still later stage of cultural development, in our own time, the discovery by Freud and his successors of the nature and importance of the fantasy life has freed dramatists from the constrictions of surface realism and encouraged them to present what are deliberately conceived of as enacted fantasies – Ionesco's *The Lesson* and much of the work of Pinter seems to be of this kind. In effect, psychoanalysis comes close to literature in giving their proper status to the passions, by directing attention away from the apparently coherent and rational patterns of the outer life to the dynamic tempests of the inner life. Art tends to be relegated to an inferior position when, as in Plato, the passions are regarded as something separable from and properly subject to reason; Freud has shown convincingly that this distinction bears little relation to psychic reality, for passion and fantasy are always at work in human behaviour and relationships.

In much the same way Fate and the supernatural, often referred to, even in the work of major dramatists, as though they were merely arbitrary devices under whose tyranny character and reader alike suffer, may be found to represent a rich variety of psychic forces that can be shown to play decisive parts in the life of the individual. Indeed, if we take as an example the fulfilment of prophecy in *Oedipus* or *Macbeth*, the pattern omnipresent in the story, and carried to its conclusion almost in the terms of a demonstration, may be found to represent that psychic determinism whose origins lie in the compulsive force of early unconscious drives. Freud remarked that Fate, in *Oedipus*, was simply the externalization of such a compulsion: what happens to the hero is presented, rightly, as neither choice nor chance, for (in Freud's words) 'the ignorance of Oedipus is a legitimate representation of the unconsciousness into which, for adults, the whole experience has fallen'.[24] Moreover, the way the pattern in any particular drama is shaped (by selection, emphasis, and the choice of this or that dramatic device) must of necessity be determined by the pattern of the inner life of the author himself. The extent to which a connection can be established between an author's life and his work will vary according to the amount of information available, including direct self-revelation; the scantiness of such information in the life of Shakespeare imposes on us the greatest caution in tracing links between the plays and the events of the life. It will also depend upon our view of the nature of the process, itself not fully understood, by which experience of whatever kind, including fantasy, is transmuted into art; clearly it is a subtle and complex business. What seems certain is that the drama of the psychic life, with its recurrent patterns more deeply significant than the drama of the outer life, must find its reflection and expression in the finished work: our plays could otherwise be written for us by computer. It is this that gives the whole of a writer's work its individual stamp and pattern; it has little to do with any conscious inclination on the writer's part to autobiography, for owing to the pressure of unconscious forces, the pattern may be as observable in the highly 'impersonal' forms of drama and fiction as in those forms that tend to direct and deliberate self-revelation. That Henry James was profoundly and personally implicated in the theme of the betrayal of children by adults, normally a parental couple, is demonstrated by the frequency with which this symbolic situation occurs in his novels and the emotional charge surrounding it. Only the unthinking modern prejudice against biographical criticism could blind the reader to this preoccupation of James and the significance it possesses for his work. The contemporary notion of the autonomy of the work of art is surely a superstition, whose origins appear to be defensive; at bottom, it is an attempt to endow art with a special kind of magic, as compensation for the shrinkage of the field of its social significance and the collapse of other, more potent, sources of magic. It does not really make sense, for as Kenneth Burke has said, 'We can eliminate biography as relevant fact about poetic organization only if we consider the work of art as if it were written neither by people nor for people, involving neither inducements nor resistances.'[25]

To say this is not of course to proclaim a direct link between known external events in a writer's life and his work, or to argue that the work cannot be understood without reference to those events (though common-sense suggests they be considered and taken into account, even if the exact impact is often obscure). We cannot always be as specific as in the case of Henry James; sometimes we can go no further than to point out what seem to be the major emotional preoccupations of a writer at a given period of his career and the effect they seem to have on his work, for better or worse. However, that the source of such preoccupations may be hidden does not militate against our sense of their existence at a level we cannot necessarily identify or describe. Ultimately the richness and variety of characterization in a play and novel must reflect, not merely observation, but an inner richness, perhaps an abnormal power of grasping and realizing what is otherwise unrealized in the self; Freud remarks that writers have a tendency 'to split up their ego by self-observation into many component egos, and in this way to personify the conflicting trends in their own mental life in many heroes'.[26] Thus it is, in the words of J. I. M. Stewart, that 'a man writes plays or novels, I conceive, partly at least because he is beset by unexpressed selves . . . elements many of which will never, except in his writing, find play in consciousness.'[27] It is this, in the great dramatist, whose 'unexpressed selves' may be presumed to be especially potent and active, that gives his characters their 'haunting suggestion of reality and of a larger, latent being unexhausted in the action immediately before us'.[28] Shakespeare is exceptional in the 'inward abundance'[29] on which he draws, but it cannot be doubted that the characteristic patterns of his work, however rich and varied, are determined by an inner activity, hard though it may be to trace a significant connection. Keats's memorable phrase is relevant here: "Shakespeare led a life of allegory: his works are the comments on it.'[30] It is easier to trace this connection in lesser contemporaries of

Shakespeare, such as Marlowe; in modern literature as a whole it is easier to see it, for in an age as self-conscious as ours the writer is more likely to be in contact, however obscurely, with the sources of his inspiration. Moreover, being no longer rooted in tradition, he is expected to spin the web out of himself – even his plots are likely to be to some degree original, and their choice and devising will consequently speak directly of his preoccupations. The principle of course remains unaltered; it may be suspected that the creative writer of any genuine talent will always draw on an unknown self for material[31] – it is a commonplace that writers feel at times their characters to be 'dissociated' from themselves and to be leading an apparently independent existence – 'I don't know what so-and-so is going to do next'. The developmental theory of personality already referred to is of profound importance in psychoanalytical criticism of literature; it both confirms and illuminates the content of literature and in so doing proclaims its continuing relevance and importance, in face of the traditional denigration of literature and art as mere relaxation and play, essentially fictional, of fundamental importance only for the man who has never learned to outgrow childish things. By demonstrating so convincingly that our adult world, in the title phrase of Melanie Klein's pamphlet already cited, does indeed have its roots in infancy, infancy and early childhood being of 'overwhelming importance as the period during which the undifferentiated psyche of the newly-born child is moulded and takes on the directions it will later follow',[32] Freud and his successors gave an altogether new status to the child at play: to outgrow the child would be to outgrow creativity itself. Just as the primitive mind underlies the civilized mind, so the child underlies the adult. It is true that in this field as in so many others Freud's work confirmed the insights of many writers and prophets in the early Romantic period, as for example De Quincey when he writes:[33]

> The bewildering romance . . . the semi-fabulous legend, truth celestial mixed with human falsehoods, these fade even of themselves as life advances . . . but the deep, deep tragedies of infancy, as when the child's hands were unlinked for ever from his mother's neck, or his lips for ever from his mother's kisses, these remain, lurking below all, and these lurk to the last.

Nothing indeed brought down on their heads so much contempt and plain ridicule as the Romantics' insistence on the importance of the child. But the detailed exploration of the content of infantile fantasy carried out by psychoanalysts has not only placed these insights on a firmer and more coherent foundation but has also opened up large new countries of the mind where basic childish patterns can be seen to operate; thus the infant's relationship to the parents, already containing sexual components, can be seen to be the foundation of later situations and relationships in adult life, while the child's basic drives, and the way in which he comes to terms with them, play a vital part in determining the nature of his adult activities, including the creative activities of literature and art. Thus the child's envy of the parents' superior strength and potency, and of their capacity to feed and care for him, may be transmuted into the kind of competitiveness that enables creative potentiality to be fully realized; the child's voyeuristic interest in parental sexuality provides the impetus that lies behind our later wish to enjoy vicarious experience through the medium of literature and art. It may also be worth noting that the Romantic 'discovery' of the child inevitably carried with it a powerful idealization of the childish state, as being close to that of the ideal primitive world unspoiled by civilization; 'wherever children are', said Novalis, 'there is the golden age.'[34] Psychoanalytical teaching, though it has directed attention with great practical effect on to the child's needs, does not suggest that childhood is a period of unalloyed goodness or happiness or argue that the child in man should dominate the adult part. Though less gross, this is as decided a distortion as the popular notion that the hypothesis of infantile sexuality, with its corollary of the importance of sexual drives throughout life, can serve to justify sexual promiscuity or as excuse for lack of restraint in adult sexual behaviour.

One aspect of the historical and developmental approach to human personality is of sufficient importance to this study to warrant reference in more detail. Melanie Klein, whose work has already been referred to in the discussion of fantasy, gained new insights into the process of development in the very earliest years of life by her work with children of two years and upwards, hitherto regarded as too young for analysis. Her researches suggest that the fundamental factor in development is the relationship, a highly ambivalent one, with the mother.[35]

> In the first few months she represents to the child the whole of the external world; therefore both good and bad come in his mind from her, and this leads to a twofold attitude toward the mother even under the best possible conditions. . . . Love and understanding are expressed through the mother's handling of her baby and lead to a certain unconscious oneness that is based on the unconscious of the mother and the child being in close relation to each other.

Recognized later as source of food, on which his life depends, as well as love, the mother in her good aspects is made part of the infant's inner world, by the process of introjection, a process by which 'the outer world, its impact, the situations the infant lives through, and the objects he encounters, is not experienced merely as external influence but is taken into the self and becomes part of his inner life'.[36] At the same time, the frustration and pain attendant upon existence also enter into his feelings about his mother and may be experienced as persecution, for 'the young infant . . . feels unconsciously every discomfort as though it were inflicted on him by hostile forces'.[37] (The Romantic idealization of the child, one-sided as it was bound to be in reaction against the blindness of previous attitudes, was thus the expression of a profound truth: that the human being's most intense happiness may be experienced in that period of early infancy when he is closest to the mother, a state of love and harmony that can yet coexist with opposite states of frustration and hostility.) Moreover, these hostile impulses – envy and destructiveness in conflict with love and gratitude – are immensely strengthened by the infant's discovery of separation and dependence, that his mother is not part of him but that she can, and does, go away, despite the fact that he is dependent upon her, in his smallness and helplessness, for food and so for life itself. This realization leads both to envy of the mother, as all-powerful object and container of all that is desired, and to greed for the food she provides, for the only way of securing enough food to ward off the starvation that threatens may be to try to seize as much as he can in excess of what he needs and even wants. Envy and greed (of which possessiveness is one aspect) are indeed crucial components of the earliest destructive impulses; I shall try to show that they are also emotions of cardinal importance in tragic drama, especially envy. Cruelty of a sadistic order, in Melanie Klein's view, has its origins in the force of early envy, which drives the child in fantasy to make spoiling attacks on the mother's body and breasts, biting and tearing his way in to the envied object. These attacks in their turn reinforce the child's feelings of being persecuted, for through identification and introjection he may experience in himself what he fantasies he has done to the mother. Moreover, he is then feeding from a breast which is not merely damaged by his attacks but actually persecutory (cf. accounts in folk tales of witches with long teeth who eat little children); for by the other basic mechanism of projection, he may seek to put out into the mother bad parts of himself and bad feelings which are unbearable to him if retained. The more successful this process, the more his mother, now a container for his own bad feelings, may become persecutory and threatening to him. Just as by introjection the external world is taken into the self and becomes part of the inner life, so by projection the child puts out unwanted parts of himself into the external world and tries to deal with them there. 'Projection', writes Melanie Klein, '. . . implies that there is a capacity in the child to attribute to other people around him feelings of various kinds, predominantly love and hate.'[38] Attacks on others in later life may thus be due to the projection on to those others of unbearably bad parts of the self; destruction is then all they deserve. Leontes in *The Winter's Tale* is a striking example of such projection, as J. I. M. Stewart points out.[39] This process is of cardinal importance in the whole history of persecution. Projection is also important in relation to greed: his greed may cause the infant to fantasy that he is actually emptying the breast, draining it dry. The desperate hunger, or fear of starvation, which supports the greed and which is therefore an essential part of it, may be got rid of by being projected into the mother, who then, empty herself, becomes even more incapable of feeding him, by a vicious circle whose operation is observable both in infancy and in many tragic situations later in life. In such ways as this the mother in her bad aspects also is made part of the infant's inner world. The processes involved in this first fundamental relationship, as seen by Melanie Klein, are very complex. Thus the urgent need to deny separation and dependence and to be rid of the hostile emotions they give rise to may lead the child to attempt to throw himself back in fantasy inside the mother's body. Not only will such an action almost certainly be felt as aggressive, because of the directing emotions of envy and greed, but any sense of success must retard and inhibit growth to the degree to which it is felt to be successful – just as the mechanism of projection, though it may bring relief to the self burdened with its own bad parts, must lead to an impoverishment of the self through loss. These processes will be referred to in more detail as and when they seem especially relevant to the discussion of particular works; one further situation of early life must be referred to here.

It was part of Melanie Klein's work to show that the intensity of the feelings centring upon the Oedipal complex is due not just to those feelings themselves but to the additional stimulus they provide to envious and destructive feelings already active in the pre-Oedipal relationship with the mother. The boy's rivalry with the father, present in many tragic situations from *Oedipus* to *Julius Caesar* and *Macbeth*, that involve the displacement of an older by a younger man, is of course a familar aspect of the Oedipus complex. One of the consequences of awareness of separation from the mother is the painful realization that the father also has claims on her and is taking her attention away from the child, while even more painful, perhaps, is the perception that the father gives the mother something that she needs and something that he, the child, cannot provide. The mouth that sucks cannot be a substitute for, or made of equal value to, the penis that satisfies her sexual needs and in a metaphorical sense sustains and supports her. In effect, the child's attempt to sexualize the relationship with the mother not only has damaging consequences for his capacity to feed from her and so grow under her care and nurture, but is also doomed to failure – a failure that is the more painful to contemplate the more it is understood. But it is clear that the hostile feelings aroused by this situation can be experienced in children of both sexes; simultaneous identification with and envy of the father, and so of men in general, leading to a degree of denial of femininity, is an important aspect of the Oedipal situation for the girl, and may be felt to be an element in the motivation of many women in tragedy, from Clytemnestra and Medea to the heroines of Ibsen and Strindberg. Moreover, the hostility may take the form, in boy or girl, of jealousy of either of the parents – for there is an attraction towards and identification with the parent of the same sex also – or of envy of the exclusive relationship they enjoy together. Children have long been observed to imagine in fantasy the sexual relationship of the parents to be basically aggressive; one source for this delusion being the envious projections the child puts into the relationship. Finally it must be stressed again that the importance of these early struggles lies in the truth, first given a new significance by Freud, that the child is never outgrown but survives into the man. How the child copes with the realization of separation and dependence, and the kind of early experience, of his parents especially, he takes into his inner life – the extent to which destructive impulses are offset by love and gratitude – these are decisive factors in his growth and development and play a determining part in his whole subsequent relationship with himself and with the external world. It will be the object of later chapters to argue that such material is the staple of tragic drama.

The objections to a psychoanalytical approach to literature are many: here I will try to answer what seem to me to be the more serious of them. First, it is often objected to any general approach, especially to one that seeks to apply to works of literature a comprehensive theory about human activity drawn from non-literary sources – political, social, religious or psychological – that it is necessarily imposing a straitjacket of theory on our direct experience of the literature itself. It must readily be acknowledged that any critic who chances his arm on the application of a general theory is in danger of failing to see the literature for the theory. The proof of the pudding can only be in the eating. This apart, it can at least be claimed for the psychoanalytical approach that by its stress on the concrete and particular – part of the kinship I have argued at the beginning of this chapter – it makes full allowance for the essentially subjective and experiential nature of the reading of literature. Just as the therapeutic benefit of psycho-analysis cannot be acquired by a study of theory and case-book histories, but only through the unique relationship of patient and analyst, so literary taste and judgment can only be acquired by the equally unique relationship of reader and work. In each case the 'working through' is what counts: it is this that gives the patient and the reader confidence that the experience has been worthwhile, and that therefore the ground of that experience is also of value. The value cannot be proved to others: it can only be demonstrated empirically – in the case of literature, where the experience itself, though not its content, is less complex, by an invitation to share the experience and thus test whether it is valid for others too. Moreover, the objections to the application of psychological theory to literature often fail to take into account that no criticism of any value can be neutral or impartial; all criticism that is not mechanical, and therefore valueless, is inevitably moulded and determined by the whole complex of attitudes, ideas and beliefs of the critic, formed as these are primarily by non-literary experience. The belief that criticism of literature can be wholly objective seems only explicable in terms of the prestige of science, and appears motivated largely by feelings of insecurity. Only those who, on grounds that I cannot myself understand, are able to believe in the complete autonomy of literature and art, can wish to ignore those insights into the nature of man provided by thinkers in whatever field; for it is not argued that the psychoanalytical approach to literature is the only valid one – there are clearly many valid approaches – although it is claimed that it is of special interest.

Second, there are what might be called historical objections. It is argued, first, that we are wrong to interpret the plays of, say, Sophocles or Shakespeare in the light of theories of human personality not propounded until our own time. It is further maintained against the psychoanalytical approach to character that 'a fundamental misconception vitiates this and most previous attempts of the kind: that of treating [Hamlet] as if he were a living man or a historical character, instead of a single figure . . . in a dramatic composition. . . .'[40] Dover Wilson adds: 'It is entirely misleading to describe Hamlet's state of mind in terms of modern psychology at all . . . because . . . Hamlet is a character in a play, not in history.'[41] Similarly, Norman Holland argues that, in all critical approaches that 'relate the play . . . to the mind of one or another of the characters . . . the psychoanalytic critic treats the character as a living human being'; whereas in fact 'a literary character is really only a tissue of words'.[42] Basically, the answer to both these objections is the same; they appear to be based on a misunderstanding of what psychoanalysis is about – that it is essentially a general theory of human personality, as valid or invalid three hundred years ago as today and as applicable to your mind and mine, and the author's, as to any single character.

The first point indeed appears to have very little substance. In so far as, say, Shakespeare deals with human nature, as he unmistakably does, 'His chief skill' in Johnson's words '[being] in Human Actions, Passions and Habits . . . so . . . that his Works may be considered as a Map of Life . . .', critics of every age are bound to interpret his plays in the light of what seem to them the most significant insights available into that human nature. The second point seeks to align psychoanalytical criticism with that kind of biographical approach to the plays through character which was fashionable in the nineteenth century and which the historical critics of our own day have tried to discredit, with some success. It is true that we cannot analyse a character in a play for a variety of compelling reasons – the most obvious being that the patient is not present, in a sense never was present, as he is a figment of the author's imagination and cannot recount his associations and dreams or provide further evidence about his actions and motives. But to argue, inferentially, that because Hamlet is a character in a play, not an actual person, we cannot speculate meaningfully about his actions and motives seems a *reductio ad absurdum* of the historical approach. It would in effect rule out all discussion of the characters of the dramatist whose 'chief Skill was in Human Actions, Passions and Habits', and could offer no possible explanation of the impact made by Hamlet and his problems on successive generations of readers and play-goers. I suspect that the objections of Dover Wilson and others, in so far as they are not based on misunderstanding, are really objections to the kind of speculation which, on insufficient evidence, seeks to relate, say, Hamlet's character to precise events either in the life of Shakespeare or the unrecorded life of Hamlet himself, for example in early childhood. Critics who employ a psychoanalytical approach are certainly under an obligation to exercise care in the connections they make, and to draw some distinction between reasonable inference from all the evidence, and speculation – as for example the relationship if any between the composition of Hamlet and the death of Shakespeare's father – which, though it may be of interest, is insufficiently supported by such evidence. There is no doubt that even very distinguished analysts who have commented on literary matters have at times been guilty of the kind of credulousness that they would not have permitted in their own field; the best known example is Freud himself, who, as Ernest Jones relates, increasingly in later life adhered to the view that Shakespeare's plays were written by the Earl of Oxford. In fact, the actual words on the page of *Hamlet* provide such a richness and wealth of evidence about the character and our, and Shakespeare's, relationship to him, that we do not need to pursue the quarry into the more doubtful areas of his creator's biography. We may of course wish to do so; there is nothing wrong in speculation provided it is clearly acknowledged as such – there is something comical about the pious horror of some historical critics as they raise their hands to heaven in protest at such heretical violation of their sacred texts as Ernest Jones's essay *The Hamlet in Shakespeare*. To say that a literary character such as Hamlet is 'really only a tissue of words' is surely to say no more than that a Beethoven violin sonata is 'really only a plucking of strings'. Perhaps the most indisputable impression made by Hamlet is of a character based on powers both of very wide observation and of a penetrating introspection, an 'inward abundance',[43] in J. I. M. Stewart's apt phrase, that so sharply distinguishes Shakespeare from his lesser contemporaries and indeed distinguishes at all times the great writer from others. This is perhaps the crucial point in answer to the biographical objection; I have suggested previously that the way the pattern of the whole work shapes itself must be determined to a great extent by the drama of the author's psychic life with its recurrent emotional patterns. The proposition that Shakespeare's inner life was exceptionally rich means, in effect, that as an artist he was able to achieve through his characters, their speech and actions, an abnormal depth and variety in the expression of emotional situations which to some extent are common to all. Freud's interpretation of Hamlet's delay in terms of the Oedipus complex would have no force or relevance were it not for the claim that this complex is part of the experience of all of us, the audience and Shakespeare himself. The pattern that reveals itself in *Hamlet* is of a whole dramatic situation shaped by internal pressures of which the most important is the hero's Oedipal situation in all its ramifications; Hamlet himself is the focal point of this pattern, but to say this is not to imply the abstraction from the whole play of a single character, who is then treated as a living human being, in effect a case-history, to the neglect of the rest of the work. That Hamlet himself has a dominating and central role in the play has so far as I know never been denied; but, as in actual life, the nature of his relationship with others is profoundly affected by their own personalities and actions as Shakespeare has depicted them, most notably his father's ghost, his mother and his uncle. In this play above all, the central figure expresses the drama's total situation, a situation in which we, the audience, participate in a largely unconscious act of apprehension and memory and which is expressed through a language which in its rhythm and imagery penetrates to unconscious levels of attention, as well as through plot and character (all are of course received simultaneously as one experience). However, he is not rendered in terms of the pseudo-historical portraiture of a single mind; Shakespeare's mode of procedure appears to be that of a psychological symbolism apt at releasing an awareness of the complexity of the forces at work within us and the deepest springs of our actions. Such a symbolism is familiar in myth and of course in dream interpretation, but is masked in Shakespeare by the realism of the treatment.

The third kind of objection to the psychoanalytical approach, in this case not to literature in general but to the special type of drama known as tragedy, is of a different order, and in my view is the most serious of the three. The argument here is, briefly, that the view of man stated or implied by psychoanalytical theory is incompatible with the tragic experience as we know it in the great tragedies of the past. Psychoanalysis presents man as, first, essentially sick and, second, as a determined, driven creature whose belief in his own freedom is a delusion. Tragedy on the other hand sees man, and must see him, as capable of greatness however flawed; such a vision of man appears to depend on a firm belief in human freedom, and is incompatible with a conviction of man's essential illness. It should be noted at the outset that this view does not necessarily carry with it any scepticism as to the findings of psychoanalysis; it may rather tend to suggest that we now see human personality in a way that is incompatible with tragic effects. Psychoanalysis would thus be a symptom, one among many, of a loss of the individual in the mass, of a general decline in the status of individual man, one of whose incidental results has been the death of tragedy. In the past, one must suppose on this view, an actual lack of awareness in writers was a strength, their ignorance making possible achievements which the increased understanding of human nature available today in effect rules out. If there is something perverse about this view, with its suggestion of an element of delusion in tragic experience, it seems less so that the alternative, which is that (whether at or about 1910 as Virginia Woolf playfully suggested or at some other date) human nature actually, not merely figuratively, changed; psychoanalytical man making his appearance on the stage as a bizarre replacement for the traditional actors. However, the question is certainly very complex. Without necessarily subscribing to the view that tragedy is dead, we may well be inclined to think that the view of human character and destiny which prevailed in fifth-century Athens or Renaissance England was more likely to be a fertile seed-bed for tragedy than that prevailing today; in particular – to take the second point of the objection first – that the determinism of psychoanalytical theory does not allow for our sense, in the great tragic characters of the past, of an almost limitless capacity for freedom, however enmeshed in fate.

Some of the wider issues involved in this whole question I shall discuss in a later chapter, when I attempt to consider the profit and loss, for the modern dramatist, of conscious psychological awareness. That psychoanalytical theory reduces the area of human freedom, at any rate as this was once conceived of, seems clear; the postulates of psychic determinism and unconscious motivation, discussed earlier in this chapter, may appear to reduce character to the level of an object entirely governed by forces out of conscious control. In answer to this I should say, first, that the paradox of human freedom on the one hand and fate or necessity on the other seems to be at the root of much traditional tragedy. If it be argued that the paradox is in truth a plain contradiction, it can only be said that, for many readers, such is the impression left powerfully upon their minds, however indefensible in logic. Second, the element of determinism in psychoanalytical theory has perhaps been somewhat exaggerated. Here again the logical or philosophical basis for our convictions may be obscure or hard to defend. But it remains true, in practice, that psychotherapy seeks to restore to the patient something of that capacity for free choice denied him by his neurosis: neurosis is essentially an imprisonment of human creativity. Nothing in fact could be more remote from the aims of psychotherapy than the reduction of the patient to the status of an object; it seeks essentially to enhance his personality. It is a central paradox of psychoanalysis that its theory is deterministic but its practice is liberating, designed to increase the subject's choice. Furthermore, we are still far from a proper understanding of the implications of psychoanalysis, in a society where resistance to its often disconcerting findings expresses itself in prejudice only surpassed by ignorance. This is a customary process with important new discoveries, a point made by Professor Carstairs in his 1962 Reith lectures in another context, that of orthodox medical resistance to psychotherapy:[44]

> I believe that here we have another instance of events (in this case the series of discoveries about the workings of the human mind which were initiated by Sigmund Freud) that outstripped the grasp of the human imagination.

If and when the human imagination comes to terms with psychoanalysis, it may be found that the problem of reconciling psychic determinism with a degree of human freedom of choice is less formidable than it may sometimes now appear.

The related though different objection, that psychoanalysis presents man as pathological, sick and needing cure, to be pitied perhaps but incapable of that heroic extension demanded by tragedy, is more easily answered. If psychoanalytical criticism seems to convert the tragic heroes of the past into pathological specimens, neurotic or even psychotic, either it is bad criticism or else the error is in the eye of the beholder, who has failed to understand the view of man postulated by psychoanalytical thought, and especially the relationship implied in that thought between art and neurosis. The ready assumption that the heroes of psychoanalytical criticism will be pathological is clearly based on the fallacious belief that psychoanalysis only has to do with the abnormal personality; in fact, to quote J. A. C. Brown, 'all psychiatrists . . . are at one in agreeing that neurotic and normal behaviour differ in degree rather than kind'.[45] The point was originally made by Freud in his famous study of Leonardo:[46]

> We no longer believe that health and disease, normal and nervous, are sharply distinguished from each other. . . .
> We know today that neurotic symptoms are substitutive

> formations for certain repressive acts . . . [and] that we
> all produce such substitutive formations. . . .

The motivational origins of this fallacy are perhaps not far to seek. If the neurotic is totally unlike the normal, then we, the presumably normal, can comfortably ignore psychoanalysis and its findings. The notion that the artist is especially neurotic, and that art, of comparable human activities, is especially closely related to neurosis, is even more widespread; it is commonly held by writers and artists themselves, and intellectuals in general. According to this view, the dramatist is indeed bound to create characters in some degree pathological; this is not however a matter for regret, but simply a recognition of reality, and psycho-analytical criticism performs an essential function in making this clear.

The belief is in fact bound up with the other notion I have discussed, that the normal and the neurotic are poles apart; for it is, obviously, only possible to believe that art stands in a peculiarly close relationship to neurosis if there are other human activities to which the whole concept of neurosis is irrelevant. We have already seen that, in the view of Freud and his successors, this belief has no foundation; true or false, it has no place in psychoanalytical theory. In his essay 'Art and Neurosis' Lionel Trilling argues trenchantly for the view that the creative part of the artist is the healthy part, and that in so far as the artist is neurotic, to that extent he will fail as an artist. 'Not only power but also failure and limitation must be accounted for by the theory of neurosis, and not merely failure or limitation in life but even failure or limitation in art.'[47] Some confusion seems to arise from a failure to distinguish between the existence of neurosis in the artist (as in other men), and the creative use to which he puts that neurosis. It may be perfectly true that in Lawrence's famous phrase he may 'shed his sickness in books'; it may even be true that his creativity is the alternative to what would be otherwise a crippling neurosis. But this is no more true of the artist than of other men – surgeons, businessmen, civil servants, teachers, engineers. The difference is simply that the artist, because of the nature of his work, is more likely to reveal directly in that work the personal stresses of his life than members of other professions in theirs.

All human creativity, in whatever sphere, must depend to some extent on the ability to come to terms with and put to creative use neurotic tendencies; anyone who believes that this principle does not apply to the more orthodox professions and avocations has totally misunderstood Freud's discoveries. It may be supposed that the belief in the special relationship of art and neurosis satisfies two psychological needs, apparently inconsistent with each other but in fact easily entertained together. On the one hand it is denigratory of art and the artist, suggesting that normal people are right to regard the artist, if not art, with some reserve and that members of respectable professions – the great majority of the cultivated – can rightly regard themselves as more balanced and healthy, even if less inspired. On the other hand it is subtly flattering to the vanity, both of the artist and, again, of those cultivated people who follow the arts and who practise them vicariously, through identification with creative artists; on this view the artist's sickness is, after all, his strength, and in both features – his illness and his genius – he is satisfactorily set apart from humdrum bourgeois ethics and attitudes. Such feelings about art and the artist have been endemic in society to some extent since the time of the Romantic movement, when the relationship of the artist to society underwent a seemingly lasting change. The ambivalence of the implied attitude is specially interesting, and perhaps explains why the picture of the sick artist is so popular with intellectuals, critics, and journalists – those whose profession employs them on the fringes of the arts, and many of whom are certainly would-be artists or artists *manqués*. In the concept of the artist as mad genius, or inspired child, we can at once mitigate our envy by an assumption of patronizing superiority ('he's obviously sick') and gratify our natural sense of identification with the artist by paying the highest tribute available ('he's obviously inspired'). It is not perhaps difficult to see the appeal of the theory to the artist himself. It is flattering to be regarded as a genius, especially if one is mediocre, and to be officially, as it were, designated sick is a licence for irresponsibility, not simply to society but to oneself and one's work.

One further point may be made here. The belief, welcome or unwelcome, that psychoanalytical criticism reduces tragic figures to a pathological level, is part of a larger conviction that Freudian discoveries have reduced the whole status of man to a kind of primitive aggressive egoism, whose real nature is disguised by a thin crust of 'civilized' behaviour which cracks all too easily. under pressure. The shock to received opinion is comparable to that administered by Darwin: and as with Darwin, time is needed before the necessary adjustments to the new view of man can be made and the picture seen for what it is, undistorted by the first powerful emotional reaction. Only familiarity can show that psychoanalytical theory is perfectly compatible with human dignity and therefore with tragedy. The blow struck at human vanity and self-esteem is a salutary, if painful one; and it is only prejudice and fear that can make a dark and hate-filled picture occupy the whole screen. Psychoanalysis shows man's capacity for love struggling constantly against his envious and destructive impulses; tragedy is born out of nothing so much as the waste of one by the other. It may seem strange, in a world that has seen in the last fifty years so much violence and terror set loose in so-called civilized societies, from the casualties on the Somme to the mass-victims of Auschwitz and Hiroshima, that the postulate of man's universal sickness and the power of his involuntary aggression and hatred should still today arouse the sort of resistance associated with unassimilated shock. As I shall try to argue in another context, only psychoanalysis offers an adequate explanation of the kind of splitting or dissociation involved in this attitude, perhaps the most disconcerting of all human characteristics.

Notes

1 L. Trilling, 'Freud and Literature' in *The Liberal Imagination* (London, 1951), p. 34. First published in *Horizon* (September 1947), vol. 16, p. 182.
2 Quoted by J. Isaacs, *An Assessment of Twentieth Century Literature* (London, 1951), p. 30.
3 Ibid.
4 Trilling, op. cit., p. 34.
5 E. E. Stoll, 'Source and Motive in *Macbeth* and *Othello*', *Review of English Studies*, xix (1943), p. 25.
6 J. A. C. Brown, *Freud and the Post-Freudians* (London, 1961), pp. 11–12.
7 Ibid., p. 6.
8 Ibid., pp. 6–7.
9 G. Groddeck, *Das Buch vom Es* (Vienna, 1923).

10 S. Freud, *The Interpretation of Dreams* (Leipzig, standard edition, London, 1953–), iv, p. 265.

11 W. W. Lawrence, 'Shakespeare's Problem Plays', *The Times Literary Supplement*, 16 July 1931, p. 554.

12 J. I. M. Stewart, *Character and Motive in Shakespeare* (London, 1949), p. 95. He argues with great cogency that the credibility gap seen by Stoll (op. cit., p. 4) as a matter of 'theatrical fancy' is really one of psychological fact.

13 Trilling, op. cit., p. 39.

14 'Such studies [psychoanalytical criticism] are not meant to explain the genius of a poet but to show the motifs that have stirred it up, and the topics imposed on it by fate.' Freud, *Preface to Marie Bonaparte, The Life and works of Poe* (standard edition, London, 1953–), p. xxii.

15 Freud, *Introductory Lectures on Psychoanalysis* (London, 1922), trans. Joan Rivière, ch. 22, pp. 283–4.

16 A. C. Bradley, *Shakespearean Tragedy* (London, 1951), pp. 337–8.

17 Stewart, op. cit., p. 94.

18 M. Klein, *Our Adult World and its Roots in Infancy* (London, 1960), p. 6. The first sentence is quoted by her from Susan Isaacs.

19 Trilling, op. cit., p. 52.

20 Ibid., p. 161. First published as 'Art and Neurosis' in *Partisan Review*, Winter, 1945.

21 Quoted in Brown, op. cit., p. 11.

22 Stewart, op. cit., p. 101.

23 E. Bentley, *The Life of the Drama* (London, 1965), p. 205.

24 S. Freud, *An Outline of Psychoanalysis* (London, 1949), p. 60.

25 Kenneth Burke, 'Freud – and the Analysis of Poetry', *American Journal of Sociology*, xlv(1939), p. 412, quoted by H. Ruitenbeek (ed.), *Psychoanalysis and Literature*, (New York, 1964), p. 133.

26 Freud, *Collected Papers* (London, 1924), iv, p. 180.

27 Stewart, op. cit., pp. 121–2.

28 Ibid.

29 Ibid.

30 Keats, *Letters*, ed. M. B. Forman (London, 1947), p. 35.

31 'The writer who possesses the creative gift owns something of which he is not always master.' Charlotte Brontë, preface to the 1850 edition of *Wuthering Heights* (1847), quoted by M. Allott, *Novelists on the Novel* (London, 1965), p. 154.

32 Brown, op. cit., p. 11.

33 Quoted D. W. Harding, 'From Blake to Byron', *The Character of Literature from Blake to Byron*, Pelican Guide to English Literature, V (London, 1957), p. 39.

34 Quoted by Irving Babbitt, *Rousseau and Romanticism* (Boston, 1919), p. 74.

35 Klein, op. cit., pp. 4–5.

36 Ibid.

37 Ibid.

38 Ibid.

39 Stewart, op. cit., pp. 30–7.

40 J. Dover Wilson (ed.), *Hamlet* (Cambridge, 1934) intro. pp. xliv–xlv.

41 J. Dover Wilson, *What Happens in Hamlet* (Cambridge, 1960), p. 218.

42 Norman K. Holland, 'Shakespearean Tragedy and the Three Ways of Psychoanalytic Criticism', *Hudson Review*, xv, 2 (1962), p. 219. Quoted by Ruitenbeek, op. cit., pp. 209–10. Kenneth Muir, 'Some Freudian Interpretations of Shakespeare', *Proceedings of the Leeds Philosophical Society*, vii, 1 (1952), pp. 43–52, discusses this and other historical objections in more detail.

43 Stewart, op. cit., p. 122.

44 G. M. Carstairs, *This Island Now* (London, 1963), p. 87.

45 Brown, op. cit., p. 9.

46 S. Freud, *Leonardo da Vinci and a Memory of his Childhood*, first published in the standard edition, vol. xi, ed. J. Strachey (1957) *Leonardo* (Penguin 1963), p. 178.

47 Trilling, 'Art and Neurosis' in *The Liberal Imagination*, pp. 171–2.

Part I

The Exploration of the Primitive

One

Euripides: The Dionysiac Experience

That tragic drama draws upon primitive and infantile material for its basic themes is the chief argument of this book; I hope to show that a great part of its power over us resides in the dramatist's capacity to perceive in the major conflicts of adult life the struggles of the human psyche in its earliest and most formative period, the child still active in the man. In literature, this capacity to see and understand is accompanied by the writer's specific gift of embodying these insights in a satisfyingly expressive representation, realistic or symbolic. One play stands out from other examples of tragic drama of all periods for the directness and force of its presentation of primitive material, *The Bacchae* of Euripides.

This play has long been recognized as being in certain ways *sui generis*. Its exceptional nature is attributed by some commentators to the fact that it was written, near the end of a long working life, in voluntary exile in Macedon. The subject of the play, the cult of Dionysus, is so far as we know new for him, and there are correspondingly novel features in the treatment, notably the central and dominant role of the god Dionysus himself. It is of course not uncommon to find in Euripides something like a rationalization of the official Olympian religion. By a brilliant insight, he is capable when his theme requires it of seeing the Greek gods as a modern reader is bound at one level to see them, as symbolic personalized representations of the great impersonal forces, instinctual urges for the most part, that govern human affairs. The clearest example is perhaps the goddess Aphrodite of the *Hippolytus*, who represents the sexual instinct and whose 'will' is the mainspring of the plot. In the prologue she announces what is to happen, the punishment of Hippolytus with the incidental destruction of Phaedra this involves; and it does happen. In this or similar ways the gods of Euripides often originate and manipulate the whole action of the plays; by a paradoxical device, their obviously impersonal significance is made compatible with a much more direct and personal interest in the events they control than the remote and largely incomprehensible powers of Aeschylus and Sophocles, who do not normally appear as persons on the stage at all.[1] The Euripidean gods can thus be said to play a central role in the theme. In the plays, however, they are normally kept in the wings – Aphrodite only appears in the prologue to the *Hippolytus,* so that her dominant role in the plot does not interfere significantly with the dramatic life of the human characters or limit our sympathetic identification with them, and this is the normal pattern. In *The Bacchae* matters are very different: here the god plays a central role, as actor not merely as pseudo-personalized fate, with the important consequence that the characters are diminished in stature and significance.

The story of the play is on the surface simple. A prophet without honour in his own country, Dionysus selects Thebes as the first city in Greece where he will make converts and, Pied-Piper-like, lead the women of the city out into the mountains as celebrants of his mysteries. Pentheus, King of Thebes, sets himself in violent opposition to the god, threatening to imprison the celebrants, including his own mother Agave, and to hang or stone to death the 'Oriental conjurer' who has seduced the women from their allegiance and who is Dionysus himself in disguise. Submitting in apparent passivity to the raging Pentheus, the god manifests his power first by destroying the stables in which he has been imprisoned and next by bringing Pentheus totally under his own control, not by violence but by a kind of hypnotic force. Under the pretext of helping him to spy out the women's presumed sexual orgies under Dionysiac influence, he leads Pentheus out to the mountains, now dressed symbolically as votary and victim in women's robes with long flowing hair and thyrsus (a kind of ritual wand) in his hand. Here Pentheus is caught by the Maenads (as the female devotees of the god are called) attempting to spy on them from the top of a pine tree; and at the prompting of their master he is torn in pieces by them, his mother Agave at their head. Agave returns in triumph cradling the head of what in her madness she believes to be a lion-cub; the play ends with the god, in his own person, restoring her sanity in

34

order to show her the terrible nature of the punishment he has inflicted on her and indeed his whole family. The two principal human characters in the play are Agave and Pentheus, and the vital relationship thus the fundamental one of mother and son. However, they are less emotionally compelling than we have a right to expect from the protagonists in tragic drama. Pentheus, the son, is a somewhat unattractive figure, mildly pathological in his early, ineffectual violence – Euripides is a master of the depiction of such states of mind – and hardly more than pathetic in the sinister scene of his possession by the god and his terrible end. Few if any readers are likely to feel that he possesses the weight and emotional complexity of the tragic hero. Agave's situation is tragic in the extreme, but her part is a very small one. More important, the divinely-induced mania under whose influence she destroys her son makes her role exclusively that of victim, in a very particular sense. Other heroines of Euripides may be portrayed as fatally driven by some overmastering impulse – Medea, Phaedra, Electra – but this reflects his astonishingly modern view of human motivation and does not necessarily diminish their complexity or their capacity to extract a full range of emotional response in the reader. Agave, on the other hand, is actually mad, as her final return to sanity makes clear; and we contemplate her, as we see her cradling her son's head, with a sort of horrified detachment. Our sympathetic identification is at another, and perhaps deeper level than with the experiences of the adult characters. It is more an identification with the total situation of the play as it is suddenly revealed to us at Agave's entrance, a situation of irretrievable ruin for both mother and son, engineered by the god who looks impassively down at the scene. Euripides is here, in my view, attempting a direct presentation of those primitive realities that, existing behind and within the more readily recognizable passions of human life, are the sources of the deepest tragedy. Hence the cold passion of the play, the detachment of feeling that does not preclude a strong and painful emotional response in the spectator. Its emotional impact comes less from sympathetic identification with the characters than from the acting out on the stage of certain primitive impulses of a destructive order, and thus the extraordinary insight it provides into the nature of those impulses. It is this interest in the direct presentation of primitive impulses that justifies the god's occupation of a central role; for basically Dionysus is simply the whole primitive constituent of the psyche, whether for good or evil, and it is this, with a tragic weighting towards evil, which is the subject of the play.

It was only in later times, in Alexandria and Rome, that Dionysus was reduced to the role of wine-god, 'plumpy Bacchus with pink eyne'. Professor E. R. Dodds writes:[2]

> To the Greeks of the classical age Dionysus was not solely, or even mainly, the god of wine; the god's cult titles confirm it: he is the Power in the tree; the blossom-bringer; the fruit-bringer; the abundance of life. His domain is not only the liquid fire in the grape, but the sap thrusting in a young tree, the blood pounding in the veins of a young animal, all the mysterious and uncontrollable tides that ebb and flow in the life of nature.

This fundamental aspect of the God has survived into our own time, in our use of the word 'Dionysiac'. He both symbolizes the *wish* to be free from restraint (in modern terms to achieve self-realization) that was the impulse behind the Romantic movement, and the *recognition* implicit in that movement of the vast and mysterious power of instinct and intuition, of the irrational in man, that Freud and his successors have confirmed and established on a new empirical basis.

The second crucial feature of Dionysus is that, unlike most of the Olympians, he is the god of a mystery religion, in Euripides' time acclimatized and tamed in organized rites of mountain dancing, but still retaining largely formalized traces of their original ecstatic and orgiastic nature.[3] Such a god is not to be revered from a distance as wholly other than man, but directly apprehended and indeed tasted and swallowed, by these magical means actually entering into man and offering him the supreme gift of identification with god. Physical possession by oral means of the longed-for divine object is thus central to the cult; the most primitive form of this sacrament is the tearing and eating raw of a god, originally perhaps in the shape of man, but as recounted in *The Bacchae* and elsewhere in the shape of the animal substitute. In civilized societies the act of eating and drinking the god, and so acquiring his substance, becomes symbolic merely – in the words of Teiresias in *The Bacchae* Dionysus, himself a god, 'is poured out in offering to the gods'.[4] By eating and drinking the god, or something like him, you become god-like yourself. The Maenads, who tear to pieces bulls and goats, and are described as eating the latter as well, are possessed of miraculous powers of various kinds – extraordinary strength, invulnerability to attack by armed men, the power to make water, wine and milk gush from the earth at a touch of the magic wand. It is interesting to note that, in the mythical account of Dionysus' birth, the child is described as born with horns, a feature that clearly asserts his animality and prefigures his transformation as sacrificial victim into an animal; he is also described as crowned with snakes – both snake handling and snake tearing are recorded in accounts of the cult. Even more striking is the legend that the Titans, on the orders of his jealous stepmother Hera, tore the child in pieces, this detail seeming to confirm that the god himself is the first, and real, object of the act of tearing and eating; in other words, that this terrible sacrament is central to the cult. In *The Bacchae* there is, of course, a human victim – Pentheus, the 'climbing beast' as Agave calls him,[5] who though dressed as a woman by Dionysus for the ritual sacrifice mistakes the god for a bull at the crucial moment when he is possessed by him and identified with him – 'I see you leading me forward – you are like a bull, you have horns growing on your head.'[6] Thus he foreshadows his coming role as animal sacrifice.

If physical possession by oral means is basic to the cult of Dionysus, another, hardly less significant feature is its ambivalence. The best illustration of this is the whole description of the behaviour of the Maenads in Euripides' play, as recounted by herdsman and messengers. In sharp contrast to the manic violence and horror that culminate in the destruction of Pentheus there is a picture of beauty, tranquillity and harmony – the herdsman reports that 'they were a sight to marvel at for modesty and comeliness'[7] emphasizing that there was no drunkenness or promiscuity among them. Dionysus is indeed both liberator and source of madness; subsuming in himself the contraries of love and hatred, peace and violence, so that possession by him may be either blessing or curse, or both, a point made by the god himself when he says of Pentheus, 'And he shall know the son of Zeus, Dionysus; who, though most gentle to mankind, can prove a god of terror irresistible'.[8] There is significant support for this violent emotional ambivalence in the psychological state of those who practise in its literal form the rite of tearing and swallowing raw an animal or human body. Professor Dodds writes,[9]

> those who practise such a rite in our time, seem to experience in it a mixture of supreme exaltation and supreme repulsion: it is at once holy and horrible, fulfilment and uncleanness, a sacrament and a pollution.

It is surely part of Euripides' power that he makes us feel something of this conflict through the metaphor of the play itself; the experience can be felt by reader or audience as in this sense Dionysiac – a celebration of the god in which we participate in combined sympathy and repulsion. This ambivalence is an essential part of our experience of the play. The view of the play that makes it a 'solemn warning against a flight from Reason', with the god 'no other than a fiend . . . not [a power] whom decent people will be prepared to worship',[10] is based on a whole series of misunderstandings – of the nature of tragedy, of the make-up of the human psyche, and more specifically of Euripides' approach to his material, essentially, here, psychological and descriptive rather than moral. In the first place, the destructive aspect of the god, though not the only one we are shown, is bound to be more prominent, given the theme and context. Second, the notion of Dionysus as a 'devil' is surely based on a failure to understand the universal force and potency, for good and evil, of the primitive elements in the human psyche. If men were for the most part reasonable ('decent people'), with the passions as a separate and inferior element ideally kept under firm control by the reason, this Dionysus would indeed be a devil. Over 2,000 years before Freud, Euripides implicitly rejects this unrealistic theory of human personality and behaviour, in which the higher rational part confronts a lower passionate part, 'the beast in man which is worse than bestial'.[11] Whatever the appearance of things, the passions, to use the traditional terminology, are always at work for good or evil in human behaviour; to attempt to relegate them to a lower sphere is to deny this essential truth. To claim that 'the horned god is no other than a fiend'[12] is also to import into the play Christian ideas that for all Euripides' human sympathies are fundamentally alien to him, based as they are on an ultimate identification of power and goodness. Euripides would have agreed with Freud in being unable to make such an identification (the two men share a certain stoical realism of outlook, accompanied by deep human understanding; the realism can be seen in Euripides' detached view of the gods as instinctual forces in human life). Thus, to him as again to many today, Dionysus, to adapt a famous phrase of D. H. Lawrence, is 'the something not ourselves that makes for life' – and for death also. In the primitive unconscious is contained the worst and best in human nature, the most creative and the most destructive potential. The impersonal force of the god is brilliantly rendered in his penultimate saying in the play: in answer to his victims' pleas for mercy and complaints that their punishment is too heavy, he merely replies 'Zeus my father ordained this from the beginning.'[13]

It is necessary now to consider the source of this deep ambivalence of feeling and experience in that primitive constituent of the psyche that Dionysus, in my view, essentially *is*. Nowhere is the conflict more strikingly illustrated in the play than in that passage of the herdsman's speech where he describes the Maenads first suckling the young of animals and then, when threatened by intruders, tearing them in pieces. Here, in these two contrasted actions, we have spelt out to us the basic polarity of the earliest primitive experiences of the infant as Melanie Klein has described them, of loving nurture and savage destructiveness; nurture received from a nourishing breast and destructiveness directed in fantasy against an envied breast, which, spoiled and damaged by the attacks, may then through identification and introjection take on a damaging, spoiling and persecutory aspect for the child.[14] Before exploring further the conflicts of the infant's inner world as revealed by psychoanalysis, and the force and relevance of Euripides' symbolic presentation of that world, it is worth mentioning certain incidents and features of the legendary history of Dionysus as recounted by classical authors, that may lend support to the view that he contains within himself the persecutory aspect of the infant's earliest struggles with the external and internal world. The penalty for resistance to Dionysus, a resistance that invariably seems to take the form of attempts at persecution of the god and his adherents, is found to include a persecutory and destructive attack on the children of the would-be persecutor, carried out not directly by the god but, as with

Agave in *The Bacchae*, by the erring parent who has been temporarily occupied and driven mad by the god as the first part of his punishment. Thus Lycurgus, King of Thrace, who had opposed and persecuted the Bacchants, in his madness kills his son Dryas with an axe in the belief that he is cutting down a vine; it is interesting to note that his fate is that of Pentheus as well as Agave – both destroyer and destroyed – as he not only kills his son but is subsequently torn in pieces by wild horses in an expiation for the crime which exactly parallels the Dionysiac ritual tearing of the sacrificial victim. (It could be said that by playing both roles he demonstrated how easily they are interchangeable in fantasy.) Again, in Argos, the Argive women are punished for rejecting the god much as the Thebans in *The Bacchae*: in particular, says Apollodorus, they destroyed their own children. Similar events occur in Boeotia, where three women, the daughters of Minyas, alone hold out against the god; they too are punished by madness in the course of which they tear to pieces the son of one of them as a sacrifice. The consistency of this pattern is further illustrated by the fragmentary accounts of the god's nurture and upbringing; they contain more than one such episode of savage infanticide under the spell either of madness or some less gross deception. The persecutory aspect of Dionysus is thus extended beyond the cult practices to the legendary context; the attacks on children that are central to the persecution suggesting in psychoanalytical terms the fantasied attacks of the infant on the mother, who because of those attacks is then experienced internally as a retaliatory and persecutory figure. It may also be thought significant that the child Dionysus only comes into being at the cost of the violent destruction of his mother; tricked by Hera's jealousy into demanding that her divine lover appear before her not in disguise but as himself, Semele is destroyed by Zeus' thunderbolt and the unborn child has to be rescued from the mother's body by the divine father. She too, like Agave and Pentheus, is thus an agent of her own destruction, though unlike them she has not been made subject at the time to the god's influence except in the peculiar sense necessary to the story. The self-inflicted nature of the punishment of those who defy Dionysus – in Agave's words, 'I have spilt the blood that is my own, torn the flesh that grew in my own womb'[15] – is very striking. Explicable in terms of the legend by the closeness of the bond between parent and child, it can also be taken as symbolizing the essentially internal nature of the struggle, the infant fantasying both that he is attacking the mother and that he is subsequently the victim of attacks by her.

It is also of interest, when considering the relationship of Dionysus to the inner physical world, to find that there are strong hints of bisexuality in the legend. He is described as being reared at first in the women's quarters disguised as a girl, and the tradition of effeminacy to which this education is said to have contributed is tellingly preserved in *The Bacchae*. Pentheus, while still free from enchantment and determined to punish the intruder, is clearly presented as attracted to Dionysus – he congratulates him on his handsome figure and seductive curls, the irony of his praise being compatible both with homosexual attraction and a significant sadism. When the god asks him what punishment he proposes to inflict on him he replies, 'First I'll cut off your scented silky hair.'[16] The god's femininity is implicit in his mastery over women, whom he both attracts as a man – hence the charge against him of being a seducer – and understands, by identi-fication, as a woman. It is noteworthy that those he enchants, with the single and peculiar exception of Pentheus, are, like his devotees, all women; the other men, even if for politic or other reasons they support him, are emotionally unaffected. That the tradition of bisexuality survived into the Renaissance is shown by Michelangelo's famous statue now in the Bargello in Florence; Ludwig Goldscheider writes that Vasari was the first to remark the hermaphroditic element in the figure – 'A marvellous blending of both sexes – combining the slenderness of a youth with the round fullness of a woman.'[17] To be animal and female as well as man of course underlines Dionysus' universality; but in the context of the psychic experiences of infancy his bisexuality may be thought to represent the infant's fantasy of a joint parental figure. Such a figure, sometimes monstrous in form, a two-backed beast, from the hostile projections the child puts into it, seems to arise from distorted notions of parental sexual intercourse.

Melanie Klein has shown how many of the infant's earliest struggles spring from his need to deny a growing awareness that he is separate from his mother and consequently wholly dependent on her for his existence; it is in this area of experience that we can look for the exploration of that violent ambivalence of feeling that, in her view, is found to characterize the first of the ages of man. The realization that his mother can go away from him and that the breast can be withdrawn may promote both a growing fear of abandonment by her, with the risk of starvation, and envious attacks upon her as reaction to his sense of his own smallness and helplessness contrasted with her power and freedom. He may therefore wish to throw himself back into the mother's body as a way of avoiding these frightening consequences, the denial of separation and loss taking the form of a fantasy that he can be reunited to her physically, so that she cannot go away from him. However, this fantasy is likely to produce results similar to those he is seeking so desperately to avoid: the wish to get into the mother's body may be based on an urgent need, first to ensure survival and second to thwart the greedy and envious attacks that may accompany an awareness of separation. However, the situation is that of a vicious circle, for the fantasied penetration is itself conditioned and controlled by the dominant emotions of envy and greed. The same envy and greed that he wishes to avoid by getting back inside her also make him a dangerous thing to put into her – in effect, a monster who can only damage her. Thus both kinds of attack lead to a persecutory situation for the child (the persecution is already fed from another source, that of claustrophobic terror). Whether it is the separable feelings of greed and envy that are projected into the mother, or the greedy and envious child himself who in fantasy projects the whole of himself, the results are similar; though objectively her behaviour is unaltered, subjectively, in the child's fantasy, she becomes both damaged and damaging, either way incapable of feeding and caring for the child. The wish for reunion is experienced as an aggressive, not just a self-preservatory, still less reparatory act; the persecution arises either through envy, in which an envied and attacked breast or body is experienced as a damaged and thus in its turn damaging and spoiling object, or through greed, under whose influence the child may fantasy that he is feeding on the breast instead of drawing nourishment from it, thus devouring it and destroying it as a nourishing source. Yet continued contact with the source of life is essential if the child is to survive, let alone grow and mature; moreover, fantasies of identification with the mother are rooted in reality, for there was a time when mother and child actually were one person.

Loving motives may in this way play their part in the fantasy, based on buried memories of such a state of harmony and nostalgia for its return. Dionysus worship can thus be related, in one of its many aspects, to the infant's deep-seated wish to restore this blissful situation of union with the mother in conditions of separation and dependence – the necessary conditions of life after birth – that make it impossible; in conditions, that is to say, where in psychic terms the attempt cannot be felt to succeed without damaging and destructive consequences. Both aspects of the infantile struggle are vividly realized by Euripides in *The Bacchae*: the ecstasy of union ('blest is the happy man who . . . joins soul with soul in mystic unity')[18] and its terrible consequences. The union is characterized, significantly, not only by a feeling of harmony with all Nature and well-being, but by a sense of omnipotence (figured here in the miracles worked by the Maenads); the madness that follows, by a total powerlessness – both Agave and Pentheus are wholly possessed by the god, their powers of resistance and understanding utterly undermined. The process is felt as essentially retributive, and bears an uncanny resemblance to the retribution the child may experience as a result of his omnipotent fantasies of entering and possessing the mother's body. The consequences in *The Bacchae*, it is true, follow only on violent and perhaps unjustifiable and unnecessary resistance to the god; but the situation as presented by Euripides in the play is a complex one, and it is to this, and to the characterization of Pentheus in particular, that I now turn.

Some critics have read the play's meaning as a warning, not against a flight from reason but against repression. Certainly it underlines, in Pentheus, the dangers of repression; but the emphasis is surely that of tragedy, not of a cautionary tale, the meaning expanding beyond such cautionary warnings to one of the fundamental sources of pain and conflict in human life. Pentheus, the voice of repressive authority and order, is himself a victim of Dionysus both literally and metaphorically, as surely driven by compulsive primitive urges as any raving Maenad. Euripides' handling of this situation shows his profound insight into a truth largely unrealized by thinkers, as opposed to artists, until Freud – that destructive primitive instincts may successfully mask themselves in all sorts of rationalizations and disguises. Indeed for civilized men especially (as Pentheus, trusted king and ruler, must be presumed to be at the beginning of the play) the greatest danger may lie precisely in the failure to see the real motives lying hidden behind and so conditioning the nature of apparently civilized behaviour. That actions are profoundly conditioned by their unconscious motivation is now widely accepted. The disguise may be relatively successful, as in a man whose aggressiveness is concealed from himself and others by the mildness of his normal behaviour, only manifesting itself, perhaps, in sadistic fantasies and in such failures of adult creativity as may be attributed to an inability to release aggressive feelings in a relatively controlled and manageable form. On the other hand, the conflict may take place nearer the surface, with self-betraying symptoms that rapidly pierce the disguise. The unavailing struggle to contain the violent impulses may reveal itself in a sudden spasmodic outburst of irrational and compulsive violence; this, of course, is Pentheus' situation in *The Bacchae*. Moreover, the field in which the mechanisms of rationalization and repression operate in the play is the field where it can be most easily observed, that of power over others and its abuse. An apparently benevolent action, in which force directed against others is justified by moral sanction and social necessity, is revealed by a symptomatic display that betrays its real motives as in essence malevolent and destructive. The judge who passes an exceptionally savage sentence on the violent criminal may be motivated to a greater or lesser extent by the same wish as his victim: a wish to exercise power sadistically. We are always entitled to suspect the motives of those who call for punishments of exceptional severity, for the more ferocious the punishment the greater gratification it will provide for secret sadistic wishes. And the policeman, judge or ruler – the man of acknowledged authority – runs the greater risk that the real nature of his act will be concealed both from himself and others, because what he does will be felt, with some justification, to be socially necessary and is sanctioned by habit and tradition. There is little doubt that those whose destructive wishes are especially powerful often seek to obtain positions of power where they can find sanctioned authority for the gratification of those wishes: if such people contented themselves with the anarchistic and criminal rebelliousness that is the most obvious and direct expression of their feelings, the world would be a safer and more peaceable place. Indeed in an ideal state only those exceptionally free from sadism, or at least judged capable of reducing their sadism to its minimal effectiveness, would be permitted to act in positions of authority. In *The Bacchae*, the situation is presented in its most dramatic and unconcealed form: the element of pathological violence in Pentheus' attempted assertion of order and discipline, and thus his unfitness to control the crisis, are immediately obvious. That this should be so is partly dictated by the legend; but Euripides exploits the traditional material to remarkable effect, demonstrating that his insight into the mechanism of repression and rationalization is as acute as is his understanding of the true nature of Dionysus. His concern is not primarily, if at all, social and political – with the consequences of the abuse of power; it is rather psychological. To read *The Bacchae* attentively is to gain an insight both into the primitive constituents of the psyche (Dionysus) and into the way in which these primitive parts still endure in the adult personality and may in favourable circumstances dominate it (Pentheus). Throughout the process by which Pentheus is converted from authoritative ruler to hypnotized victim, we are constantly reminded of the nature of the primitive forces working in him like yeast, with their logical culmination in the dreadful confrontation of mother and son; like Shakespeare after him, and perhaps most great dramatic artists before modern times, Euripides takes the accepted, familiar material and turns it to dazzling psychological account.

Pentheus' initial reaction to the scandal is significantly violent, as I have mentioned. It shows how powerful his aggressive impulses are – the herdsman confirms later in the play that he has the reputation of being hot-tempered. In his first speech he announces that, when caught, the women, including his mother and sisters, will be put into irons: the 'Oriental conjurer' he threatens with 'the worst of punishments, hanging'.[19] Next, in answer to Teiresias' pleas for prudence, moderation, and, significantly, self-control, his violence increases. He sends his guards literally to smash the priest's place of augury, and declares he will stone the stranger to death – his wishes are now taking a more primitive form.[20] In this way Euripides shifts the emphasis to the inner, psychological conflict while retaining all the external features of the legend; a lesser dramatist might have shown Pentheus as relatively sane and normal until his occupation by the god. Euripides' handling of Pentheus under the god's influence is no less striking, and adds immeasurably to the depth and richness of the portrayal of his sickness. The achievement here is to place the violent wishes where in terms of infantile pathology they clearly belong, in a sexual context. To try to sexualize the relationship with the mother is another way, seemingly less dramatic than an attempted reunion, of denying dependence and smallness and, in the Oedipal situation, of challenging the father. It carries a comparable penalty, for since the mother is thus reduced to the status of sexual object, due to the envious and greedy feelings accompanying the attempt, she will seem to the child less able to nurture and protect him. At first Pentheus sustains the note of straightforward violence; when Dionysus urges him to control his rage and sacrifice to the god, he replies, 'Sacrifice! I will indeed – an offering of women's blood, slaughtered as they deserve . . .'.[21] A few moments later, under Dionysus' prompting, this sadism has been extended into voyeurism:[22]

> *Dionysus* . . . . Would you like to *see* those women,
> sitting together, there in the mountains?
> *Pentheus* Yes, indeed; I would give a large sum of gold
> to see them.

The hostility is now to take the form of sexual spying, ostensibly justified by Dionysus on the grounds of the women's invulnerability to direct attack; however, the suggestion is clearly offered by the god, and eagerly accepted by Pentheus, as enjoyable for its own sake:[23]

> *Dionysus* . . . Yes! You shall find the right hiding-place
> . . . coming like a crafty spy to watch the
> Maenads!
> *Pentheus* Yes, I can picture them – like birds in the
> thickets, wrapped in the sweet snare of love.
> *Dionysus* *That is the very thing you are going to look for* . . .

Again, it is in order to gratify this wish – the wish of 'a perverse man, greedy for sights you should not see'[24] – that Dionysus justifies his device of dressing Pentheus as a woman. But the bisexuality has a deeper significance; it is part of his growing identification with Dionysus, an identification that culminates in his enactment of the god's own original role of sacrificial victim. Moreover, in a significant reference to Agave, Euripides hints

46

at the essentially inner nature of the struggle that culminates in Pentheus' death:[25]

> *Pentheus* (he enters dressed as a woman)   Well, how do
> I look? Do you think I stand like Ino or like
> my mother Agave?
> *Dionysus* I think you are their very image.

The voyeurism is thus shown, correctly, to be based on a sexual identification with the mother; that Pentheus is ironically hailed as a woman may be interpreted in the context of a fantasy by which the child succeeds not only in sexualizing his relationship with his mother but actually in merging his identity with her.

The voyeuristic emphasis is sustained in the messenger's account of Pentheus' end. He climbs a towering pine tree in order to 'have a proper view of their [the women's] shameful behaviour',[26] Agave's reaction demonstrating that they have divined his wish accurately – 'We must catch this climbing beast, or he will reveal the secret dances of Dionysus.'[27] Throughout this part of the play the infantile material is very striking, and gives great authority to the account of Pentheus' developing mania. It is common enough knowledge that the child may obtain satisfaction and excitement from actual or fantasy attempts to spy on the parents' sexual activities. Sufficient evidence that this child's trait, like other psychological traits of childhood, survives into adult life can be found in the immense contemporary popularity of strip-tease clubs and scenes of voyeuristic fantasy on film and in literature. It is also clear from a great deal of clinical evidence that the wish to penetrate with the eyes into the mother's breasts and body, her whole sexuality in fact, and also to penetrate the joint sexual activity of the parents, is essentially a denigratory and spoiling activity in the child, motivated by an inability to tolerate a state of dependence, separation and smallness, and the greed and envy to which this gives rise. It seems that the denigration is an integral part of the pleasure obtained in voyeurism. The fantasies accompanying it are likely to emphasize the role of the woman as sexual object, for use as a receptacle for various feelings and wishes. In contrast, there seems little doubt that a satisfactory sexual relationship will be based on some real recognition of the needs of the woman, and therefore of the man also, as a wholly separate person, in the same way that the child must learn he is separate from the mother, with the implication in each case of love and dependence rather than use or possession. Lawrence's most valuable insight into sexual relationships seems to have been just this.

Both the sexual interest and the denigration are clearly present in Pentheus' attitude; his secret wish, revealed to us by Dionysus, is for an envious penetration and possession of the feminine mysteries, to be achieved by means of an identification with his mother. The envy and denigration naturally colour the whole view taken of the envied object or activity; in a paradoxical way this justifies the voyeurism, for if sex is dirty, all it deserves is the hostile denigration inherent in spying. To conceive of sex as dirty also bridges the otherwise unbridgeable gap between the sexually impotent infant and the sexually potent father: in his smallness and helplessness, he cannot perform the father's sexual role for the mother any more than he can produce milk, but he can, and does, produce dirt in ample quantities, just as he can bite and kick. Thus we get the deluded fantasy of the sexual act both as violence done to the woman (instead of pleasure experienced by her), and as dirty and despicable. In his first speech Pentheus imagines the women, drunk, 'go creeping off this way and that to lonely places to give themselves to lecherous men',[28] a denigratory view of their activities which serves to justify his savagery and which is anyhow baseless: the herdsman who brings the first account of the 'strange and terrible doings' on Cithaeron insists that there was no drunkenness or love-making.[29] The modesty, harmony and joy of the Maenads, until they are provoked by male hostility, may be taken as hinting at the essential, and tragic, element of spoiled love in all these envious attacks. It is interesting that on the second occasion when their activities are described, when the deluded and degraded Pentheus has gone out to Cithaeron to spy on them, they have reverted once more from the savage violence of their attacks on cattle and villagers to their former tranquillity: the messenger who brings the news of Pentheus' death describes the Maenads as 'busy at their happy tasks' while others 'were singing holy songs to each other. . . .'[30] Pentheus, too, shows some awareness of how close the hatred lies to love; when Dionysus teasingly enquires what has betrayed him into such eagerness to see the women, he first replies that he is 'not eager to see them drunk; that would be a painful sight'; but pressed on this score –

48

'Yet you would be glad to see a sight that would pain you?' – he admits that he would in fact enjoy this 'if I could sit quietly under the pine-trees and watch'.[31]

Voyeurism, then, as an aspect of the wish to penetrate into and become part of the woman's body, is grounded ultimately in the denial of separation and dependence. Denial, leading quickly to actual delusion, is central to Pentheus' situation and indeed personality: he is the type of barely repressed Puritan – it is the most obvious thing about him – engaged in a desperate attempt to deal with his own violence and envy, indeed the whole complex structure of destructive primitive forces, by putting it into others and punishing it there. The mechanism of control is breaking down from the start, as his fury at Cadmus and Teiresias, elders whose advice he might have been expected at least to ponder, shows. It is true that he is faced, as ruler, with an extraordinary outbreak on the part of his subjects, if not of violence then of abandonment of self-control, but it is just this lack of self-control that betrays him so quickly. His instantaneous, and violent, reaction to the first news of the Bacchic dances demonstrates clearly that loss of control in others is the one problem he cannot deal with, for he has too inadequate a control over himself. He is rapidly defeated by the impulses he is trying to suppress, a fact illustrated by the ease with which Dionysus later obtains total control over him. In their second interview the god mocks him – teases him almost – on this score: 'You are angry. Now control yourself';[32] indeed nothing is more striking in the play than the contrast between Pentheus' mania and Dionysus' calm. While Pentheus threatens and rages, Dionysus is quiet and controlled, seldom raising his voice and apparently, like Christ before his judges, complying with human authority; he consents to be taken away to prison,[33] and promises not to run away during the herdsman's account of the activities on Cithaeron.[34] In their first interview he quietly warns Pentheus that he is deluded – 'You do not know what life you live, or what you do, or who you are' and states plainly, 'I am sane, you are mad.'[35] It is a powerful irony that, as Pentheus rationalizes his mania as the need to preserve decency and civilization, so Dionysus enacts his terrible revenge under the guise of cool, calm self-control. The irony reaches to the heart of the play: Pentheus – the adult destructively dominated by primitive parts of himself – is indeed mad, aberrant;

Dionysus – the whole primitive constituent of the psyche – is thus source of madness but is not himself mad; he is agent and essence, not victim as the mad must always be. His power is overwhelming, indeed irresistible, a fact symbolized by the helplessness of his human victims. He can only be controlled through contact, never through the kind of denial or splitting attempted by Pentheus. By splitting off the Dionysiac part of himself Pentheus denies it the possibility of any creative outlet, such as that enjoyed by the Maenads in their sane moments, and ensures that it will ultimately destroy him.

With Agave's arrival, cradling her dead son's head, and demanding, in her delusion, the congratulations of the chorus, the full metaphorical meaning of the play is revealed. The demonstration of the adult personality submerged and destroyed by a more primitive part has a relentless logic about it: Agave and Pentheus have done more than submit to the god's influence; true to the earliest primitive mechanisms, they have actually absorbed him into themselves. Together, as suggested, their fate may be taken as representing one of the most powerful of primitive fantasies, the attack on the mother, out of envy, greed, and the need to deny dependence, and the subsequent experience of a retributive persecutory attack by her as an internalized, and now torn and damaged figure. The isolation of the mother/son relationship in the penultimate scene of the play is crucial, and enables the audience to respond at an unconscious level to a long buried and suppressed situation reactivated for them in mythical and dramatic form. The disturbing quality of Euripides' presentation of the material was clear from the reaction of the audience at the performance at the Mermaid Theatre in London in 1964. It would be hard to explain this reaction simply on the grounds of the unpleasantness or painfulness of the spectacle depicted. There is in fact an element of identification; as Kenneth Burke argues, in discussing the emotional effects of ritual drama, its appeal is not purely as spectacle: 'Would it not be more likely that the fate of the sacrificial king was also the fate of the audience "writ large"?'[36] The whole presentation is uncanny in its accuracy, especially of those mechanisms of projection, introjection and identification by which the infant may fantasy that he is victimized internally by the mother he has himself in fantasy attacked. Pentheus had wished to smash up his enemies and he is, literally, smashed to pieces by his mother; as a necessary part of the process that leads him to his fate, he had turned himself into a female travesty, the 'very image' of his mother Agave, in Dionysus' words.[37] When Agave appears with Pentheus' head, she believes herself to be carrying a young creature, the 'lion cub' and 'calf' of her rhapsody.[38] Our attention has already been drawn to the world, not simply of mother and son, but of mother and infant, by the sinister final dialogue between Dionysus and Pentheus before the king is led out to where his mother, unawares, is waiting for him:[39]

Dionysus	. . . another shall bring you home.
Pentheus	You mean my mother?
Dionysus	A sight for all to see.
Pentheus	It is for that I am going.
Dionysus	You will be carried home –
Pentheus	What splendour that will be!
Dionysus	– in your mother's arms.
Pentheus	Why, you make a weakling of me!
Dionysus	That is – one way of putting it.
Pentheus	Yet it is what I deserve.

Agave, celebrating her triumphant capture of the 'lion-cub', invites the chorus to 'join in the feast' – in effect an invitation to cannibalism as their reaction, horrified in spite of themselves, shows: 'What, wretched woman? *Feast?*'[40] This of course recalls the god who is eaten by his worshippers as a sacrament; but in primitive infantile terms it also recalls pathological fantasies of actually devouring the breast and body of the mother, and then being devoured, both as a retributive act and through identification. Though actual cannibalism is just avoided, on stage at any rate, there is a terrible sense in which mother and child are again at one. As Agave says when her sanity is restored, in the lines I have quoted before, 'I have spilt the blood that is my own, torn the flesh that grew in my own womb.' She expresses too the whole tragic ambivalence of the situation in her farewell to her son's mangled remains; for there would be no tragedy but for spoiled love. In a passage that recalls Theseus' farewell to the dying Hippolytus she asks for her son's forgiveness[41]

for what I did, not knowing what I did, and for what I
do now, touching you with unholy hands – at once your
cruellest enemy and your dearest lover.

51

Her ignorance of what she was doing, like the ignorance of Oedipus, symbolizes the unconscious nature of primitive fantasies. They are part of that 'unseen world' spoken of by Cadmus in his grief at the end of the play – a statement that, freshly interpreted, may serve as epigraph for Euripides' remarkable work: 'If there be any man who derides the unseen world, let him consider the death of Pentheus, and acknowledge the gods.'[42]

Notes

1 An exception to this, the Apollo of the *Eumenides*, singularly fails to impress as a god, being neither all-powerful force nor just ruler.
2 Euripides, *The Bacchae*, ed. E. R. Dodds (Oxford, 1944), pp. xi–xii.
3 Cf. E. R. Dodds, *The Greeks and the Irrational* (Berkeley, Los Angeles, 1951), Appendix I (Maenadism), pp. 270–8.
4 Euripides, *The Bacchae and Other Plays*, trans. P. Vellacott (Penguin, 1954), p. 190. Translations are from this version unless otherwise indicated.
5 Ibid., p. 216.
6 Ibid., p. 210.
7 Ibid., p. 203.
8 Ibid., p. 208.
9 Dodds, op. cit., p. 277.
10 Euripides, trans. P. Vellacott, pp. 25, 29.
11 Ibid., p. 29.
12 See above.
13 Euripides, trans. P. Vellacott, p. 226.
14 See above, pp. 15–19.
15 Euripides, trans. P. Vellacott, p. 223.
16 Ibid., p. 196.
17 L. Goldscheider, *The Sculpture of Michelangelo* (London, 1950), p. 151.
18 Euripides, trans. P. Vellacott, pp. 183–4.
19 Ibid., pp. 188–9.
20 Ibid., p. 192.
21 Ibid., p. 205.
22 Ibid., p. 206.
23 Ibid., p. 211 (my italics).
24 Ibid., p. 210.
25 Ibid.
26 Ibid., p. 215.
27 Ibid., p. 216.
28 Ibid., p. 188.
29 Ibid., p. 202.
30 Ibid., p. 215.
31 Ibid., p. 206.

32 Ibid., p. 201.
33 Ibid., p. 197.
34 Ibid., p. 202.
35 Ibid., p. 197.
36 K. Burke, 'Freud – and the Analysis of Poetry', *American Journal of Sociology*, xlv(1939), p. 405. Quoted by H. M. Ruitenbeek (ed.), *Psychoanalysis and Literature* (New York, 1964), p. 271.
37 Euripides, trans. P. Vellacott, p. 210.
38 Ibid., pp. 218–19.
39 Ibid., p. 212.
40 Ibid., p. 219.
41 Ibid., p. 224.
42 Ibid., p. 223.

Two

Strindberg: The Strong and Cruel Struggle

In two important respects modern drama has shown an under-standing of the nature of the primitive: first, in its awareness of the force and ubiquity of those primitive instincts which in their barbarity civilized man was supposed to have outgrown; and second, in the realization that such instincts, first manifest in early childhood, are dynamically active in normal adult life but in a concealed and condensed form. Here the parallel with psychoanalytical findings is very close. If we look at the cultural history of the last decades of the nineteenth century and the first decades of the twentieth century, we find many examples of a phenomenon often observable at times of intellectual revolution and ferment – of parallel insights in related but different fields of human activity, for example, literature and psychology, where no direct influence is traceable. In the fiction of this period, Dostoevsky and Kafka would be outstanding names; in the drama, Strindberg. One of the clearest examples is the explanatory note he wrote for *A Dream Play* (1902), in which he notes[1]

> In this dream play . . . the author has tried to reproduce the disjointed but apparently logical form of a dream. Anything can happen; everything is possible and probable. . . . The characters are split, doubled, and multiplied: they evaporate and are condensed, are diffused and concentrated. But a single consciousness holds sway over them all – that of the dreamer; for him there are no secrets, no incongruities, no scruples and no law. . . .

As Eric Bentley points out[2] this was written several years after *The Interpretation of Dreams,* but there is no evidence that at this time Strindberg had read, or even heard of, Freud. The case is the same with Strindberg's handling of the primitive. In the preface to *Miss Julie* he writes, in answer to the criticism that his tragedy *The Father* was too grim and lacked 'joy of life', that 'I myself find the joy of life in its strong and cruel struggles, and my pleasure in learning, in adding to my knowledge'.[3] Those who know Strindberg are likely to agree that there is an element of defiance and denial in his assertion that he enjoys seeing the weaker swept aside by the stronger, in particular a denial of his own persecutory fears by an indulgence in omnipotent fantasy. His plays of this period show clearly enough that the denial was only partially successful: in *The Father*, it is the man who is destroyed by the predatory woman while in *Miss Julie* the woman, though defeated, is much the more sympathetic character, to Strindberg as well as to the reader. In his life, as in his work, the predominant note is one of often acute suffering. However, his remark in the preface to *Miss Julie* does hint at his uncanny understanding of the satisfaction that can be obtained in the infliction and suffering of pain. It also speaks of that inch of detachment which enabled him by the barest of margins to dramatize his own violent conflicts in works which, directly or indirectly autobiographical, possess independent life, in the sense that their significance does not depend upon a knowledge of Strindberg's biography, though it is greatly enriched by such knowledge. Elsewhere, in a comment on *The Father*, he demonstrates his understanding of the truth that such violence may be purely psychological: that however powerful and ultimately effective the instinct to attack and destroy, or the fear of being persecuted and destroyed, may be, such primitive drives, physical in origin, take on disguises compatible with the needs of a 'civilized' social context, and based on the force of repression. '*The Father*', he writes,[4]

> is the realization of modern drama, and as such is something very curious. Very curious because the struggle takes place between souls. It is a battle of brains, not a dagger fight or a poisoning with raspberry juice. . . .

It is of course true that the 'strong and cruel struggles', especially those between man and woman, are very openly and directly portrayed throughout Strindberg's work. This may be attributed in part to the form – drama, with its brevity, calls for concentration and exaggeration – and in part to Strindberg's temperament, in which need for others, women especially, was only paralleled in force by the resentment bred by that need. Indeed the constant urge to exposure of others seems in him to be rooted in a markedly paranoid tendency, which imperatively sought an outlet in attacks on the oppressive father or elder brother, the predatory wife or mother, the devouring parents. But this leaves the essential insight unimpaired; the battle is 'between souls', and violence is not the prerogative only of those who can be seen openly to employ it, and who as a result are likely to be excluded from civilized society. In *The Father* an insight of this nature is combined, as often in Strindberg, with a paranoid resentment against women likely, one would have supposed, to exercise a very distorting influence. Though Laura, the wife, admits to her husband in private that as a woman she is his enemy, her final triumph over him leaves her role as long-enduring wife and devoted mother unimpaired in the eyes of society. Hypocrisy, like the other vices of this repellent creature, is justified by 'instinct' and the will to dominate and defeat the male.

Most significantly of all, the Captain's old nurse combines with Laura to betray and destroy her Adolf. This of course greatly reinforces the audience's sense of women, in Strindberg's presentation of them, as the predatory and ruthless sex. To herself, however, the Nurse in cajoling the Captain into his straitjacket seems to be performing a task of painful self-denial, the last dutiful service but one she can do for him in defiance of natural inclination. The men in the play, doctor and parson, are given some of Strindberg's own insight, as he felt it to be, into Laura's true motives. But this is a tacit admission of her superior strength – one may be sure that out of cowardice and self-interest they will keep their own counsel, for they are very thoroughly gelded.

It is very characteristic of Strindberg that a paranoia likely, one would have supposed, to have prevented him writing drama at all should have been turned to a kind of creative use. Conceived after the break-up of his first marriage, the figure of Laura in *The Father*, the first of many vampire women who out of greed and envy batten on the happiness of others, is full of Strindberg's hostile projections. It is the parts of himself that he puts into her that make her into the monster we see on the stage, a creature who has Strindberg's own wish to dominate and destroy in projected form. Yet her impact on us as a character study – and she makes a striking impact in her own right – derives from her creator's understanding of psychological violence and the eagerness of 'instinct' to satisfy its needs at the expense of others. A living Laura would surely be a more neurotic personality than the Laura of the play. However, to have emphasized this would not have answered Strindberg's need at the time to portray woman, in the sexual relationship, as the stronger as well as the more destructive partner. To have shown her as more neurotic would not, of course, have meant a less implacably destructive character; burdened as we are with the terrible historical experience of our time, we are less likely than Strindberg's contemporaries to disbelieve in the existence of 'civilized' monsters. But Laura must be seen in the whole context of the relationship between husband and wife, which affords perhaps the best evidence of Strindberg's psychological understanding, and demonstrates how brilliantly he turned his own neurotic illness to account in his art. Our first reaction to Laura's destruction of her husband may be simply to feel, as I have suggested, that this woman is not merely a killer but is a sick creature as well. It is easy to dismiss Strindberg's implicit claim that she is normal, and that this is what the relationship of husband and wife is like, as symptomatic of a paranoid misogyny, always latent in him and in powerful spate at the time of his composition of *The Father*, soon after his parting with his first wife. Indeed if the play is viewed realistically this conclusion seems inevitable. However, if we look at the way Strindberg has presented the relationship between the pair we can see that he has expressed in terms of an adult relationship a very powerful and prevalent infantile fantasy: that there is, in effect, an intentional element of psychological symbolism in the play. Basically, the husband's situation is that of a child whose mother's love towards him has been turned to hostility by his attempt to sexualize the relationship. In the great duologue between them in Act Two, Strindberg spells this out in so many words. Turning from abuse to a desperate appeal (the immediate occasion of the scene is the doubt sown in the husband's mind over his paternity of their daughter), the Captain says to Laura, 'Can't you see I'm as helpless as a child? Can't you hear me crying to my mother that I'm hurt?' Her response is initially favourable, though she has to be cajoled into it: 'Weep then my child and *you shall have your mother again*' [my italics]. 'Remember, it was as your second mother that I came into your life. You were big and strong, yet not fully a man. . . .' The Captain at once acknowledges the truth of this – 'Born without a will', he says, 'I looked up to you . . . and listened to you as if I were your foolish little boy.' Laura replies:[5]

> Yes, that's how it was, and I loved you as if you were my little boy. But didn't you see, how *when your feelings changed and you came to me as a lover*, I was ashamed? My very blood seemed tainted. The mother became the mistress – horrible! . . . That was your mistake. The mother was your friend, you see, but the mistress was your enemy.

At the end of the scene, before the final hostile exchange that culminates in the lamp throwing, the situation is summed up:

> *Captain* Just one thing more – a fact. Do you hate me?
> *Laura* Sometimes – as a man.[6]

That the child in fantasy does seek to turn his dependent relationship to the mother into a sexual relationship is widely supported in clinical experience. His motive for this, as I have suggested in an earlier chapter, has to do with the need to deny his total dependence upon her, with its frightening implications, and, at a later stage, with jealousy of the father: why should his relationship to his mother be limited to feeding from her, at her whim? Why should not he enjoy the right over her body claimed by the father, a usurper who has pushed him out of the place where he has first claim, for he was there from the beginning? The very factors which serve to promote such an omnipotent fantasy – smallness, dependence, consequential envy and jealousy – also serve to check it. Reality makes clear to him that he is too small and weak to serve his mother in this way, and, more important still, she does not want him in this role ('when your feelings changed and you came to me as a lover . . . my very blood seemed tainted'.)[7] He is permitted to feed but that is all, and his father is admitted to her body when he is excluded. The bitter sense of his total dependence on her may even provide an inkling of the most radical psychological difficulty of all in the path of the child who has sexual designs on his mother – that the function of the father's penis is not simply to gain satisfaction, like the child at the breast, but also to give it. More broadly, the father's role in relation to the mother extends beyond the giving and taking of sexual satisfaction to essential functions of support and succour, whereas the child at first gives nothing whatever to the mother, other than an opportunity to exercise her own capacity to feed and care for him, a situation that only changes slowly as the child grows and develops its own capacity to give. The consequence of the checking of the fantasy may be serious; the child, if his advances are rejected (the situation will be experienced as rejection just as the mother's attempts to teach the child to be separate from her will be experienced in the same way), may feel his only recourse is to fling himself back inside her, not now in love but in envious and resentful aggression. In *The Father*, the Captain's wish as a husband to remain united with the mother is shown by his wish to be dominated by Laura and to be a 'foolish little boy'[8] in relation to her. In a later scene, he is even more specific: complaining that he has nothing to live for, now that he has been robbed of the children of both body and mind (his work), he says:[9]

I grafted my right arm and half my brain and spinal cord on to another stem. I believed they would unite and grow into a single, more perfect tree. . . .

This is an image that, set alongside his openly infantile wishes, shows a concept of marriage suggestive of the reforging of the original physical link with the mother. The wife, we recollect, had come into his life as a 'second mother'. Very strikingly, this is followed at once by a scene with his daughter where he demands that she sink her identity in his – 'You must only have one soul or you'll have no peace . . . you must have only one mind, fruit of my mind. You must have only one will – mine.'[10] When the daughter – here clearly a substitute for the now implacably hostile wife, just as the wife is substitute for the mother – rejects this appeal – 'No, no! I want to be myself' – her father replies[11]

Never! I am a cannibal, you see, and I'm going to eat you! Your mother wanted to eat me, but she didn't succeed. To eat or be eaten, that is the question. If I don't eat you, you will eat me – you've shown your teeth already.

Just as in the earlier scene Strindberg shows an uncannily accurate knowledge of the child's sexual fantasies about his mother, so here he shows how the sense of rejection and persecution will lead rapidly to sadism, deflected now from the too powerful wife to the weaker daughter. Later sadistic fantasies about women have been commonly traced by psychoanalysts to the infantile experience of rejection, obliquely referred to in this scene at a point in the play where the Captain's pleas have been decisively rejected by Laura. Once the fantasy of a sexual relationship has been checked, the emotions accompanying the child's attempt to get back inside the mother – envy, greed, and the anger of resentment – may well turn that attempt into a tearing, biting attack of a sadistic nature. Oral fantasies, such as the Captain's here ('I am a cannibal', etc.) are the most likely, owing to the primacy of the mouth in the earliest stages of life and the likely confusion of feeding with sexual intercourse. There is a further important point in Strindberg's depiction of this fantasy, which links, as so often, his paranoid feelings about women to his astonishing insight. 'The mother was your friend but the mistress was your enemy.'[12] The child's envious and resentful feelings, which he needs urgently to evacuate, are thus projected into the mother. By this process she is turned into the monstrous figure so common in fantasy concepts of women, from the ogresses and witches of legend onwards, and of which Strindberg's Laura is a worthy example. The child's voracious appetite, as well as his savagery, may be projected into, and so go to create, this monstrous figure. Infantile greed, we may suppose, animates the fantasy of the sexually insatiable woman, and also of such a devouring mother-figure as the Cook in Strindberg's *The Ghost Sonata*. In this play, both parent figures are vampires; but whereas the father, Hummel, is exposed and defeated, the bad mother in the shape of the cook who 'drains the children, and the food, of sap',[13] proves significantly undefeatable. The sadism that may accompany the projection into the mother of envious and greedy feelings is bound to reinforce and deepen the projective process, which then takes the familiar form of a vicious circle, in which every projected attack increases the mother's fantasied hostility and every increase in her hostility necessitates a still more violent attack in order to penetrate further and win the battle for control of her. The process known as splitting may be employed in an attempt to preserve in the mother what is felt to be good, and more than that necessary for sheer survival, while rejecting what is felt to be bad; in Strindberg's life, as well as in his plays, Madonna worship alternates with misogyny. Whereas *The Father* is exclusively misogynistic, other plays, *Easter* for example, are characterized by unalloyed sentiment about the woman, reflective of the opposite feeling. As Strindberg himself clearly realized, Madonna worship is an idealization of the mother, just as misogyny of the ferocious type we see in *The Father* and elsewhere is the corresponding denigration; both are implicit in the attempt to split off the good from the bad. The difficulty, of course, is that both idealization and denigration are experienced in relation to the same woman, originally the mother. Again, Strindberg's insight is shown in his understanding of this – it is the same woman, the mother, who is friend and enemy, angel and devil, Madonna and whore; the splitting process is therefore bound to fail, relatively speaking, and the man, really the child, bound to be defeated. Strindberg's early history is a classical demonstration of how the child's original trauma at being separated from the mother's body at birth may be reactivated and exacerbated, in his case by what he felt to be her neglect – she had thirteen children – followed by her death in his early adolescence; in his own words, 'This feeling of . . . longing after his mother followed him all through his life. . . . He never became himself, never a complete individual.'[14] This exceptionally strong emotional bond to his mother, reinforced in early childhood by a total rejection of his harsh and unsympathetic father, is the most important source of Strindberg's attraction towards and resentment against the opposite sex. A striking instance of his attempt to preserve harmonious contact with the woman as mother although he is now in a sexual relationship with her as wife or mistress, is found in his insistence that woman should not enjoy the sexual act. Her sole source of pleasure, he argued, should be pregnancy and childbirth, and subsequent child-rearing. Supported as this view was to some extent by his pietistic upbringing and by the sexual attitudes of the period, its origins must also be sought in the incestuous fantasies of the personal life – there are striking instances throughout Strindberg's autobiographical writings. If the mother's image is so powerful as to be experienced in subsequent intimate relations with other women, the accompanying sense that sex is incestuous will threaten a taboo against sexual intercourse altogether; the guilt that follows the inevitable breaking of the taboo was a fertile source of Strindberg's misogyny. To deny the woman sexual pleasure is thus clearly a way of coming to terms with the taboo, of playing along with it; the breach is then in some ways robbed of its consequential terrors. The child's concept of a sexual relationship with the mother is essentially a kind of masturbatory evacuation; in fantasy, he discharges himself into her as into a passive receptacle. It is therefore wholly appropriate that she should not derive pleasure from it. This idea of her indifference to sexual activity can be seen as a distorted and softened down version of the more frightening belief that the mother violently rejects the child's sexual advances. By declaring that all is well, provided the woman does not enjoy it, he simultaneously robs the situation of its terrors and gratifies the omnipotent fantasy, based on envy, that sees the woman merely as a sexual object with which to gratify himself.

In *The Father* the conclusion is irresistible that Laura, the wife, is really a substitute for the mother who was the first source and centre of these violently conflicting feelings; her superior strength alone would suggest this. Further confirmation is to be found in Strindberg's use of the Nurse, where a figure apparently maternal in a benevolent sense, and who has no other conflicting role of a sexual nature in relation to 'her Adolf', joins forces with Laura and betrays him at the end, tricking him into the straitjacket and so bringing about his collapse and presumed death. There is a fine irony in the Captain's dying devotion to the woman who has betrayed him:[15]

> Let me put my head on your lap. Ah, that's warmer. . . .
> Goodnight, Margaret. Blessed art thou among women.
> (He raises himself, then with a cry falls back.)

In this way, the play can be seen as presenting not just the adult sexual conflict, but, more deeply, the inevitable defeat of the child who distorts both his own and his mother's role, and, rejecting childish dependence, seeks to form an adult pseudo-sexual relationship with her. That Strindberg survived the pressure of these early conflicts, so acute and seemingly destructive, is remarkable; from time to time he did endure spells of madness.

It is equally remarkable that he should have possessed such acute insight into the nature of these conflicts – the insight that alone makes tolerable the savage partiality of his depiction of marital relations in *The Father*.

If *The Father* contains these remarkable insights into infantile sexuality, on a realistic level it presents the 'strong and cruel struggles' of the sexes very directly, almost crudely. (In general it may be noted that the baffling impression made on many audiences by Strindberg's early plays seems to be due to the combination of a surface naturalism with rich psychological symbolism at a deeper level.) Strindberg's second realistic play, *Miss Julie*, is much subtler in its presentation of sexual conflict in the adult here-and-now. It too contains remarkable insights into the primitive constituents of the psyche and their power to direct the conscious life of the adult. In this play, where the servant possesses and in so doing destroys the 'decadent' upper-class woman, the aggressive feelings against women take a more thoroughly sadistic form, culminating in the beheading of the finch and Miss Julie's suicide. Although Jean does not consciously wish for Julie's death, there is a coarseness and cruelty in him that allow him to derive satisfaction from bringing Julie down to his level, and from the subsequent survival of the fittest; more-over, he directly incites her to her death. At this level the play appears to be a riposte to *The Father*; if women are potentially stronger, and wish to dominate and destroy us, then we must hoist them with their own petard. There is an identification here with Strindberg's father, who seems to have dominated the women in his life. However, the impression the play makes on us is very different from this; it is as though the triumph over the woman releases Strindberg's sympathy with her, and enables him to portray her as a tragic victim, despite his talk (in the foreword) about the 'degeneracy of the half-woman, the man-hater'.[16] If there is an element of self-portraiture in Jean – like Strindberg the servant's son who seduces the aristocratic girl but 'sexually is himself the aristocrat because of his virility'[17] – there is more of Strindberg in Julie, the child fatally divided by the divisions between her parents; and whereas Jean is described by Strindberg in his introduction to the play, correctly, as callous, vulgar, and with a slave mentality,[18] Julie as presented by him is a tragic figure, unconsciously bent on self-destruction. Just as

Strindberg himself was a woman-hater who at the same time was powerfully drawn towards women, a conflict originating as he himself was aware in his attitude towards his mother, so Julie is portrayed as a man-hater whose sexual urge, as powerful as Strindberg's, is similarly and even more fatally turned to self-destructive ends. For Jean is more the occasion than the cause of her ruin, whose origins, as the play specifically demonstrates – Julie is given a passage of recollection acute in its self-analysis[19] – lie far in the past, in the child's relations with her parents. It is here that we find Strindberg's finest insight into primitive aggression and persecution: Julie's sexual initiative towards Jean, seemingly based on appetite, supported by the accident of physical circumstances, is really self-destructive in nature and design. Although she believes herself to be in love, and although their situation, admittedly difficult, is not desperate, she kills herself when her father returns, because (to quote Strindberg himself in the foreword) her 'repressed instincts break out uncontrollably'.[20] What these repressed instincts are is shown partly in description and partly in action: her sexual intercourse with Jean is experienced by her in the fantasy light of her original incestuous feelings for a father defeated and humiliated in the sexual struggle with her mother. Miss Julie had been brought up by her mother 'to loathe the whole male sex'; more recently, her breach with her fiancé has been brought about by her insistence on 'training' him, an activity that involved sexual humiliation. To give herself to a man is thus an act undertaken against powerful resistance, and is experienced as an enactment of this forbidden incestuous passion for the father; to give herself to her father's servant is felt as an act of defiance and revenge against him, the fruit, perhaps, of envy and a sense of rejection. As she says to Jean near the end:[21]

> My father will come back . . . find his desk broken open
> [at Jean's prompting she has stolen some of her father's
> money so that they may elope together to Italy, but
> nothing comes of the idea] . . . then he'll ring the bell . . .
> send for the police . . . and I shall tell him everything.
> Everything. Oh how wonderful to make an end of it
> all – a real end! He has a stroke and dies and that's the
> end of all of us. . . .

Both aspects of her sexual union with Jean – the enactment of an incestuous wish and the act of revenge against her father whom, in her own words, she 'loved deeply but hated too, unconsciously' – provoke in her an overwhelming sense of guilt. In the passage quoted above, Strindberg shows how closely she is identified with her father. He will die, she says, from the shock of what she has done 'and that's the end of all of *us*' [my italics]. By a similar process of identification, his sexual defeat has imposed a like defeat on her. (At the same time Strindberg shows her identification with the mother, when she says, contemplating what she has done and what she has yet to do, '. . . my mother is revenged again, through me'.) She is herself the desk that should have been kept closed for her father but has been broken open and violated – in this image the two contradictory aspects of her sexual guilt are simultaneously expressed. When the bell finally rings, warning her that her father is in the house, and she prepares in a trance-like state for the final act of suicide, she says to Jean,[22]

> . . . the whole room has turned to smoke – and you look like a stove – a stove like a man in black with a tall hat – your eyes are glowing like coals when the fire is low – and your face is a white patch like ashes.

In this superb image of destructive sexuality father and lover coalesce as a single avenging persecutory figure. The figure also beckons her to peace – the peace of death, suggesting the seemingly reparatory aspect of suicide, and thus the magnitude of the preceding guilt. It is very striking that she needs Jean's help in order to perform the act. He has to instruct her 'like a hypnotist at the theatre'[23] and actually puts the razor into her hand; no less striking is the timing, and nature, of her appeal to Kristin, the elder woman. In revulsion against Jean at the killing of the goldfinch (she rightly identifies herself with the bird) she appeals frantically to Kristin for protection against him. The tone and manner of her speech is that of a frightened child, repelled by and terrified of a brutal father, whose desperate pleas to a hostile, jealous mother fall on deaf ears. It may be noted that the cold hypocritical pietism of Kristin's final dismissal of Julie's appeal recalls the pietism of Strindberg's parents, especially his mother, against which he rebelled so violently in adolescence. Significantly, Strindberg has made Kristin Jean's regular mistress, and made Julie aware of this fact; the child in Julie is thus appealing to a woman who, like her (or any child's) mother is in sexual relation to the man in her life. Julie's failure to placate Kristin leads directly to the despair which culminates in suicide once her father's bell is heard. Her first open reference to suicide immediately follows Kristin's smug departure. Rejected by the mother, she is left alone with the man in black – lover and father – whose persecutory threat derives both from guilt and from her own hostile projections, stimulated as these have been by Jean's cruelty to the finch: 'I should like to see the whole of your sex swimming . . . in a sea of blood',[24] she says to Jean after he has killed the bird. Her suicide is both reparation and identification; her death is what the avenging male figure desires – Jean puts the razor into her hand – for in so acting she both makes amends for what she has done – obtaining what she calls the 'gift of grace' – and joins him in his defeat and disgrace. The father, whose 'unhappy spirit is kept above and behind the action',[25] in the words of the author's foreword, had earlier attempted to shoot himself. It is insights such as these that give *Miss Julie* so deservedly honoured a place in the beginnings of modern drama. They demonstrate Strindberg's understanding of some of the mechanisms of aggression and persecution, as yet unexplored by psychoanalysis, whose nature he divined by an introspective understanding of his own experience, with its conflicts and obsessions. He had something of the analyst's gift for 'examining the box with the false bottom', to use his own metaphor again from the foreword to *Miss Julie*.[26] Explaining his concentration on the two characters of Julie and Jean, he remarks that he has done this 'because it seems to me that the psychological process is what interests people most today. [We] are no longer satisfied with seeing a thing happen; we must also know how it happens.'[27]

The understanding of 'how it happens' implies an awareness of the complexity of human beings, their obscurities of motivation and vacillations of conduct, that anticipates Freudian thought and is comparable on a smaller scale to the insights of Dostoevsky. In the preface to *Miss Julie* Strindberg explains ironically that in order to avoid the stereotype of the 'fixed and finished character' popular on the stage of his time he had made his people 'somewhat characterless';[28] what he is claiming for his own method is made clear in the last sentence of the paragraph: ' . . . the summary judgement of authors . . . should be challenged by the Naturalists who know the richness of the soul-complex and realize that vice has a reverse side very much like virtue'.[29] He adds, 'Because they are modern characters . . . I have drawn my figures vacillating, disintegrated, a blend of old and new.'[30] This attempt to 'modernize the form', in his own expression, that was to prove so influential, is reflected in dialogue as well as in characterization. Later in the same preface he remarks that, in regard to the dialogue, he has 'let people's minds work irregularly as they do in real life where . . . no topic is drained to the dregs' and 'the dialogue wanders'.[31] As the reference to 'real life' makes clear, Strindberg regarded this departure from tradition as basically realistic. However, he has surely gone further than the liberation of the dialogue from an artificial symmetry. Part of the strange effect of the play is due, I believe, to Strindberg's allowing the unconscious or part-conscious thoughts and feelings of the characters, especially Julie, to find a more coherent outward expression than would be found in actual life, without its being made obvious that this is what he is doing. If this is right, it means that the element of psychological symbolism even at this early naturalistic stage of Strindberg's career is present in the dialogue as well as more obviously in plot and character. Strindberg's method may create certain unresolved problems so far as the dialogue is concerned. We recollect that he was to abandon naturalism for expressionism, a form in which he attempts a direct and open transposition into dramatic scenes and events of all the rich confusion of the inner life. But it nevertheless adds greatly to the play's penetrative power into the recesses of the personality. After sixty-odd years of modern drama, there has been no one to surpass Strindberg in intimate understanding of 'the psychological process', especially in the vital sphere of the relations between the sexes.

Notes

1 A. Strindberg, *A Dream Play*, trans E. Sprigge (New York, 1955), p. 193, author's prefatory note.
2 E. Bentley, *The Modern Theatre* (London, 1948), p. 59.
3 A. Strindberg, *Miss Julie*, trans. E. Sprigge (New York, 1955,) p. 63, author's foreword.

4 Quoted by Bentley, op. cit., p. 143.
5 A. Strindberg, *The Father*, trans. E. Sprigge (New York, 1955), pp. 41–2.
6 Ibid., p. 43.
7 Ibid., p. 41.
8 See above, p. 58.
9 *The Father*, ed. cit., p. 51.
10 Ibid., p. 52.
11 Ibid.
12 Ibid., p. 42.
13 Strindberg, *The Ghost Sonata* (Stockholm, 1907), Scene 3.
14 Quoted by Bentley, op. cit., p. 140.
15 *The Father*, ed. cit., p. 56.
16 *Miss Julie*, ed. cit., p. 65.
17 Ibid., p. 67.
18 Ibid., pp. 67–8.
19 Ibid., pp. 97–9.
20 Ibid., p. 65.
21 Ibid., pp. 107–8.
22 Ibid., p. 113.
23 Ibid.
24 Ibid., p. 107.
25 Ibid., p. 69.
26 Ibid.
27 Ibid.
28 Ibid., pp. 64–5.
29 Ibid.
30 Ibid.
31 Ibid., p. 69.

Three

Pinter: The Roots of the Relationship

The theatre will never find itself again . . . except by
furnishing the spectator with the truthful precipitate of
dreams, in which his taste for crime, his erotic obsessions,
his savagery, his chimeras, his utopian sense . . . even his
cannibalism pour out on a level not counterfeit and
illusory, but interior.[1]

Two people in a room – I am dealing a great deal of the
time with this image of two people in a room. The curtain
goes up on the stage, and I see it as a very potent question:
What is going to happen to these two people in the room?
Is someone going to open the door and come in?[2]

In this and the following chapters I wish to discuss some contemporary dramatists all of whom in different ways have developed
a new freedom and flexibility in the expression of primitive
instincts of infantile origins. Like Strindberg, they are concerned
to show the power of such instincts as they are seen to operate in
the adult personality, that is in a disguised or displaced manner;
nevertheless without adopting an expressionist or openly allegori-
cal form they retain far less of a realistic content than Strindberg
in *The Father* or *Miss Julie*, and thus tend to present their material
in a form that corresponds more closely to the structure of
infantile fantasy. This is especially true of Pinter, whose interest
in people is very much at the level of the basic primitive stuff that
he sees as the deepest stratum, enigmatic and threatening, of our
lives, and of Ionesco, with his urge to 'create a theatre of violence,
violently comic, violently dramatic',[3] the dominating image of
whose plays is a world full of endlessly proliferating forms which
appear phantasmal and unreal. In both these writers, as also in
Beckett, there is to be found a characteristic doubt or confusion

over identity, accompanied by a sense of the unreality of the self and others and a conviction of the futility of attempts at communication; like other haunting psychic experiences of adult life, this sense of unreality and emptiness may be found to take its origins from early experiences and fantasies. The same is true of a tendency to present situation rather than plot, a dramatic image of compulsive repetition where talk and action pursue circular, seemingly purposeless patterns in place of the steady development to a climax of traditional drama, and there is little or no time sense; this is especially common in Beckett, but is also found in Pinter and indeed throughout experimental modern drama. Primitive violence and savagery, sustained in a manner of grotesque incongruity, as in Ionesco, or breaking through decisively at moments of crisis, as in Pinter, is perhaps the most immediately striking of all such expressions of the primitive. Indeed, in Pinter, a blind violence is often the alternative to the sense of unreality; the principal object of talk seems to be to provide an illusion of meaningfulness and identity and so protect the characters against the blankness and violence that is the reality 'at the root of their relationship'.[4] This phrase comes from a radio interview in the course of which Pinter remarked, 'I feel that instead of any inability to communicate there is a deliberate evasion of communication. Communication itself between people is so frightening that rather than do that there is continual cross-talk, a continual talking about other things, rather than what is at the root of their relationship.'

A noteworthy example of the handling of themes of primitive savagery is the recent work of a playwright very different in style and approach from those hitherto mentioned, Peter Weiss. His *Marat Sade* play[5] sets the debate between the anarchic destructive individualism of Sade and the equally violent but ostensibly creative collectivism of Marat in the ironical context of a therapeutic drama performed under controlled conditions by the inmates of an asylum. Though the debate itself is of great interest, the power of the play lies principally in its picture of the 'appalling existential reality' of human existence as seen by Sade, with his claim that what is most 'real' is the freedom of the individual to explore to the limit his own basic primitive drives ('There is nothing I could not do and everything fills me with horror').[6] It is a reality that he sees enacted in the world around him, the

France of the Revolution in its cruelty and violence confirming his own private fantasies. Weiss has thus added a new dimension of interest by showing these sadistic interests, whose infantile origins I have discussed in an earlier chapter,[7] enacted not in the private life but in a familiar and fearful public context, and also by calling in aid, in a free interpretation of his thought, the extraordinary historical personage whose name has been preserved in the word sadism. Weiss's attempt in this play to extend the psychological understanding of man's primitive feelings to their enactment in the public sphere, however admirable, fails to surmount entirely the inherent risk of overloading and confusion; the variety of kinds of material a single play can handle directly seem to be limited except in the hands of a genius by the physical limitations of the dramatic form. The *Marat Sade* is technically brilliant, but it lacks, I think, that final assurance and control. The difference in emphasis between the public and private spheres reflects in part a familiar difference of approach between British and Continental dramatists. Political debate tends inevitably to the abstract, and British writers are traditionally wary of the kind of abstraction found in Weiss, as well as, for example, in Beckett, who is unconcerned with politics. It is part of Pinter's strength that he concentrates so directly and detachedly on the private life and the concrete experience; the concentration may be limiting, but it gives him a unique position among contemporary theatrical explorers of the primitive.

The basic image in his plays to date, representing what is clearly a fundamental preoccupation, is of a safe place whose safety is threatened and finally penetrated by a hostile external force. This is a situation of great importance in the early world of the infant, before the passionate fears and desires that are a feature of the ego-centred fantasy of this period of life are partially overlaid by the influences of education and social relationships; the safe place must originally be the mother's body, while the threat must arise from the injuries the infant, in fantasy, inflicts on that body. It can indeed be said that many of Pinter's characters, possibly all of them at the level at which they are most real to us, represent alternating bad aspects – aggressive and threatening or lost and persecuted – of that primitive infantile self which Pinter rightly sees surviving concealed but unimpaired into adult life; this basic primitive self is the dominating part of his adult character's everyday lives. It is thus, in dramatic terms, un-historical and timeless, though the psychoanalyst would trace its historical origins in the early life of the individual. This is surely the reason why Pinter likes to isolate his characters from the wide social context which is an inevitable part of life in the actual world, presenting them in a timeless social and psychological vacuum where only the present seems real; though characters come and go, there is a sense in which there is no way out of the room we see on the stage into the Goldhawk Road or on to the sea front. At the most real level, there is nowhere to go, for outside is not a place but a state of mind (šource primarily of persecutory invasion), an impression that adds greatly to the claustrophobic intensity of the plays and in one instance, *The Caretaker*, provides a climax of tragic power. Similarly, information about the charac-ters' lives at the observable historical level, their antecedents, occupations, and family and social relationships, is either with-held altogether or offered in a fragmentary form; his people normally possess only a single name, as in *The Birthday Party*, *The Caretaker*, *A Slight Ache*, and are often defined by age alone, a man in his sixties, a girl in her twenties, etc. This isolation and lack of definition in his characters and their environment is especially marked in his work up to 1960; since then, especially in *The Collection* and *The Homecoming*, he has shown rather more concern with the social surface, which had indeed been the staple of at least one earlier play, *A Night Out*, probably the most realistic and least obviously mysterious of his plays to date. However, it is doubtful whether his basic preoccupation has changed much; in his most successful work there is a subtle blend of what Pinter himself has called the 'recognizable reality of the absurdity of what we do and how we behave and how we speak'[8] with an exposure of the more primitive and basic levels of existence. As one would expect, Pinter has shown himself well aware of this central feature of his work; in answer to a complaint of Kenneth Tynan's that he wrote plays 'unconcerned with ideas and showing only a very limited aspect of the life of their characters, omitting their politics, ideas, and even their sex life', Pinter replied that he was 'dealing with his characters at the extreme edge of their living, where they are living very much alone'.[9] The lack of a past or future in their lives he defends in a similar way: 'We are only concerned with what is happening then, in this particular moment of these people's lives. There is no reason to suppose that at one time they did not listen at a political meeting . . . or that they haven't ever had girl friends.'[10] If this seems to concede rather too much of his opponent's assumptions, still it makes the point clearly enough: 'The point is, who are you? Not why or how, not even what . . .'[11]

The plays up to *The Homecoming* thus unfold a metaphor of the primitive self, in direct, concrete terms that avoid the abstractions of deliberate allegory, a self dominated by the basic drives of hunger, rivalry, the need for love, the intolerance of dependence; its key activity the struggle for possession, its key method of relationship a tense evasion of communication, its key image that of two people in a safe place and a threatening presence without, leading to the expulsion of the victim and a successful take-over by the intruder of the valued place or object, the room in the play of that name and in *The Caretaker*, the room and the woman together in *A Slight Ache* and *The Birthday Party*. There are of course many variations in the pattern – in *The Room* the blind negro who is the victim of the final savage attack seems to be an intruder but is clearly staking an earlier claim – but it is none the less extraordinarily consistent; the roll-call of victims and their persecutors includes Riley, the negro, kicked into insensibility by Mr Hudd in *The Room*, Stanley driven into insanity and taken away in the Rolls by Goldberg and McCann in *The Birthday Party*, and Gus stripped and presumably shot by his fellow-conspirator Ben in *The Dumb Waiter*. With less violence and more subtlety, Teddy is forced to abandon his wife to his predatory family in *The Homecoming*, a subtlety that is at its best in *The Caretaker*, where Aston mourns the lost happiness of his hallucinatory visions before 'they put the pincers on his head' and Davies, the tramp, is quietly but finally expelled from his haven, the lumber-room which may have offered a special security because of the absence, in this play, of female characters; rivalry for the woman, in Pinter, provokes a particularly destructive competitiveness. The image of the safe place must be taken to represent fundamentally the woman as mother; in the plays of this period in which she appears, woman seems to occupy one of the complex primary roles she fills in infantile fantasy, that of a mother figure whose protectiveness towards the child is undermined in various ways by the child's greedy or envious attacks. *The Caretaker* is the most human of Pinter's plays not only in the greater fullness and richness of character relationship it deploys but also in that the expulsion is due in part to the victim's own vanity and treachery; it may indeed be thought that it alone of Pinter's plays transcends the limits set by his seemingly obsessional concern with primitive realities, and so achieves something of the complex human effect of traditional tragedy. For this reason, however, these realities – what Pinter has called 'the root of the relationship' – are more clearly exposed in the earlier, cruder, plays, and it is to one of these, Pinter's first full-length play, *The Birthday Party*, that I now turn.

In the first act we are rapidly introduced to what is clearly the basic family situation of mother, father and child (we remember the two people in the room and the one who is going to open the door and come in). In the child's role is Stanley, described as 'a man in his late thirties',[12] who for some time now has been occupying a room in the house of an elderly couple, Meg and Petey, in a seaside town. As is common form in Pinter, obscurity surrounds Stanley's situation; he seems on rather dubious evidence to have been a pianist – at one point he indulges in a reverie about past success as a concert pianist, which, however, seems primarily designed to deceive the credulous Meg – but his life with Meg and Petey is characterized by almost total inactivity; we get the impression that, like a very small child, he seldom if ever goes out. (Later he tells McCann, '. . . all those years I lived in Basingstoke I never stepped outside the door.')[13] What is soon clear enough, however, is the nature of his relationship with the couple, especially Meg. Petey, a deck-chair attendant, is the character least affected by the nightmare world evoked in the play; a decent, inarticulate man, he is drawn into it only so far as to be unable to resist its destruction of Stanley. With Meg, a muddled, feeble-minded creature, almost a 'natural', Stanley occupies the role of favoured only son, resentful of his dependence on a woman who oppresses him with her affection and repels him by the obvious excitement she derives from the relationship. A coy, flirtatious archness characterizes her talk with him; as she says in her speech celebrating his birthday, ' . . . He's my Stanley now. And I think he's a good boy, although sometimes he's bad. . . . I know him better than all the world, although he doesn't think so.'[14] In the first scene, in a typical Pinter exchange where he plays her up unmercifully – not difficult as she is so simple-minded – over the repulsive breakfast she insists he is enjoying, she concludes by telling him, 'You deserve the strap', and 'ruffles his hair as she passes'; from this and other more amorous displays of her feeling for him, such as 'a sensual stroking of his arm', he recoils in disgust.[15] The crucial development in their relationship comes when two strangers 'open the door and come in'; apparently 'two gentlemen who want a room for a couple of nights' in 'a very good boarding house . . . a house on the list',[16] Meg's description, although her house up to now had only one visitor, Stanley. They turn out to be sinister figures, a heady blend of savagery and false bonhomie, who with the unwilling, partly unconscious connivance of the rest of the cast set about the destruction of Stanley, the favoured child – significantly enough, on a day they claim to be his birthday: the inference may be drawn that his crime, in their eyes, is simply to have been born. 'There's a gentleman living here . . . who's got a birthday today, and he's forgotten all about it. So we're going to remind him',[17] says the senior of the two men, Goldberg. No other reason need thus be given for their hostility, and none is given; with brilliant economy, Pinter simultaneously suggests the implacable jealousy of the excluded children to the favoured one, and, at a different level, draws on our recollections of the millions victimized in our own time simply for being what they were, by birth and race.

Why cannot Meg protect her favourite, when she recognizes, however vaguely, that he is menaced by the strangers' presence, attempting to offer reassurance to his anxiety ('Stan, they won't wake you up, I promise. I'll tell them they must be quiet. They won't be here long, Stan. I'll still bring up your early morning tea')?[18] On one level of course she is simply not their match – a foolish, at times almost imbecile, elderly woman faced by a secret conspiracy of which she has no conscious inkling; this gives them an overwhelming advantage, especially in Pinter's claustrophobic world, where there is no help from without. Indeed, one of the few moments in the play when we are aware of an awkward tension between the actual and the metaphorical occurs when Petey, who unlike the major characters inhabits the real world and who unlike Meg realizes what is being done to Stanley, proves equally helpless; it is momentarily impossible to suspend disbelief. However, on any reading of the text there is more to it than this. Stanley's resentment of Meg's possessiveness and naïve eroticism has already been noted. When he discovers she has bought him a child's drum for a birthday present, he at first gratifies her whim and like the good little boy part of himself for whom the present is intended kisses her in thanks and 'marches round the table, beating it regularly'. But on his second march round the table there is a dramatic instance of that violent ambivalence of feeling I have already noted in chapter two as characteristic of infantile experience: 'the beat becomes erratic, uncontrolled' and by the time he arrives back at her chair, to her dismay 'his face and the drumbeat [are] now savage and possessed'.[19] The climax comes in the play's central act, the birthday party itself, when in a scene of hysterical confusion Stanley, blindfold, seizes Meg by the throat and tries to strangle her. As he advances on Meg McCann places the drum in his way, so that he 'falls over with his foot caught in it'. Rising, 'he begins to move towards Meg, dragging the drum on his foot.' The child's drum is thus associated with the attack; moreover, with the drum on his foot Stanley suddenly appears before our eyes as Oedipus, Swellfoot.[20] The party game, blind man's buff, has been chosen by Meg, abetted by Stanley's would-be girl friend, Lulu; it is perhaps suggestive of an answering hostility, unconscious though it be, that she should choose the activity that leads directly to his ruin. Another curious piece of evidence suggests that she shares with him a dim foreknowledge of his death, and perhaps entertains an unconscious wish for it. In the first act, immediately after she has created an intense anxiety in Stanley by her news that 'two gentlemen' are coming to stay (an anxiety he attempts to deny by his grandiose fantasy of success as a concert pianist), the two of them participate in one of Pinter's tense question and answer games; Stanley rapidly excites Meg to a pitch of terrified anticipation. The burden of his news is that 'they' are 'coming today' with a 'wheelbarrow in a van'; they 'wheel it up the garden path and knock at the front door' because 'they're looking for someone. A certain person.'[21] Later, in Act Three, the morning after the débâcle of the party, Meg innocently supposes Stan to be simply late down to breakfast, as usual, when in fact he has already been reduced to a gibbering wreck by the two visitors, Goldberg and McCann. At a deeper level, however, she shows an awareness of what has happened and of what is yet to happen. A large car is parked outside – the car in whose boot, it is implied by Goldberg, Stanley is shortly to be removed – and she asks Petey in a tense whisper, '. . . is there a wheelbarrow in it?';[22] she has clearly not forgotten the earlier talk with Stanley, or its meaning. Finally, her reaction to the horrible events of the party is curious and striking: we learn from Petey that 'she slept like a log'.[23] Attributable perhaps to shock, this fact, and her amnesia over the whole affair of Stanley's attack on her and his subsequent fate, suggests also the satisfaction of some need, especially when she concludes, in talking over the affair with Petey at breakfast, that Goldberg and McCann are 'old friends' of Stanley's. There is thus a level at which not only the intruding couple but mother and son also may be felt to be engaged in a conspiracy of their own, the purpose of which is to undermine and subvert a good relationship between them.

The pattern of the inner psychic meaning of the play can now perhaps be discerned. As I have suggested in a previous chapter, clinical experience in psychoanalysis suggests that the child may attempt in unconscious fantasy to sexualize his relationship with the mother in order to deny his painful awareness of smallness and dependence and, in the Oedipal situation, be in a position to challenge the father, and possibly other male rivals, for possession of her. Envy of the mother's independence and capacity to feed him, greed for her bounty, and anxiety over what will happen to him if she abandons him, combine to make this fantasy aggressive, liable to damage the mother and reduce her to the status of an object for the evacuation of his sexual feelings. She is now felt to be under his control, her freedom no longer a potent source of anxiety; but his sense of her capacity to feed and care for him has been severely affected. (It may be taken as symptomatic that the milk Meg provides for Stanley's cornflakes in the opening scene of the play is 'off', as he bitterly notes.[24]) The situation can thus rapidly become persecutory for the child, first through identification with the damaged mother figure, the object, it must be remembered, of his love and gratitude as well as his envious attacks. The persecution may then be experienced as retributive punishment for the fantasied attack. Sadism and masochism are thus experienced in the same consciousness, a sufficient reason, it may be thought, for the curiously close and dependent relationship of aggressor and victim throughout Pinter's plays. Furthermore, the hostile feelings accompanying the act may be projected into the parent, who then becomes herself a persecutory figure. In *The Birthday Party*, the first source of persecution is clearly the more important; Meg is a damaged rather than a directly persecutory figure, this role being reserved for others. Projection, however, may be supposed to play a part in the sexualization of the relationship of mother and child. In the play as we have it it is Meg who makes the sexual advances to Stanley; in the given circumstances of their two characters this is perfectly convincing. However, it is also possible to see this attitude of Meg's, in terms of the play's inner meaning, as a projection into the mother of the child's own sexual wishes in order to deny his ownership of them. Stanley, it will be recollected, is a very repressed personality, to whom denial must be a central activity; in one of his rare expansive moments there is a tacit acknowledgment of such denial, at this point, of Meg's importance to him. 'Look at her. You're just an old piece of rock cake, aren't you?'[25] Strikingly enough, what may be called the characteristic negative components in the child's attitude to the mother – his possessiveness, his sexual fantasies and his hostility, are all attitudes found in Meg, the last at an appropriately unconscious level; that she herself is a figure of childlike innocence surely adds to the convincingness of a psychic situation that can be experienced both directly and in terms of a projected reversal of roles. It is also true that the child's unconscious fantasies about the mother are likely to be greatly stimulated by finding an actual response, in fact not fantasy, from her; fantasies that find support from the facts, as they are bound often to do, simply take a firmer root. It is part of Pinter's achievement to blend without effort what may be described as the literal and metaphorical meanings of the play, which thus enrich rather than contradict each other. The simultaneous existence of the plays at both a realistic and expressionistic level may recall a comparable achievement in the poetic drama of the past; the work of Pinter, Beckett, and others is perhaps more truly the successor of such drama than deliberate attempts to revive the verse form.

Persecution, on any possible interpretation, is the central theme of *The Birthday Party*. The main, many would feel the only, source of this persecution is not Meg but the two strangers, of the same sex as their victim, one older and one younger, conspirators who Iago-like establish a nearly absolute control over the action as the play develops. In the play's inner meaning, their part is surely that of the hostile jealous siblings who deal out condign punishment to the usurping child, whose chief crime in their eyes is simply to exist. Once again, fantasy may be supported by reality. The younger child may sense the objective hostility and resentment of the other siblings whose place with the mother he has in some degree taken over; but the persecutory quality of this variant of the Oedipal situation may be immensely reinforced by his guilt over fantasied attacks on the mother. The siblings' attack may then be experienced as further retribution not only for his attempts to deny them their rights by an exclusive possession of the mother but also, and more seriously, for his savage attacks upon her, which on his own showing can only merit punishment. Herein lies the importance of Pinter's presentation of the ambivalent hostile relationship of Meg and Stanley that I have tried to describe; it is the essential foundation, very accurately presented, for the persecution that develops out of it. There may again be an element of projection in the child's fear of persecution, in fact or fantasy, by sibling rivals; his own feelings of envious or jealous hatred may be put out into the siblings by a kind of deflection from their principal objects, the parents. Certainly, Stanley's savage though frustrated attacks upon Meg (the drum scene and the party scene) find an exact correspondence in the savagery meted out to him, a fact that might suggest an element of projection as well as retribution in the process.

Stanley's attitude when he hears of the intruders' approach and his whole subsequent relationship with them, and also their relationship with the parental couple, may be thought to provide striking support for this view of the inner psychic meaning of *The Birthday Party*. The weakness of the parents in contrast to the strength of the siblings suggests a situation in which the child is left naked and exposed to the siblings' attack precisely because his own attacks on the parents have enfeebled them and left them impotent to protect him. Meg from the outset is a pathetic, partly ruined figure, strongly suggestive of a mother damaged in fantasy by the child's attacks; she is close cousin in this respect to Rose of *The Room*, an earlier play by Pinter. Petey, the father-figure, is a benevolent but ineffectual character whose helplessness in the final scene, where he realizes that Stanley is being tormented but proves powerless to intervene, has been prepared for throughout the play by his inferior status *vis-à-vis* the other men. Meg, though clearly dependent on him, as clearly prefers Stanley, a preference later extended to Goldberg and McCann, whose presence excites her and causes her to behave with a girlish coquetry. She has no breakfast for Petey the morning after the party – not even cornflakes and sour milk – for 'the two gentlemen had the last of the fry this morning'.[26] Admittedly, he connives with her attitude by asking nothing for himself; at the end of the play he is still protecting her against the truth of what has happened to Stan. As a study in simple but ineffectual goodness he anticipates in some ways Aston in *The Caretaker*. Ineffectuality in a practical sense is the hallmark of the couple as such; it is in the strongest possible contrast to the resistlessness of the intruding siblings, who alternately seduce, deceive, and badger them into total submission. Goodness in Pinter is normally ineffectual, just as strength is normally violent and sadistic; the most meaningful relationships in his plays are sado-masochistic in nature.

Stanley's reaction when he hears of the 'two gentlemen' who are coming to stay immediately presents us with an aspect of him as threatened child. He is immediately anxious, an anxiety itself suggestive of guilt in the absence of any objective evidence as to why he should fear them; when straightforward denial ('They won't come')[27] fails to calm his fears, he attempts to assert his rights over Meg as though in defiance of the challenge to come ('Tell me, Mrs Boles, when you address yourself to me, do you ever ask yourself who exactly you are talking to? Eh?'). Meg's placatory mention of his skill as a pianist immediately offers another way out – the indulgence already mentioned in a grandiose fantasy about his past success as a concert pianist. The way the fantasy develops is noteworthy: first the dazzling success '(Champagne we had that night, the lot'),[28] then the sudden malignant attack that robs him of the fruits of triumph ('Then after that, you know what they did? They carved me up.').[29] The omnipotent fantasy that is designed to render the child invulnerable to attack is shot through by paranoid fears that suggest the child's own aggression coming back at him in projected form, an aggression that is likely to be further stimulated in its turn by the omnipotence. In this context, we may recall the savage outburst at Meg. The

paranoia emerges directly in the question-and-answer sequence
with Meg about the wheelbarrow which 'they' are 'bringing in
a van' because 'they're looking for someone. A certain person . . .';[30]
Stanley's pretty exact anticipation of what is to be done to him
suggests that there is in fact a reason for it, a reason that must be
sought not in the world of external fact but in the exact correspondences of the inner world, where a fantasied attack may
provoke a precisely similar punishment. Two aspects of the
relationship of Goldberg and McCann with Stanley lend incidental
support to the view that their role is essentially that of siblings.
First, though we are left in ignorance of when and even whether
they have met before, there is a hint that Stanley recognizes
Goldberg; when Meg asks, 'Do you know them?' he does not
answer. Later, when he first meets McCann, he asks him in an
agitated whisper, 'Has [Goldberg] told you anything? Do you
know what you're here for? Tell me.'[31] Second, both Goldberg
and McCann show signs of nervous agitation and stress after
Stanley has been effectively destroyed. Tension steadily rises in
Goldberg during a scene[32] where Petey, uneasy about Stanley, is
met with an equally uneasy evasiveness; on Petey's departure the
tension is suddenly released in a 'murderous' attack on McCann,
whose own manifest agitation has provoked him to an obscure
insult to his partner. McCann is forced to expiate this insult in a
homosexual episode in which he blows into Goldberg's mouth.
Both the conspirators seem unable to face the evidence of their
crime; McCann is desperately eager to '. . . get it over and go. . . .
Let's finish the bloody thing . . . go and get him'[33] (the wreck of
Stanley is upstairs in the bedroom); Goldberg procrastinates. On
the realistic level, their reaction may indicate simply that they
are not so hardened that they can torment and destroy a fellow
human being without remorse; it may also suggest, on the metaphorical level, guilt over the attack on a brother about whom
feelings are likely to be ambivalent, however consciously hostile.

In Act Two, Stanley has already come face to face with the
intruders, who submit him to a softening-up process in preparation
for the *coup de grâce* at the party. In a preliminary skirmish he
attempts alternate placation and defiance of his tormentors; the
combination of feebleness and violence in his challenge provokes
from them an increasingly rapid pressure of questions and insults
until the desired response is obtained – a scream, a desperate

thwarted attack on Goldberg. The content of their persecutory sequence is striking: Stanley is accused of 'force[ing] that old man out to play chess' and 'driving that old lady off her conk'; he is a 'Mother defiler' whose 'old mum' is 'in the sanatorium' (this, apparently, on his own admission).[34] The accuracy of these charges in terms of what I have suggested the play's inner meaning to be will be noted; this is the possessive predatory child who thrusts the father out of doors and drives the mother mad with his Oedipal sexual assaults. The punishment is made to fit the crime, a symbolic castration by blinding that savagely disposes of the child's vaunted sexuality. During the sequence Stanley's glasses are snatched off; later he recovers them, only to lose them again to McCann at the climax of the party when he is forced to take his turn at blind-man's-buff. McCann's deliberate breaking of his glasses while Stanley is blindfold marks the beginning of their final assault on him;[35] at his last appearance in Act Three, a wordless wreck who can only mouth meaningless sounds, he carries his broken glasses in his hand.[36] The two conditions of blindness and castration are verbally associated in the persecutory sequence of the second act: 'Wake him up,' says McCann. 'Stick a needle in his eye', to which Goldberg adds a moment later, 'We can sterilize you. . . . What makes you think you exist?'[37] In Act Three Stanley, now broken and passive, is subjected to another mocking verbal assault in which they openly exult over his condition, 'wooing him gently and with relish'.[38]

Goldberg	Between you and me, Stan, it's about time you had a new pair of glasses.
McCann	You can't see straight.
Goldberg	It's true. You've been cockeyed for years.[39]
McCann	Now you're even more cockeyed.
Goldberg	He's right. You've gone from bad to worse.

The point is made clearly enough, though with characteristic economy and unobtrusiveness. The predatory child is violently extruded from the safe place by his rivals, who in their ruthlessness echo his own wishes and fantasies in magnified form; in literal terms the safe place is, of course, the boarding house, while symbolically it must represent the interior of the mother's body he has damaged with his spoiling attacks.

Meg, the symbolic mother, plays the principal woman's role

in this fantasy, but she is given appropriate support by Lulu, Stanley's girl friend. At the climactic scene of the party Lulu is the subject of an hysterical appeal by Stanley that threatens to take the form of a sexual assault on her. Following immediately on his attack on Meg, this act is the appropriate signal for the persecutors to close in on their victim; it is the last time we see Stanley sane. Later that night Lulu is seduced by Goldberg. Stanley's attack on her, followed by her betrayal of him with a rival, reinforces our sense of the nature of his crime and corresponding punishment; the woman he looks to for succour – mother or mate – who is, however, also the destined victim of his aggressive sexual designs, is the occasion of his ruin. In her last appearance Lulu summarizes the theme of the play in a phrase applicable both to its external events and its inner meaning; 'An old woman nearly killed and a man gone mad.'[40] Displayed before us in the play we thus find 'at the root of their relationship' an enacted fantasy of early life, with the exact correspondences which in fantasy and dream betray the unconscious intentions behind them. The child's aggressive designs on the mother, sexualized by the denial of dependence and powered by greed and envy, return on him with interest. They are experienced first in the form of a masked hostility from her and then, directly, as a ferocious retribution from the rival siblings, the father having been rendered effectually impotent. The act of retribution is part of the fantasy, through projection and identification, though it may be reinforced by the presence of an external hostility displayed by rivals of the same sex.

To interpret the play in the way I have suggested does not preclude interpretation in other terms; it is part of its strength that it exists adequately, if strangely, at a realistic level, a confirmation perhaps of Pinter's remark, in speaking of his characters, that '[these] people always remain for me quite real; if they were not, the play could not be written'.[41] Pinter is skilful at maintaining the kind of relationship between the actual world and the 'Pinter' world of compulsive fantasy that prevents any permanent gap opening up between them. Some other interpretations are considered by Martin Esslin in *The Theatre of the Absurd*. He speculates whether the two strangers are 'emissaries of a secret organization he [Stanley] has betrayed? Or male nurses sent to fetch him back to an asylum . . . ? Or emissaries from another world?' and of the play as a whole remarks that it has been seen as an allegory of conformity, and also of death: 'man snatched away from the home he has built for himself by the dark angels of nothingness. . . . ' Dissatisfied with these interpretations, he continues:[42]

> a play like this . . . explores a situation that, in itself, is a valid poetic image that is immediately seen as relevant and true. It speaks plainly of the individual's pathetic search for security; of secret dreads and anxieties; of the terrorism of our world, so often embodied in false bonhomie and bigoted brutality; of the tragedy that arises from lack of understanding. . . .

Esslin is surely right in suggesting that conscious allegorizing, in the expressionist vein, is alien to Pinter: 'I think it is impossible – and certainly for me – to start writing a play from any kind of abstract idea. . . .'[43] However, an interpretation in analytical terms allows us to be more specific than Esslin judges to be possible, without any such assumption of the author working consciously to a preconceived idea. I would argue that we enrich our experience of the play and come nearest to an understanding of its emotional effect when we see how clearly it expresses the pattern of a paranoid fantasy whose origins are in the infantile world. A dramatic experience that has the force that inheres in the concrete and the actual is seen to possess also a meaningful pattern; the paradox of seemingly inconsequential material, especially in the dialogue, that yet rivets the attention, is resolved. There is admittedly a price to pay for the fullness and concentration with which the fantasy of persecutory anxiety is presented. In the first place, the characters retain so close a link with their primitive selves that as adult human beings their appeal is limited; Meg's feebleness of mind and lack of understanding, and Stanley's repressed apathy, allow only so much scope for sympathetic identification. Second, the primitive self that is displayed is largely, though not entirely, negative and destructive. Though love is present, in Meg and Petey, it is enfeebled and easily defeated, from internal weakness as much as external pressure. Similarly, the guilt that temporarily affects Goldberg and McCann is easily put aside; in the context of the finale, a paean of sadistic triumph over Stanley and, by implication, over Meg and Petey also, it is totally ineffectual and leads to no sort of reparation. For both reasons – and they are closely connected – the aggressive and destructive impulses are not mitigated or restrained by any love and understanding, as they must be in life if the infant is to survive or the adult to retain his sanity. In one way, this concentration is part of the play's strength. But it may be doubted whether *The Birthday Party* fully attains the peculiar emotional effect of tragedy, since though the material contains both pity and terror, the range of feeling it commands is so narrowly negative.

This limitation is perhaps characteristic of Pinter's work as a whole to date, with the single but significant exception of *The Caretaker*. In this play, which followed *The Birthday Party* in 1960, three years later, he achieves a much more complex human effect while retaining and developing the characteristic themes and preoccupations of his earlier work. A meaningful contact is established between two victims of life, both prisoners of their own natures: Davies, the tramp, traditional outcast of society, and Aston, the maimed man, victim of society's currently fashionable method of physical treatment of mental illness. The failure of this relationship, and Davies's subsequent expulsion from the lumber room that is the play's only setting, provide a climax that in its reverberative pathos may be truly called tragic. It is perhaps significant that the play is considerably more realistic than *The Birthday Party*; the gap between the actual world and the 'Pinter' world has been sensibly reduced, in that the point of balance has been moved away from what seems arbitrary and inexplicable in terms other than those of primitive symbolism and closer to what is normally observable in daily social and personal life. Both in its realism and in its moral complexity *The Caretaker* is closer to later, that is adult, experience, than the earlier plays; the behaviour and attitudes of the characters are less dominated by infantile fantasies. The unexplained murderous violence has been replaced, at the play's most significant point, by an act of rejection, more explicable in terms of all that has gone before and more tragic in its implications; a change, as Pinter has explained, from the original plan: 'The original idea . . . . was . . . to end the play with the violent death of the tramp. . . . It suddenly struck me that it was not necessary. And I think that in this play . . . I have developed. . . .'[44] Moreover, although the lumber room, cluttered up with useless or misused[45] machines, is an effective symbol of the fragmentariness and disconnectedness of human experience, two of the three characters are provided with historical antecedents which go some way to explain their conduct. It is in keeping with this that the characters, less confined to their primitive roles, are more fully and richly conceived and so more capable of exacting a wide range of emotional response – amusement, pity, anger, identification. Aston is perhaps the only fully-drawn portrait of potential human goodness in Pinter's work. He is shown as genuinely capable of benevolent impulses, impulses frustrated by the stupidity and ingratitude of Davies; with a queer honesty he recognizes Davies's faults as incurable, at any rate by him. The sympathy we feel for him is the greater in that he is without self-pity. His words and actions tell of a ruined man who has endured his crisis long before the duration of the play and who maintains a precarious hold on life and identity by certain repeated rituals, tinkering purposively but to no apparent effect with electrical gadgets, 'working with . . . good wood', taking a walk down the Goldhawk Road. His stability – and he impresses us as an exceptionally solid and stable character for Pinter – like his benevolence and honesty, seems paradoxically associated with the fact of his illness; as 'normal' characters in Pinter behave for the most part in a primitive and irrational fashion, it is the less surprising than an 'abnormal' character should appear relatively civilized and rational. Implicit perhaps in the characterization of Aston is the suggestion that the despised and rejected – fools, madmen, the mentally sick – are really the salt of the earth; this is the traditional outsider's claim, and it might be expected to appeal to Pinter, with his preference, as an artist, for the primitive over the civilized.

Davies, the central figure of *The Caretaker*, is Pinter's most Shakespearean character, an Everyman of the Drama of the Absurd who transcends its limits to become, like Falstaff or Parolles, a figure of comedy in the most serious sense of the word; he achieves universality through his personification of human weaknesses – vanity, stupid cunning, ingratitude, a pathetic capacity for self-deception. A realistic study, he is also at home in the dramatist's unmistakably personal world of fantasy; his creation is a remarkable feat, the most striking piece of character-ization Pinter has yet achieved. Mick, Aston's enigmatic younger brother, concludes his recital of Davies's faults with the words: 'And to put the tin lid on it, you stink from arse-hole to breakfast time.'[46] The accusation is obviously well-founded; the human stinks – but none the less in Davies it remains the human, in the attempt to retain dignity and self-respect in circumstances of oppressive humiliation, in the capacity for genuine if fragmentary contact with others, in the pathos of the self-defeating search for a safe place, a room of one's own.

The third person of the play, Mick, Aston's younger brother, is a less satisfactory character precisely to the degree in which he belongs to the earlier, more primitive world of *The Room* and *The Birthday Party*. As dramatic material, he is inadequately assimilated to the world of *The Caretaker*, a sufficient explanation of the uneasiness we feel about him. His attitude to Davies is sadistic in a way familiar from the earlier plays, though it is not clear how seriously the persecution is intended; often he seems merely to be playing with him. At their first meeting he terrorizes the old man as though he were a dangerous intruder rather than his brother's guest; subsequently he teases him by alternating bouts of genteel mock-politeness (Goldberg's tone in *The Birthday Party*) laced with semi-nonsensical reminiscence, and savage practical jokes. Finally with a more subtle sadism he deceives him into believing that he will support him against Aston, Davies's real protector and friend; he thus brings out the worst in Davies, exploiting all his pitiful moral weaknesses merely in order to trip him up with them and cast him brutally out. The lack of explanation and suggested motive for his mischief-making actions throws him into sharp contrast with the other two: why does he treat Davies in this manner? ('You've been playing me about, you know. I don't know why. I never done you no harm'[47]) What are we to make of this enigmatic attitude towards Aston? Or of his sudden modulation to a tone of seriousness, even passion, at the moment of Davies's expulsion, when he breaks the statue of the Buddha? In one production of the play[48] an attempt was made to get over the difficulty by an interpretation in terms of neurotic stress. It was an interpretation that underlined the split in the conception of the character, for it could offer only a partial explanation of his words and actions; with the part as we have it, the cool mocking self-assurance so characteristic of Mick cannot comfortably be interpreted in this way. Pinter does not seem to have provided a consistent foundation for the character in the context of the play as a whole; a way of portraying character that proved triumphantly successful when consistently applied in *The Birthday Party* sticks out here like the proverbial sore thumb. There is perhaps an explanation for the curious effect he produces: that, far from being, like his brother, a neurotic victim, he is in fact in control of the whole action of the play. At the beginning, he is shown alone on the stage, as though waiting silently for the play to begin; at the end, he engineers the climax of Davies's fall from pride to humiliation. In watching the play I have had the sense, from time to time, that Mick's actions are explicable less in terms of the sadistic control he exercises over Davies in the play, than of the aesthetic control the dramatist exercises over his characters in composing the play. In other words, he enjoys a special relationship to his creator, his privileged role representing perhaps to Pinter a concentration of that primitive interest in 'the roots of the relationship' which inspired *The Birthday Party*. Characters who are close to the dramatist in the special sense of being, so to speak, in his confidence, and thus enjoying a secret understanding of and power over the rest of the cast, are found, of course, in earlier drama; Iago is an obvious example. It is then the business of the dramatist to assimilate such characters to the general life of the play; when this assimilation is successful, as with Iago, the character can exist without strain at two levels and move freely between them. As I have suggested, Pinter seems to me to fail with Mick here; the failure, it must be emphasized, is not in the role, which is brilliantly conceived and necessary to the total effect, but in the characterization. There is a kind of transparency in the character, as though he were simultaneously within and without the framework of the play; he impresses me as acting the part of a man who enjoys sadistic teasing rather than actually being, fictionally and dramatically speaking, such a man. Some of Mick's talk recalls strongly the style of cabaret and revue sketches, a genre at which Pinter has tried his hand; in such sketches, a character may be in as direct relationship with the audience as with other members of the cast. There is perhaps a risk that Pinter's extraordinary virtuosity in dialogue should flourish at the expense of more serious effects; the dialogue he writes for Mick, though undoubtedly entertaining, has the quality at times of a virtuoso solo performance undertaken at the expense of the other instruments of the trio and of the total aesthetic effect.

If in ways such as I have outlined *The Caretaker* achieves its effects on a more adult and less primitive level, the themes of the play retain a force that derives from the close contact preserved with primitive impulses and ways of feeling. This may be seen first in the shape of the play, which has a balance and symmetry, and also a polarization between good and evil, characteristic of fundamental relationships. The duration of the play is a fortnight; its plot could be described, simply, as the process of first taking Davies in and then getting him out. Its central rhythm is of a fragile human contact that, under the impact of Davies's moral fragility and its exploitation by Mick for unexplained purposes of his own, rapidly dissipates itself; its central action sees the attainment by Davies of the safe place and his subsequent expulsion from it. (His marriage, we recall, also lasted a fortnight.) The sense of security, of belonging somewhere, that Davies begins to enjoy is undermined and finally wrecked by his own greedy and envious impulses: greed provokes him to ask for more than he can hope to receive, and so lose what little he has gained; envy makes Aston's goodness repugnant to him in itself, simply for being what it is. In psychoanalytical terms this recalls the basic relationship of the dependent child to the mother, and the harm that may be done to the relationship by such hostile impulses; the struggle in the dependent child between loving and hostile impulses towards the protecting parent is mirrored in Davies's see-saw relationship to Aston. The finale gains its tragic force not only from its enactment of the damaging consequences of greed and envy but from the victim's own awareness of how much he has contributed to the disaster. His final appeal to Aston breaks through the barriers of evasiveness and self-pity to base itself clearly on an acknowledgment of guilt and responsibility; it is an attempt to undo the damage he has done. To be capable of such an acknowledgment is evidence that the good impulses are still alive in him and that he is still in contact with them; we thus have here a classical tragic situation in which we contemplate not simply the destruction of the victim but the fall of the hero through his own *hamartia*, the tragic waste of a potentially good relationship. There is a marked contrast to *The Birthday Party*;

though there are clear indications of Stanley's savage feelings towards Meg, the more virulent aggression is projected into the two intruders, so that Stanley is seen increasingly in the victim's role. Here the aggression is much more fully contained within the central character, Davies; despite Mick's more primitively aggressive role, it is in Davies that the main battle between good and evil in the play is deployed. It could be said that the situation in *The Caretaker* is less persecutory and more depressive; Melanie Klein has argued that very early in life the child becomes afraid of the damage his destructive feelings may have done to his loved objects, and so 'experiences feelings of guilt and the urge to preserve these objects and to make reparation to them for harm done'.[49] The anxiety and depression he experiences at a later stage of development than persecutory anxiety thus has a a creative potential, for the capacity to make reparation is an important part of successful relationships in later life. There is a kind of hope at the end of *The Caretaker*, not so much in spite of but because of the tragic pathos; the experience is essentially that of loss, and to feel loss it is necessary to remain in touch with the lost object and accept its value. A sense of spiritual enlargement that can only arise from positive feelings such as hope is sometimes held to be a central feature of tragic experience; *The Caretaker* is closer to this traditional concept of tragedy, as it is found in Greek drama, Shakespeare and Ibsen, than is at all common in modern drama.

There is one other feature of *The Caretaker* that perhaps supports the view that Pinter intends an effect closer to traditional tragedy in this play. Conversation in his plays, if not directly sado-masochistic, seems for the most part to serve two contrasting but related purposes; repetitive, wary, often circling interminably round a topic without coming to grips with it, it embodies first a need to get into contact with the other in order to relieve isolation, a reaching out from the deeply ego-centred self which Pinter sees, dramatically speaking, as the protective core of personality. However, it is also a device for evading the reality of relationship with the other, as the very failure to make effective contact shows, for fear of what real contact would reveal.[50] In much of Pinter talk, and indeed activity, is an ineffectual defence against the thinly concealed violence 'at the roots of their relationship', a way, in the words of Davies in another context, of 'keeping the

Blacks at bay'. The second purpose is usually felt to be the more pressing; better, it seems, to use talk in order to avoid communication and suffer the ensuing isolation, than get into real contact by a breakthrough in communication and have to face the frightening primitive reality that lurks below the surface. In *The Caretaker* talk does indeed possess this primary defensive function, notably in Davies's evasions and withdrawals and Aston's strained hesitancies; the dangerous moment for their relationship, full of harm for the future, comes with Aston's great speech describing his illness and its treatment, where he temporarily abandons his halting, inconsequential style of speech to reveal something of his 'real' self to Davies.[51] However, there is also the feeling, more powerfully conveyed than elsewhere in Pinter, of talk used successfully for genuine human contact; in the exchanges between Davies and Aston in the first act, we have the impression of a growing relationship between the two based on mutual needs. Aston's silences are of the same order; in his patient, fatherly refusal to respond to Davies's childish lies and complaints he is concerned to protect not himself but Davies. It may, finally, be significant that the humour in this play, especially in these early exchanges, is so delightful; in its own way, it suggests a greater awareness of human potentiality.

Five years after *The Caretaker*, in 1965, another full-length play by Pinter appeared, *The Homecoming*; this play shows both a continuity with his past work and striking new developments in the handling of familiar themes and images. It possesses the primitive directness and uninhibitedness of *The Birthday Party* but is concerned, like *The Caretaker*, with a more adult level of relationship. The nature of the relationships within the play are admittedly bleak and brutal enough, without the humanity and pathos of *The Caretaker*; but there is less concern with persecutory terrors and more direct adult competition for the desired object, here once again a woman. The basic Pinter image – the safe place whose security is threatened by a hostile external force – is here modified in an interesting way. The desirable objects, room and woman, are still in the centre of the stage, but there is now open competition for them between the males – father and brothers – of an actual family; the woman is also a member of the family, being the wife of the brother who has made a life for himself away from the family home but who returns to it for a visit. The struggle is now specific and literal rather than hidden and symbolic, as it is in the siblings' attack on the possessive child in *The Birthday Party*. We see them manœuvring, more or less on equal terms, for mastery of the living space – coexistent, as Ronald Bryden points out, with the stage itself, 'the actual area on which they battle'[52] – and subsequently for the woman. In terms of the basic image, the married couple represent the two people in the safe place and the rest of the males of the family, with the exception of the enfeebled Uncle Sam, the hostile intruders. There is a curious reversal here, in that Teddy and Ruth, the couple who seem to be safely protected within the redoubt of a civilized middle-class marriage, are dramatically speaking the intruders who disturb the lives of their more primitive relations.

The naked primitive impulses thus show themselves more in the method than the mere fact of competition; Ronald Bryden[53] argues cogently that much light is cast on the structure and meaning of the play if we see it in zoological terms, as of a group or family of male animals who bicker and snarl among themselves but who share a firmly established if surly cohabitation; the appearance of a female, property of one of them who has been away from the lair, creates jealous tensions in the group, but tribal feeling survives the strain. The defeated male, owner of the woman, is forced to withdraw, while the others decide to share her, on what they intend shall be their terms, but which turn out, not surprisingly, to be hers. The violent 'blue' language and total sexual amorality supports the impression both of animality and of group loyalty. The open and continuous indulgence of all but one of the male characters in such verbal violence – expletives, insults, a wide range of vernacular obscenities – makes it seem less menacing and more animal than in the earlier plays; its suggests that this is their habitual way of communication. The unconcealed physical violence also suggests the wild animal, as does the indifference with which the collapse of one of their number, Uncle Sam, is received.[54] The animality of the characters is ironically pointed in the dialogue: Max, the father, says of his family, 'They walk in here every time of the day and night like bloody animals',[55] and later enquires of his daughter-in-law 'Where's the whore? Still in bed? She'll make us all animals.'[56]

The central character in this menagerie is the woman, Ruth,

and her role is of crucial significance. To all appearances she is simply a sexual object to be competed for by, and finally shared among, the males, her sexuality thus being put to different uses according to the different needs of members of the tribe. However, as the only female, young and attractive, among a group of males, she possesses scarcity value, so that her apparent passivity is misleading; as 'owner of the property to be developed' she is able to make her own conditions, which they are forced to accept, and she ends with the mastery. What is striking here is the combination of inferiority and superiority, the woman as sexual object and the woman as dominant; the wives in Pinter's plays (*The Collection*, *The Lover*, *The Homecoming*), with their enigmatic sexuality, confirm the impression gained from his elder women, possessive but damaged maternal figures, such as Rose and Meg: that woman in general occupies in his plays one of the primary roles she fulfils in the infantile imagination. In discussing *The Birthday Party* I have suggested that it is relevant to recall how the child in fantasy may reduce the mother to the status of an object into which his sexual feelings may be evacuated and which, in contradiction to the facts, is felt to be subject to his control. In fantasy the woman is thus dominated by her conversion into a sexual object, in compensation for her superiority on all other scores – size, strength, capacity, independence – to the infant. Thus we see here, in one aspect of a very early relationship of mother and infant, the salient features of the relationship of Ruth to the four men in *The Homecoming*: apparently made over, in the most direct and crude way imaginable, as a sexual object for their use and convenience, but in truth the dominant partner in her relationship with all of them. Her sexuality is the most obvious thing about Ruth; there seems to be little, if anything, of the maternal about her. However, if we look closely at her attitude to the men, and theirs to her, we shall find supporting evidence for the view that the primary role she occupies betrays maternal features, being originally that of the mother. (Pinter has given her real children, left behind in America.) Consider first Lenny, the elder of her two brothers-in-law, by profession a pimp; it is he who is instrumental in procuring Ruth for his younger brother, Joey, the sexual athlete of the family, quietly participating in their sexual relationship by caressing Ruth's hair and touching her with his feet while Joey embraces her. It is he, too, who makes the suggestion that, to relieve the family's economic problem of an 'extra mouth to feed', he should 'take her up to Greek Street . . . put her on the game' so that 'she can earn the money herself – on her back'.[57] Her first meeting with Lenny takes place on her arrival at the family home late at night, her husband, Teddy, having gone unwillingly to bed without her. After the exchange of a few enigmatic courtesies, he offers her a glass of water. She accepts; he pours himself out a glass, following this up with an account of his brutal dealings with two women, one young, one old, clearly designed to impress her with his male prowess, in effect a 'mating display', in Bryden's phrase.[58] The scene between them ends with perhaps the most absorbing exchange in the play.[59] When he offers to relieve her of her glass, she deftly seizes the opportunity for a counter-attack. In the course of a brief argument over the question whether she has or has not had enough water – Lenny's insistence that 'you've consumed quite enough, in my opinion' invests the emotionally neutral water with some of the associative potency of alcohol or milk – she disconcerts him by using the name 'Leonard': 'Don't call me that, please. That's the name my mother gave me.' His threat to remove the glass by force if she will not surrender it is countered by the enigmatic assertion 'If you take the glass . . . I'll take you'; ignoring his protests – 'You're in love . . . with another man. . . . Then you come here without a word of warning and start to make trouble' – she quietly increases the pressure, suggesting that he sit on her lap and have 'a long cool sip' from her glass. There is a touch of panic in his response: 'Take that glass away from me.' Again she plays a higher card: 'Lie on the floor. Go on. I'll pour it down your throat.' 'What was that supposed to be? Some kind of proposal?' he shouts angrily after her as she effortlessly drains her own glass – 'Oh, I was thirsty' – and leaves him, mounting the stairs to bed.

This little scene is most compelling to watch on the stage; I would suggest that what is really happening between them is something like this. Lenny seeks to extend his dominance over Ruth by reactivating an infantile fantasy of omnipotence; by relieving her of her unfinished glass of water, he will effectively rob her of her female, maternal capacity to feed and acquire it for himself. Her counter-attack consists, essentially, in an assertion that the power is hers and hers alone, in her own right, as sexualized mother and even, by a raid on his territory, as potent male. Returning the glass, she offers him a sip and then, in counterbalance to his own fantasy of usurping the woman's role, she confidently seizes the man's role too: 'I'll pour it down your throat.' To the maternal nipple in her armoury has been added the male penis; no wonder that, threatened with the loss of both reality and fantasy, he blusters and panics. Her easy mastery in this scene – she simply ignores him when it suits her – itself suggests the adult's capacity to ignore the infant. It is also worth noting that Lenny, as he watches her take her first sip of water, remarks, 'Isn't it funny? I've got my pyjamas on and you're fully dressed?' This is the normal situation of the mother and child after dark. It is also of interest that, immediately after her departure, his mind goes back to his own beginnings. In a spirit of vindictive mock-enquiry, he asks his father, who has been disturbed by the noise and who is angrily demanding whom he has got concealed, 'That night . . . you got me . . . that night with Mum, what was it like? Eh? When I was just a glint in your eye.'[60]

This episode between Ruth and Lenny is another example of Pinter's extraordinary ability to penetrate to the deeper levels of relationship while retaining sufficient links with observable reality. First, their behaviour in this scene prepares us for Ruth's later promiscuity and Lenny's part in encouraging it. Second, as is well known, couples do indulge in fantasies of occupying each other's sexual roles; they may also portion out the original mother/child relationship – to feed or be fed – or dispute it between them. The exchanges between Lenny and Ruth, like those of Stanley and Meg in *The Birthday Party*, thus retain a certain plausibility in realistic terms; the difference from run-of-the-mill scenes of realistic sexual fantasy, so common on the contemporary stage, lies in the boldness and freedom with which Pinter awakes the echoes of that deeper, buried life, so that what we are invited to witness vibrates with meaning. Ruth's relationship with the younger son, Joey, though less varied and subtle than that with Lenny, goes to confirm our impression of her primary role. She seems wholly passive in face of his sexual demands, which are supported by the father and Lenny ('He's irresistible. He's one of the few and far between' is Lenny's tribute);[61] but in an important respect she establishes a dominion over him which is not solely or primarily sexual. Joey, demolition worker and part-timer boxer, a man of seemingly crude and simple sexual appetites, is delighted to find that Ruth is ' . . . wide open . . . a tart . . . just up my street';[62] after a mimed act of copulation before the others, he takes her upstairs with him. However, on his reappearance he has to report to Lenny, to the latter's sardonic indignation, that although he's 'had her up there for two hours' he 'didn't get all the way.'[63] Expansively, Lenny chides the husband, Teddy, a silent observer of the scene, for introducing into the family home a wife who is a tease, but Joey demurs: 'I've been the whole hog plenty of times. Sometimes . . . you can be happy . . . and not go the whole hog. Now and again . . . you can be happy . . . without going any hog.'[64] There is an obscure recognition here of a different order of relationship, of the child in himself and the mother in Ruth, and specifically of the loss involved in the sexualization of the mother: Ruth appears, not as the unsatisfactory mate who offers and then withdraws her favours, but as the protective woman who bestows an unexpected happiness 'without going any hog'. At the same time Joey retains the sense of her sexuality, as his violent jealousy of her husband shows.[65] In the play's final tableau the maternal role is again emphasized; Joey 'kneels at her chair' and 'puts his head in her lap' while she 'touches his head, lightly'.[66] It is a role ironically at variance with the demands of the profession that is being mapped out for her, where Joey, to his dismay, must share her with an anonymity of lovers; but its significance is unmistakable. The signs of tender sentiment that Joey, an indiscriminately promiscuous man, displays towards Ruth emphasize the special role that this woman, with her ambiguous attitude to his sexual needs, is made to occupy in his life.

There is another besides Joey who makes a child's appeal to her in the final scene. This is Max, the father, a man in his seventies, well described by Bryden as 'a mangy old bull . . . failing . . . but still powerful enough to provide food and occasionally to savage the two young bulls of his engendering who also use the lair'.[67] His rivalry with his sons is ferociously direct and open, in animal fashion, but in spite of the bellowing vituperation with which he responds to Lenny's mockery we have the impression at first of a mutual if grudging tolerance. Not until the woman, Ruth, is introduced into the family by Teddy, the returning prodigal, does he match violence of word with that of act. The discovery of the presence of a nubile young female in the house, the property of one of his sons, arouses all his jealous possessiveness. His feelings first express themselves in violent verbal resentment – 'who asked you to bring dirty tarts into this house?'; when Joey tries patronizingly to excuse his behaviour – 'He's an old man' – Max strikes him with all his strength in the stomach with his stick.[68] It is the one moment of effective assertion of power by a man who only maintains a fragile authority as head of the family by a constant effort of self-projection; the way the character is conceived shows Pinter to be a natural dramatist, for its intense theatricality is thus grounded in psychological truth. This act of physical violence is in a way a sign of defeat; the dissension caused by Ruth's appearance can now only be resolved by admitting her, and the old man's insults now give place to a flamboyant gallantry. It is clear from a number of touches that he had hitherto maintained his mastery by a variety of means; not only has he hitherto successfully denied his sons the right to bring women into the family home, but he also acts as mother to his thankless brood. Several earlier hints are confirmed in a complaining speech to Ruth in Act Two; he does the cooking, and resents being 'driven out of the kitchen' by his feebler brother, Sam, whom he despises.[69] When pressed to produce a meal, he replies indignantly, 'Who do you think I am, your mother?';[70] but it is clear that this is just how he does see himself, his omnipotent fantasies fed by fear of displacement. He complains to Ruth that he has slaved all his life 'to keep my family in luxury', adding significantly, 'My mother was bedridden, my brothers were all invalids. . . . A crippled family, three bastard sons, a slutbitch of a wife – don't talk to me about the pangs of childbirth – I suffered the pain, I've still got the pangs – when I give a little cough my back collapses. . . .'[71]

At the end of the play he seems to have secured his position by a cunning blend of assertion and concession. Ruth, on his initiative, is to be kept in the family circle for the mutual benefit of its members, the only exception being her husband, Teddy, the original culprit, whom Max has the satisfaction of seeing withdraw, defeated. However, betrayal comes from an unexpected quarter, in the final minutes of the play. Teddy has gone; Joey sits with his head in Ruth's lap while Lenny watches, satisfied. Suddenly Max echoes the phrase of Joey's which had provoked his earlier outburst of violence. 'I'm too old, I suppose. She thinks I'm an old man.'[72] Anxiety and longing well up in him; he attempts to deal with it indirectly, in expressing doubts to Lenny about Ruth's trustworthiness as a business partner; she mustn't think she can just have Joey all the time. But the direct need is too strong. 'He falls to his knees, whimpers, begins to moan and sob.' Then, crawling round to where Ruth is sitting, he looks up at her: 'I'm not an old man, do you hear me?' and in a final bellow of entreaty that ends the play 'Kiss me.'[73] She ignores him as serenely as she had earlier ignored Lenny's outburst over her play with the glass of water; the final stage direction reads, 'She continues to touch Joey's head, lightly. Lenny stands watching.'[74] The ferocious old man, who has taken over the role of the dead mother, finds himself with perfect appropriateness reduced to the position of the unwanted child, begging unheeded for love, or food, from a woman whose role is that of sexualized mother. There is an exact correspondence about Max's situation, like Ruth's riposte to Lenny over the glass of water, or the nature of Stanley's punishment in *The Birthday Party*, that sorts well with what we know of the inner world of the infant, where omnipotent fantasies, returning with interest on the head of their perpetrator, only serve to emphasize helplessness and dependence. It is as though Max has claimed: 'I am the father, all-powerful; you, the children, are nothing in comparison. What's more, I am the mother too.' She replies: 'Not only are you not the mother, you are yourself the child whom you despise as inferior, and the unwanted child at that, the child who is himself nothing.' Once again, in *The Homecoming*, Pinter has shown his understanding of this inner world, in offering us a situation where the woman, contrary now to surface appearances and expectations, occupies a primary role that contains, as it must, maternal features. In effect the men, father and sons, are sexualized children, while the woman is a sexualized mother. There is an impressive accuracy in the picture.[75]

In my analysis of these three plays I have tried to show the truth and cogency with which Pinter explores primitive levels of relationship, while at the same time achieving 'this recognizable reality of the absurdity of what we do and how we behave and how we speak'[76] that makes his work accessible to a relatively wide audience. In this blend of the two levels of experience he writes in the finest tradition of poetic drama. His virtuosity is remarkable, so much so that, on the strength of his recent work, some critics have wondered whether it is becoming his master, not his servant. Thus Bryden, for all his admiration of *The Homecoming*, concludes that Pinter 'has elected to exploit his metaphor's exoticism. He has written a stylish entertainment, but not much more. All that remains at the end is a flavour.'[77] I have argued that there is a great deal more to the play than Bryden suggests – that in the relationship of Ruth and Max and his sons he has extended the grasp of primary psychological roles he had earlier displayed in *The Birthday Party*. I would however share some of the reservations that have been expressed about Pinter's development, but on rather different grounds. In all his major plays except *The Caretaker* there is a limitation of emotional range and depth that, in the early *Birthday Party*, could be seen as a necessary condition of the achievement. *The Caretaker*, however, showed that without abandoning his insight into the primitive he was capable of pathetic and tragic effects that were enlarging and liberating. *The Homecoming* is a play rich in meaning and technically brilliant, but it does not recapture effects like these. This, then, is perhaps the major question about Pinter's future. His admirers may allow themselves to feel encouraged by the superiority in technique of *The Homecoming*; this might suggest that, having achieved this mastery of the medium, he may be free now to extend and deepen the human and moral aspects of his work without loss of power.[78]

Notes

1 Antonin Artaud, *The Theatre and its Double*, trans. M. C. Richards (New York, 1958), p. 7.

2 Harold Pinter, interview with Hallam Tennyson, BBC General Overseas Services, August 1960 (quoted by Martin Esslin, *The Theatre of the Absurd* (New York, 1961), p. 199).

3 E. Ionesco, 'Expérience du Théâtre', *Nouvelle Revue Française* (Paris, 1 February 1958), pp. 258–9.

4 Harold Pinter, interview with Kenneth Tynan (BBC Home Service, 28 October 1960). I owe this and other quotations from broadcast interviews with Pinter to Martin Esslin, *The Theatre of the Absurd*, ch. 5.

5 Peter Weiss, *The Persecution and Assassination of Marat as Performed by the*

Inmates of the Asylum of Charenton under the Direction of the Marquis de Sade, trans. G. Skelton and A. Mitchell (London, 1965).

6 Ibid., p. 40.
7 See Introduction and Chapter One.
8 Pinter, interview with Hallam Tennyson (see note 2).
9 Pinter, interview with Tynan (see note 4).
10 Ibid.
11 Pinter, *The Dwarfs*, in *A Slight Ache and Other Plays* (London, 1961), p. 116.
12 Pinter, *The Birthday Party and Other Plays* (London, 1960), p. 8.
13 Ibid., p. 45.
14 Ibid., p. 58.
15 Ibid., p. 18.
16 Ibid., p. 13.
17 Ibid., p. 35.
18 Ibid., p. 38.
19 Ibid., p. 39.
20 Ibid., p. 66.
21 Ibid., pp. 24–5.
22 Ibid., p. 71.
23 Ibid., p. 69.
24 Ibid., p. 15.
25 Ibid., p. 24.
26 Ibid., p. 69.
27 Ibid., pp. 22–3.
28 Ibid., p. 25.
29 Ibid.
30 Ibid.
31 Ibid., p. 45.
32 Ibid., pp. 72–83.
33 Ibid., p. 79.
34 Ibid., pp. 50–4.
35 Ibid., p. 66.
36 Ibid., p. 85.
37 Ibid., p. 55.
38 Ibid., p. 86.
39 The use of this expression seems significant.
40 Ibid., p. 84.
41 Pinter, BBC interview with Tynan (see note 4).
42 Esslin, op. cit., pp. 204–5.
43 Pinter, BBC interview with Tynan.
44 Ibid.
45 For example, the electrolux used to terrify Davies.
46 Pinter, *The Caretaker* (London, 1960), p. 74.
47 Ibid., p. 47.
48 BBC Television, 1966.
49 Melanie Klein, *Our Adult World and its Roots in Infancy* (London, 1960), p. 9.
50 Cf. p. 70 above.
51 *The Caretaker*, pp. 54–7.

52 Ronald Bryden, 'A Stink of Pinter', *New Statesman* (11 June 1965), p. 928.
53 Ibid.
54 Pinter, *The Homecoming* (London, 1965), p. 79.
55 Ibid., p. 17.
56 Ibid., p. 69.
57 Ibid., pp. 71–3.
58 Bryden, op. cit.
59 *The Homecoming*, pp. 34–5.
60 Ibid., p. 36.
61 Ibid., p. 67.
62 Ibid., pp. 58–9.
63 Ibid., p. 66.
64 Ibid., p. 69.
65 Ibid., pp. 69–70.
66 Ibid., p. 81.
67 Bryden, op. cit.
68 *The Homecoming*, p. 43.
69 Ibid., p. 38.
70 Ibid., p. 17.
71 Ibid., p. 47.
72 Ibid., p. 81.
73 Ibid., pp. 82–3.
74 Ibid.
75 A peculiar enigma surrounds the relationship of Ruth and Teddy, the married couple. Why does she behave towards him as she does, and why does he passively tolerate it? What is the significance of her final remark, 'Don't become a stranger'? It seems possible that Teddy unconsciously wishes to be rid of his wife. He is drawn back to the primitive family he seems to have outgrown, but which he can rely on to absorb her, even at the cost of expelling him. At the same time, like the other males of the family, he wants to be dominated by the sexualized mother. A similarity between Teddy and his father, not obvious in their behaviour, is pointed by the similar pattern of relationship: Teddy, like Max, is to bring up three boys, as mother to them as well as father.
76 Pinter, interview with Hallam Tennyson (see note 2).
77 Bryden, op. cit.
78 Since *The Homecoming* Pinter's more significant work has developed in a new direction, towards what might be called Chamber Dramas. In *Landscape* and *Silence* (1968), and *Old Times* (1971), the theme becomes more diffused, concerned with the privacy of our memories and imaginations, with imprisonment in the past and in dream-like shadows cast on the present. There is still challenge for possession, and the characters still play sexual games, now in a lighter spirit (first seen in *The Collection* of 1961); but there is a new, poetical concern with Beckett's 'suffering of being'. The inner world, instead of controlling the external, observable world of everyday, has effectively taken its place as dramatic image. These plays are of great interest, but are less relevant to my theme of the primitive in modern drama.

Four

Ionesco: Paroxysm and Proliferation

Eugene Ionesco, writing of his own theatrical ambitions, argues as follows:[1]

> What was needed . . . was to go right down to the very basis of the grotesque, the realm of caricature . . . to push everything to paroxysm, to the point where the sources of the tragic lie. To create a theatre of violence – violently comic, violently dramatic.

The path to the 'basis of the grotesque' lay through introspection, an examination of the inner life: defending himself in the *Observer* against Kenneth Tynan's attack on his subjectivism, he wrote:[2]

> To discover the fundamental problem common to all mankind I must ask myself what *my* fundamental problem is, what my most ineradicable fear is. I am certain then to find the problems and fears of literally everyone. That is the true road into my own darkness, our darkness, which I try to bring to the light of day. . . .

This darkness lies in the common inheritance of the primitive and irrational, a perception of which conditions the structure as well as the meaning of Ionesco's plays. Two aspects of the 'fundamental problem', as illustrated in his theatre, are of especial relevance to my theme. First, there is an element of paroxysm and intensification; the characteristic movement of the plays is one of acceleration, of instinctual urges ever more frenziedly and maniacally released. As Ionesco's comment on the grotesque shows, this makes for comedy; in place of Pinter's enigmatic slow-burning menace, Ionesco offers us a feverish dance of incongruity, in which the contrary elements of anarchic protest against order on the one hand, and the fear of chaos and nothingness on the other, are held in dramatic balance. Something that can properly be called comedy, in spite of powerful tragic over-tones, is also ensured by a certain lightness of tone and temperament which distinguishes Ionesco from other major practitioners of 'Absurd' drama; the amiably helpless hero is in a well-established comic tradition, as is the taste for parodistic fantasy.

Intensification is of the essence of Ionesco's plots. *The Lesson* develops feverishly from a conventional beginning – the small change of talk between hesitant Professor and eager pupil – to rape and murder; in *The Chairs*, more and more chairs fill the scene as the old couple welcome invisible guests; in *Amédée*, the corpse in the next room gets bigger and bigger as the play proceeds. In these two plays the second aspect of the 'fundamental problem' is even more prominent: proliferation. 'The horror of prolifer-ation', in Esslin's words, 'is one of the most characteristic images we find in Ionesco's plays.'[3] Ionesco himself calls it 'the point of departure', along with its opposite and complement, a feeling of emptiness and unreality:[4]

> Two fundamental states of consciousness are at the root of all my plays. These two basic feelings are those of . . . emptiness and of an overabundance of presence; of the unreal transparency of the world, and of its opaqueness. . . . The sensation of evanescence results in a feeling of anguish, a sort of dizziness. But all of this can just as well become euphoric; anguish is suddenly transformed into liberty. . . . This state of consciousness is very rare, to be sure. . . . I am most often under the dominion of the opposite feeling: lightness changes to heaviness, transparency to thickness; the world weighs heavily; the universe crushes me. . . . Matter fills everything, takes up all space. . . . Speech crumbles. . . .

This is a very revealing statement of Ionesco. We are certainly made more aware in the plays of the proliferating tyranny of matter than of any sense of liberation: the growing corpse in *Amédée* which is beginning to sprout mushrooms; the bread and coffee cups that fill the stage in *Victims of Duty*; the encirclement of Bérenger by rhinoceros heads in *Rhinocéros;* the ever-increasing flood of furniture which pours into the room of *The New Tenant*. Moreover, the persecutory threat represented by the oppressive density of matter is liable to be intensified, not relieved, by its alternating aspect of unreality; the sensation of the 'unreal transparency' of the world causes vertigo, dizziness. Ionesco describes his sensations while writing his first play, *The Bald Prima Donna*, apparently almost by accident while learning English by the Assimil method:[5]

> While writing the play . . . I felt sick, dizzy, nauseated. I had to interrupt my work . . . and, wondering all the time what demon was prodding me on, lie down on my couch for fear of seeing my work sink into nothingness, and me with it.

However, 'anguish is suddenly transformed into liberty'; it is important to see that the lightness and euphoria which this sense of evanescence occasionally induces may themselves be associated with proliferation. Thus the writing of *The Bald Prima Donna* was at first experienced by Ionesco as an unexpected and extraordinary proliferation of original words and characters out of the bare clichés of the Assimil primer. Words began to behave like the spreading objects that were to fill the plays:[6]

> The very simple, luminously clear statements I had copied diligently into my . . . notebook, left to themselves, fermented after a while, lost their original identity, expanded and overflowed.

The experience, though disconcerting in the way described, was also stimulating; Ionesco conveys vividly the excitement he felt at seeing, for the first time, his word-creations coming to life through the interpretation of actors and the response of an audience:[7]

> To incarnate phantasms, to give them life, is a prodigious irreplaceable adventure, to such an extent that I myself was overcome when, during rehearsals of my first play, I suddenly saw characters move on the stage who had come out of myself. I was frightened. By what right had I been able to do this? Was this allowed? . . . It was almost diabolical.

He seems to be describing here a kind of creative proliferation of the self, successful perhaps in counteracting the destructive proliferation of matter; its similarity to the persecutory experience makes it ambivalent, at once exciting and appalling. The end of *Amédée*, where the anonymous hero floats off into the air, drawn up out of reach of his oppressors by the oppressing corpse itself which now 'seems to have opened out like a sail or huge parachute' seems to symbolize this ambivalent feeling of the author; the source of persecution, the growing corpse, becomes itself the means of liberation. Though Amédée claims he is being carried off involuntarily, there is a lightness of spirit and euphoric excitement about the conclusion: 'Forgive me, Ladies and Gentlemen, I'm terribly sorry! Forgive me! Oh, dear! But I feel so frisky, so frisky. (He disappears.)'[8] His disappearance is signalized by brilliant lights and flashes in the sky, 'comets, shooting stars, etc.'; he is deaf to his wife's plea that he can 'come home, the mushrooms have bloomed'.[9] The blooming mushrooms recall the grotesquely blossoming corpse (both travesties of true growth); in contrast to these oppressive presences, the lights in the sky are liberating, celebratory of Amédée's triumphant release from earthbound matter. The contrasting images seem clearly to represent the opposite poles of Ionesco's 'fundamental states of consciousness', of heaviness and lightness, overabundance and transparency.

Paroxysm, or intensification; fullness, with its inevitable complement of emptiness. These two aspects of Ionesco's inner drama exemplify in a striking manner part of the basic structure of infantile fantasy as explored by psychoanalysis. Ionesco's account, quoted above, of how he came to write his first play, shows clearly how close he has kept to unconscious sources of feeling; he emphasizes both the semi-voluntary nature of the activity – as though his conscious self were being taken over by something deeper – and the powerful physical reaction, of dizziness and nausea, that suggests an involvement of the personality at a deep level. Like Pinter, he does not write from an abstract idea, but because he is possessed by an image, the pictorial or fictional representation of a feeling:[10]

I have no ideas before I write a play. I have them when I have written the play or while I am not writing at all. I believe that artistic creation is spontaneous. It certainly is so for me.

Both the undoubted emotional reality of the underlying experience, and its sources in some of the earliest and most primitive psychic situations, go far to explain the lasting impression made on us by Ionesco's plays; we apprehend intuitively a meaningful pattern in what may appear on the surface merely whimsical and arbitrary. Thus the power of the image of proliferation, with its associated feelings of fullness and emptiness, heaviness and lightness, seems to be clearly related to infantile greed.

In discussing *The Bacchae* I sought to show how easily greed may produce anxiety in the infant. First, there is anxiety springing from the realization that the breast can be withdrawn; even though he may be receiving ample food, the greedy baby's gratification may be so short-lived that this anxiety, basically a fear of starvation, is very readily activated. Second, there is anxiety over what his greed in its excess may do to the mother, in emptying her breast and so rendering her incapable of feeding him. The greed is itself likely to be stimulated by anxiety, so that a vicious circle is set up, the greed producing anxiety and the anxiety in its turn further increasing the greed. This situation may cause the baby to seek to get rid of the unwanted feelings by putting them into the mother, projecting his greed and anxiety into the person who represents to him, in the very earliest stage of life, the greater part if not the whole of the external world. The more successful this mechanism the more dangerous and disturbing it is likely to prove. Just as by introjection the outer world may be taken into the self, and so experienced as part of the inner life, so by projection that outer world may be experienced as actually endowed with those parts of the self that are put into it. Thus the mother is now felt to contain the baby's greedy and anxious impulses; not only may she then be believed incapable of feeding him adequately, but through the identification or confusion of child with mother which is an essential part of the mechanism of projection she may now be experienced as a restless devouring creature who threatens to stifle the child with his own greed. If it be accepted that the mother represents, at this early stage, the greater part of the external world to the child, then the later fear of invasion by proliferating objects can be seen as an extension of this original experience.

Proliferation may thus be taken to represent, at one level, the invasiveness of the infantile self experienced, through projective identification, as a hostile external force attacking and persecuting its victims. Ionesco shows an intuitive understanding of the vital part played by identification in this process; the victims appear as in some way responsible for, or at any rate very closely related to, the proliferating objects. A stage direction in *Amédée* makes the point with peculiar precision. As Amédée succeeds, with a 'superhuman effort', in pulling the now vastly extended body up on to the window-sill, at the moment it yields to him 'the impression should be given that . . . it is dragging the whole house with it and tugging at the entrails of the two principal characters'.[11] A typical confusion of identity between mother and child, represented here by the corpse and the two characters, has occurred. Moreover, the intimate relationship of mother to child makes the situation profoundly claustrophobic. The child may attempt in fantasy to project the whole of himself into the mother in order to restore the prenatal organic unity between them and so put an end to the damaging attacks brought about by subsequent separation. Again, the more this fantasy succeeds the more dangerous it will prove to be; finally separate now, the child cannot re-enter the safe place without the risk of suffocation. It is thus right that we should have the impression that Ionesco's characters are in danger of being actually swallowed up by the monstrous proliferation of matter that surrounds them. ('Matter fills everything, takes up all space.') The child's greedy and invasive projections have already made of the mother a monster who will envelop, suffocate, and finally absorb him.

It will be recalled that Ionesco sees, as the contrasting and complementary 'fundamental state of consciousness' to overabundance of presence, emptiness: a condition both agonizing and, more rarely, exhilarating. Emptiness again suggests greed: if the 'overabundance of presence' suggests the greedy child who projects his greed into the mother, the emptiness suggests the child who for the same reason is no longer able to receive nourishment from her. The painfulness of this very common experience of emptiness and unreality, in the self and the external world, is explicable in psychoanalytical terms as the result of a projection of too great a part of the self, leading inevitably to a sense of impoverishment. Unreality is experienced because a great part of the self has been temporarily lost; the anxiety over identity inherent in this condition (am I a real person?) may well be exacerbated by the suppressed awareness that the 'real' self that has been projected is hostile and invasive, a threat to peace. Ionesco gives a moving and penetrating account of having experienced this state of consciousness in childhood:[12]

> When I was a child I lived near the Square de Vaugiraud. I remember – it was so long ago! – the badly lit street on an autumn or winter evening. My mother held me by the hand; I was afraid, as children are afraid; we were out shopping, for the evening meal. On the sidewalks sombre silhouettes in agitated movement . . . phantomlike, hallucinatory shadows. When that image of that street comes to life again in my memory, when I think that almost all those people are now dead, everything seems a shadow, evanescence. I am seized by a vertigo of anxiety. . . .

The contrasting state of exhilaration, in which 'anguish is suddenly transformed into liberty', may be thought to signalize a counteracting fantasy of omnipotence. In place of the experience of impoverishment and loss, the self, free of its hostile and invasive parts, enjoys an exhilarating if dangerous sense of liberation that may be felt to transcend normal physical limits. It will be recalled that in the third and final act of *Amédée*, matter, that had threatened to fill everything, is left behind altogether as the hero soars triumphantly into the upper air; that this is a child's dream of freedom is emphasized by the language of the watching crowd:[13]

> *Madeleine* (to the sky)   Come along now, Amédée, won't
> you ever be serious?
> *Second Policeman*   (looking up at the sky and wagging
> his finger at Amédée as one would at
> a child)   You little rascal, you!
> *Soldier*   Why Junior, you bad boy!

Under the spell of this feeling happiness seems unqualified, absolute. In another play, *The Killer*, Bérenger, the typical Ionesco hero, describes it as 'a blazing fire inside me . . . youth-fulness, a spring no autumn could touch; a source of light, glowing wells of joy that seemed inexhaustible'.[14] Later – he is describing a landscape so beautiful it makes him forget everything else – he speaks significantly of 'that deep sky and that sun, which seemed to be coming nearer, within my grasp, in a world that was made for me'.[15] Not only does the world exist for his gratification but he fills the world with himself: 'My own peace and light spread in their turn throughout the world, I was filling the universe with a kind of ethereal energy.'[16] The image is surely that of an identification with the mother as source of all goodness and nourishment. In place of emptiness and unreality, there is a superabundance of reality; all other experiences, and even existence, are validated by the fantasy fulfilment of this first and most profound wish: 'I walked and ran and cried I *am*, I *am, everything* is, everything *is*. . . .'[17] The experience is comparable to the ecstasy of union celebrated by the Bacchants; the re-forging of the physical link with the mother that is so often described, as Bérenger describes it here, as both familiar and new. The description is apt, for it is the buried life that is being rediscovered: 'Everything was virgin, purified, discovered anew. I had a feeling of inexpressible surprise, yet at the same time it was all quite familiar to me.'[18] As these quotations show, the experience possesses a perhaps unique value as the rediscovery of the deepest and most real happiness known to the self; but it is the urge to maintain this happiness pure and undiluted that stimulates the omnipotence, the denial of pain and loss that is ultimately damaging. Death itself is denied – inevitably, for the magic reunion with the mother has been substituted for the separation and growing away from her that is the condition of health and maturity, but must end finally in death: 'A song of triumph rose from the depths of my being: I *was*, I realized I had always *been*, that I was no longer going to die.'[19] It is also worth noting that in the imagery expressive of this mood there is a sexual colouring; the triumphant union with the mother may be experienced, it is implied, as a sexual possession of her. The fireworks and shooting stars of *Amédée* which accompany the hero's apotheosis suggest orgasm, while the language of *The Killer*, though still metaphorical, is more direct; Bérenger speaks of 'glowing wells of joy' and of 'filling the Universe with an ethereal energy'.[20] The sense of omnipotence is complete.

Alternating with liberty, anguish; an accurate recognition of the price to be paid for the fantasy of omnipotence is enacted in the plays. There is the Icarus-like fall into dizziness and emptiness, as the reality of the infant's helplessness and hunger breaks through the fantasy. There is also the pain of separation, part of a recognition that in the process of rapturous identification with and possession of the mother in fantasy, the real mother is lost. Bérenger in *The Killer* describes both aspects of the feeling, in a passage that follows immediately the long evocation of ecstasy from which I have already quoted. There is a change of mood:[21]

> And suddenly, or rather gradually . . . no, it was all at once, I don't know, I only know that everything went grey and pale and neutral again. Not really, of course, the sky was still pure, but it wasn't the same purity. . . . It was like a conjuring trick.

Fantasies of omnipotence do indeed partake of the nature of conjuring tricks. Bérenger continues:[22]

> There was a kind of chaotic vacuum inside me, I was overcome with the immense sadness you feel at a moment of tragic and intolerable separation . . . I felt lost among all those people, all those *things*. . . .

As soon as the sense of omnipotence fades, objects begin to threaten again. The play ends with Bérenger's submission to the knife of the 'Tueur sans Gages',[23] the gratuitous killer, in appearance a shambling one-eyed dwarf, giggling and imbecile; the murderous dwarf here suggests the death-dealing aspects of the omnipotent child. Movingly and tragically, the finale presents the inevitability of death, in contrast to the fantasy of freedom and happiness; in the words of the short story, 'La Photo du Colonel', from which the play was later elaborated:[24]

> No words, friendly or authoritative, could have convinced him; all the promise of happiness, all the love in the world, could not have reached him; beauty would not have made him relent, nor irony have shamed him. . . .

Death is the more intolerable and absurd, not because the happiness had been so real, but because there had been a certain unreality about it. To argue, as Esslin does, that *The Killer* portrays not only the inevitability and unacceptability of death but the absurdity of human existence itself – 'No argument of morality or expediency can prevail against the half-witted, idiotic futility of the human condition. . . .'[25] is surely to impose an alien philosophy of despair on Ionesco's subtle, poetic presentation of experience. Esslin makes a similar point when he argues that even in the radiant city of the first act (seemingly a representation in objective terms of Bérenger's private happiness) 'the presence of death makes life futile and absurd'.[26] It is rather the unreality of the radiant city that produces this effect – the unreality of a world where all human needs are catered for by perfect planning, where 'it's all calculated, all intentional. Nothing . . . left to chance', not even the weather; the climate is of everlasting spring sunshine, 'in this district it never rains at all'.[27] It is appropriate that the killer should walk in this city whose inhabitants have deserted it or, if unable to leave, stay hidden within their beautiful flats (Bérenger is puzzled by the city's abandoned air); in its unreal perfection it is already empty, a place of fantasy not reality, a place of the dead. Bérenger fails to see this, in his rapturous acclamation of the city in the first act, just as he fails to see the elements of omnipotent yearning and denial of loss in his own memories of transcendent happiness. Ionesco's heroes are so sympathetic that the extent of their surrender to overmastering fantasy may well be missed; this surrender is surely the central preoccupation of a writer who has described his theatre as 'the projection on to the stage of the world within – my dreams, my anguish, my dark desires, my inner contradictions. . . .'[28] *The Killer* is a more powerful play than *Amédée* not because it testifies to the supposed meaninglessness of existence but because it suggests a fuller recognition of the truth about fantasy. The dissatisfaction expressed by critics about the third act of *Amédée* – that there is a decline of tension, that the transition from heaviness to lightness cannot be adequately realized in dramatic terms – may be symptomatic of an uneasiness about the hero's apotheosis at the end of the play, with its implications of an uninhibited triumph of fantasy. The ambivalence conveyed by Amédée's guilt at abandoning his earth-bound companions, and by the crucial role played by the corpse in his escape, does little to offset the euphoria. The euphoria is very appealing, but it does not altogether ring true. However, if there is an element of indulgence in the finale of *Amédée*, for the most part Ionesco displays a penetrating and lucid understanding of the crucial role played by unconscious fantasy in normal life, as 'an activity of the mind that accompanies every impulse . . .';[29] without such understanding he could not evoke so well the darker and more damaging aspects of its mastery over us. (The darkness is usually relieved by a certain instinctive human sympathy and, often, an infectious gaiety; love and affection always exist as a possibility, however remote, in the relationships of Ionesco's characters.) He recognizes, notably in *The Killer* and *The Chairs*, how fantasy embodies our daydreams of happiness and our longing for peace and security as well as our invasive and destructive wishes; above all, he sees the tragic link that may be forged between the two.

It is in such ways as this that the feeling of emptiness and evanescence is experienced as profoundly ambivalent, Janus-faced in its contrasting anguish and euphoria. It will be recalled that the act of artistic creation itself and its consequences are described by Ionesco as partaking of this ambivalence; to see 'characters move on the stage who had come out of myself' is both frightening and exhilarating, 'a prodigious, irreplaceable adventure'.[30] The adventure is rightly felt to be dangerous; polarized between fulfilment (fulfilled achievement) and omnipotence (omnipotent fantasy), what I have called the creative proliferation of writing seems to Ionesco to partake of a Faustian bargain – 'Was this allowed? . . . It was almost diabolical.'[31] (Images of procreation often occur in Ionesco in the context of fantasies of proliferation: the corpse in *Amédée* which produces blossoming mushrooms, the unceasing basketsful of eggs hatched by Roberte at the end of another play, *The Future is in Eggs*.) In thus conceiving of art as an extension of the self, its material the artist's own fantasies and conflicts, Ionesco is firmly in the Romantic tradition; he makes the large claim that, as Professor Sutherland notes, is implicit in the attitude of the early Romantic poets – 'This was important to me; it must therefore be so to all men.'[32] At the same time, the justification of the claim lies in the Romantic artist's perception of the universal revealed through the experience of a single consciousness:[33]

> For me, the theatre is the projection on to the stage of the world within – it is in my dreams, my anguish, my dark desires, my inner contradictions that I reserve the right to find the stuff of my plays. As I am not alone in

the world – as each one of us, in the depths of his being, is at the same time everyone else – my dreams and desires, my anguish and my obsessions do not belong to myself alone; they are part of the heritage of my ancestors, a very ancient deposit to which all mankind may lay claim.

The response to Ionesco's plays shows that his judgment here is right; he speaks to us so effectively through his profound understanding of the inner life, supported by the ability to find compelling dramatic images in which to express it. In a defence of the free employment of fantastic or magical effects on the stage he writes:[34]

> I personally would like to bring a tortoise on to the stage, turn it into a race horse, then into a hat, a song, a dragon, and a fountain of water. One can dare anything in the theatre. . . . Let the playwright be accused of being arbitrary. Yes, the theatre is the place where one *can* be arbitrary. As a matter of fact, it *is not arbitrary. The imagination is not arbitrary, it is revealing.* . . . [my italics]

The apparent chaos of the inner life of fantasy is found to possess an inner meaning and coherence. This discovery, the truth of which Ionesco expresses in the cogent final sentence of this passage, is central to psychoanalytical thinking; his own theatre bears it out.

One of Ionesco's subtlest treatments of the 'two fundamental states of consciousness', of overabundance and emptiness, is *The Chairs*. Here the emptiness lies at the heart of the overabundance, for the ever increasing number of chairs are set out by the old couple for non-existent guests, while the stream of polite conversation is addressed to the ears of the audience alone. The central theme of the play, as Ionesco defines it, in a letter to the director of the first production, Sylvain Dhomme, is emptiness and unreality; it is unusually close to Beckett in mood:[35]

> The subject of the play is not the message, nor the failure of life, nor the moral disaster of the two old people, but the chairs themselves; that is to say, the absence of

people . . . the unreality of the world, metaphysical emptiness. The theme of the play is nothingness. . . .

Ionesco also calls it a 'tragic farce'. It will be remembered that Bérenger in *The Killer* experiences a 'chaotic vacuum' of loss and unreality: 'I felt lost among all those people, all those things'. In *The Chairs* the unreality that, in certain states of consciousness, seems to be a property of the external world as well as of the self, is conveyed through an image of great power – 'the chairs themselves'.[36] By means of this image the experience of unreality is embodied directly in the drama; in place of the hero being unable to communicate his feelings and needs to other characters who exist independently of him, as in *Amédée* or *The Killer* – the normal way of expressing this situation – the two chief figures people the stage with characters with whom they communicate freely but who exist only in their imagination. In terms of psychological symbolism, it may be said that the external world has been reduced to their own projections into it. There is always a possibility that the infant through his projective and omnipotent fantasies may experience a loss both of self and real mother so complete that a sense of total isolation results, his need for love and understanding completely frustrated. Such an early situation seems to be represented in the predicament of the old couple, which Ionesco interestingly refers to in the passage quoted above as a 'moral disaster'[37] though they do retain a certain reality to each other. It is noteworthy that the maternal aspect of the old woman's attitude to her husband is emphasized: 'Mummy's with you, what are you afraid of?'[38] she declares when he is distressed at the thought of having wrecked his career. He for his part sobs for his mother 'with his mouth wide open, like a baby',[39] in the accents of a child who has broken a toy; she rocks him backwards and forwards on her knee to comfort him, but at first he sulkily refuses to accept her in the maternal role – 'you're not my real Mummy'.[40] However, their relationship is very much that of spoiled child and indulgent mother, he looking to her for continuous consolation and support; towards the end of the play she echoes, exactly, his speeches, and he remarks to an old flame of his, a Mrs Lovely, one of the imaginary guests, 'My worthy spouse, Semiramis, has taken the place of my mother.'[41] The dialogue at various points impresses on us that the old man is also a child; thus, he describes how the revelation he is about to dispense to his guests came to him when, at the age of forty, he was sitting on his father's lap before going to bed. (Some visitors laugh at him and tell him he's a man, but he thinks 'But I'm not married yet. So I must still be a child.') In another passage, evocative of the tragedy of the parent/child relationship, the old woman informs one of the guests that they had had a child who abandoned his grief-stricken parents because 'they killed all the birds' and whom they never saw again; simultaneously, the old man tells another guest that they never had a child, but that *he* had abandoned *his* mother, leaving her to die in a ditch. The confusion of identities here suggests that it is the child part of the old man who is the hero of both these incidents: a child whose guilt over his fantasied cruelty to the parents is assuaged by a projection of that cruelty into them – 'Daddy, mummy, you're wicked, wicked! . . . The streets are full of the birds you've killed and the little children dying.'[42]

A sense of frustrated omnipotence, again reminiscent of an early infantile situation, is also prominent in the old man's talk. He feels that he is singled out from the mass of men by the achievements that might have been his 'if he had had a little ambition in Life', by the extent of his humiliation and sufferings – he describes himself as having been 'a lightning conductor for catastrophe' – and above all by his role as a saviour:[43]

> And then, no one ever took any notice of me . . . and yet it was I, I tell you, it was I and I alone who could have saved mankind, suffering, sick mankind . . . I haven't given up hope of saving mankind, there is still time, and my plan is ready.

This conviction is actually responsible for the drama presented to us: the guests have been summoned in order that they may listen to the old man's message, the fruit of a lifetime's experience. He has hired a professional orator to deliver the message 'who'll answer for me, who'll explain to you exactly how we feel about everything . . . he'll make it all clear. . . .'[44] The arrival of the Orator is the consummation of the old couple's lives; he 'really exists. In flesh and blood. . . . It's not a dream.'[45] As they now have nothing more to ask of life, they leap out of the window to their deaths in the sea. Their disappearance is the signal for the hitherto silent and impassive Orator to face the rows of empty chairs and attempt to speak. However, he is deaf and dumb; his desperate efforts to make himself understood only produce 'moans and groans and the sort of guttural sounds made by deaf mutes'. The resourceful idea occurs to him of writing his message on the blackboard, but the result is likewise gibberish, along with the single word 'Angepain' (Angelbread). Thus the message the old man could not speak himself remains unspoken. There is a hint, in the fact that he disappears as soon as the Orator appears, that he is to recover his lost identity in the identity of the Orator; but the sense of unreality remains undimmed. Indeed, finally it is only the unreal that has reality; a magnificent final image conveys this to us when, at the Orator's departure, 'for the first time human noises seem to be coming from the invisible crowd; snatches of laughter, whisperings . . . little sarcastic coughs'.[46] As Ionesco recognizes, it is a familiar theatrical paradox – the baseless fabric of the stage's vision – presented in a new context:[47]

> The invisible elements must be more and more clearly present, more and more real (to give unreality to reality one must give reality to the unreal) until the point is reached . . . when the unreal elements speak and move . . . and nothingness can be heard, is made concrete. . . .

The paradox is pushed to the point where the author succeeds in communicating to the audience his conviction of incommunicability and nothingness. The non-existent 'human noises', the stage direction continues, 'should last just long enough for the real and visible public to go away with this ending firmly fixed in their minds'.[48] The empty chairs, as has been pointed out, do of themselves suggest a theatre, and the Orator's inability to deliver the precious message hints at the difficulties and discouragement the artist may experience in the effort to reach his public if, like Ionesco, he 'projects on to the stage the world within'. There is no doubt that he has succeeded in reaching them in *The Chairs*.

In the opening paragraph of this section I suggested that there were two features of Ionesco's drama of especial relevance to my subject: first, proliferation and all that is associated with it; second, intensification. *The Lesson*, the play of Ionesco which provides an exceptionally concentrated and powerful example of this second feature, also embodies in an unusually direct form the content of an infantile fantasy. There are three characters: The Professor, aged between fifty and sixty, the Girl Pupil of eighteen, and the Maid of forty-five to fifty. The pattern of the play is a reversal of roles by Professor and Pupil. At the outset the Professor is 'excessively polite, very shy, a voice subdued by its timidity', while the Pupil is described as 'vivacious, dynamic, and of a cheerful disposition'. As the play proceeds, however, '[he] will grow more and more sure of himself, excitable, aggressive, domineering', while 'she will become more and more passive, until she is nothing more than an object, limp and inert . . . in the hands of the Professor'. Ionesco explains carefully, in this long stage direction with which he introduces his characters to us, how every feature of appearance and behaviour is to correspond to this change; thus the Professor's voice should change 'from thin and piping at the start . . . to an extremely powerful, braying, sonorous instrument at the end; whereas the Pupil's voice, after being very clear and resonant... will fade almost into inaudibility'. The 'prurient gleam' that at first 'now and again . . . quickly dismissed, lights up his eyes . . . will end by blazing into an insistent, lecherous, devouring flame'.[49]

It is characteristic of infantile sadistic fantasies that while under their spell the infant should lose to a great extent his sense of the mother as a person and retain only the sense of her as an object, receptacle for the spoiling sadistic attacks. Indeed this sense of the woman as merely object, present for the gratification of own's own needs but without needs of her own, remains the single most typical feature of adult male sadism. I have previously tried to show how sadism, in Melanie Klein's view, has its origins in infantile envy.[50] The envy is experienced as a result of the infant's awareness of his own helplessness and dependence in contrast to the mother's independence and freedom:[51]

> whenever he is hungry or feels neglected, the child's frustration leads to the phantasy that the milk and love are deliberately withheld from him, or kept by the mother for her own benefit.

Envy is essentially spoiling in nature; the urge to possess the loved object, normally the breast, is characterized by powerful feelings of frustration and resentment. I have already mentioned how the projection of bad parts of the child into the mother may lead to a persecutory situation. In a context of sadistic fantasy, projection is likely to play its part in the denigration of the coveted object, the mother's body or breast. Containing the bad envious parts of the child, the breast is experienced as a bad as well as a good object and can thus be attacked with the less guilt. However, the sadistic fantasy at its most intense may try to avoid the persecutory consequences of projection by experiencing the mother's body as exclusively object, to be freely used for the satisfaction and containment of envious impulses; the infant is thus defended against the potentially threatening and persecutory aspects of the mother as a person into whom such feelings have been projected.

It is this extreme situation, pathological if acted out but very common in fantasy, that Ionesco presents in *The Lesson*. The reversal of rules by which the vivacious and charming girl pupil is transformed into an inert and limp object suggests both the root of sadism in envy and the compulsive nature of the urge to spoil and destroy. The climax is of a simultaneous rape and murder, confirmation that the sadistic fantasy is at its purest and most intense; as the Professor 'kills the Pupil with a spectacular thrust of the knife' he first cries out in satisfaction, then[52]

> She too cries out, then falls, crumpling into an immodest position on the chair . . . : they both cry out, murderer and victim, at the same moment.

It is an accurately rendered parody of sexual intercourse, the woman's body being used simply as receptacle for the knife, or penis. Even at the climax of a sadistic fantasy some sense of the real function of the woman's body must be retained, as provider first of food and subsequently of mutual sexual satisfaction, if it is to continue to be desired and coveted. It is thus appropriate that the murderous act should be experienced as orgasm: 'after the first blow, he gives the dead Pupil a second thrust of the knife, with an upward movement; and then he starts visibly and his whole body shudders'.[53] His next words – the first he speaks after the act of rape – show the mechanism of projection at work; the projection has resulted in a denigration of the envied object, so that a retrospective justification is available for the sadistic attack and the welcome release of tension enjoyed, at first, without guilt:[54]

> *Professor* (out of breath, stammering)   Trollop. . . . She
> asked for it. . . . Now I feel better. . . . Ah! . . .
> I'm tired. . . .

I mentioned that sadistic fantasies at their most intense may lose sight of the woman as a person, as the Professor virtually loses sight of the Girl Pupil except as a vehicle for his sadism. However, *The Lesson* is greatly strengthened by the introduction of a different, and less pathological, relationship between the man and another woman. In the person of the Maid Ionesco has given us the kind of disapproving but indulgent mother figure who might be expected to support and encourage the child's sadistic fantasies. The relationship between her and the Professor, deployed in the epilogue that, after the climax of the murder, closes the play, is demonstrably that of mother and child. At the climax itself there is a subtle anticipation of the Professor's child self; as Professor and Pupil approach the moment of truth, he enjoins her to repeat after him the word 'Knife': 'Say it again, watch it. (Like a child) Knifey . . . Knifey.'[55] After the murder, the Professor, in a reaction of horror at finding the body of a pupil on his hands, calls in panic for the Maid. She is at first severe and unsympathetic: 'Aren't you ashamed of yourself, at your age too!'[56] Vexed at her reproaches, he defends himself by accusing the dead girl of being 'a bad pupil'; Professor and Maid then enact with remarkable precision the parts of a nasty child turning on its mother and the mother responding with interest:[57]

> *Professor* (approaching the maid slyly, his knife behind
> his back)   It's none of your business! (He tries
> to strike her a terrific blow, but she seizes his
> wrist and twists it; the Professor drops his knife).
> . . . Forgive me!
> (The Maid strikes the Professor twice, forcibly
> and noisily, so that he falls to the ground on his
> behind, snivelling.)
> *Maid*   You little murderer! Revolting little swine!
> Wanted to do that to me, did you! I'm not one
> of your blessed pupils!

> (She hauls him up by the back of his collar. . . .
> He is afraid of being hit again and protects
> himself with his elbow, like a child.)

Having thus established her ascendancy, she relents. It is already clear from an earlier scene that she has known all the time what is going to happen and has allowed it to happen; she warns the Professor not to go too far – 'Philology is the worst of all . . . you won't say I didn't warn you!'[58] Later, however, although she recognizes that with the toothache induced in the Pupil by the philology lesson 'the worst symptom'[59] has arrived, she leaves the two alone together. Now, with the body of the Pupil between them, she responds to the Professor's sobs and protestations with something like sympathy, as soon as he has admitted he is sorry:

> Maid   At least you're sorry you did it?
> Professor Oh yes, Marie, I swear I am.
> Maid   I can't help feeling for you. Come now! You're
>   not a bad boy after all! . . .

She exacts a promise that he won't do it again, significantly because it might be bad for him ('it would give you heart trouble . . .'); she then helps him to plan the funeral and advises him how best to protect himself, finally assisting him to carry the body off stage.[60]

This fine scene suggests in almost every particular the mother who overlooks the murderous pranks of the child because she is too big to be seriously threatened by them; the initial violence of her response combines with the absence of any real disapproval on her part to stimulate his sadism, which is effectively displaced on to the more vulnerable target of the girl pupil. Structurally the scene is integral to the meaning of the play, which presents us both with the roots of sadism in infantile fantasy and with a cogent example of a later, indirect manifestation of the impulse in the exploitation of language for the purposes of sadistic domination. The adult teacher who forces a parody of learning down the pupil's throat and the child caught out by its mother in a nasty sadistic game are linked by the enacted fantasy of the rape cum murder. Ionesco is careful to preserve a sense of fantasy throughout the grotesque climax; the knife with which the Professor kills the

Pupil, and with which he later threatens the Maid, is invisible. Moreover, when the Professor asks, of the coffins which the Maid is to order for him 'What if anyone asks us what's inside?' she replies, ' . . . We'll say they're empty. Besides, no one will ask any questions. *They're used to it*'[61] [my italics].

We are, indeed, all used to it, although it is not often recognized for what it is. *The Lesson* is not a morality play, but none the less it embodies a valuable and neglected truth: that primitive sadistic instincts do not only, or indeed normally, find gross physical expression, but find effective release in many less obvious and more subtle ways. Ionesco's choice of the teaching situation is an apt one for this purpose. The educative process can degenerate into an exercise of power at the expense of the pupil, a power that is sadistic in origin in that it reflects in displaced form an early sadistic impulse. *The Lesson* shows how the urge to dominate and control may at first take the milder form of a metaphorical seduction and if this proves unsuccessful develop into metaphorical rape. (It must be remembered that the design of the play requires that the seduction remain metaphorical while the rape is presented as literal and actual.) Both processes concern themselves with the needs of the teacher and not with those of the taught. The student may be seduced into believing that he is learning when he is really serving the teacher's ego, whether by acting as willing receptacle for an exhibitionist display on the teacher's part or by himself making such a display of prowess in response to flattery and encouragement by the teacher; both processes are a substitute for the mutual effort of learning. In terms of early experience, a narcissistic and exhibitionistic activity, involving masturbatory fantasies or at a later state fantasies of intercourse with the mother, has been substituted for feeding. Rape, in terms of the metaphor, suggests the bludgeoning of the pupil into an acceptance of what is arbitrarily prescribed by the teacher; it is a penetration by force – the psychological force at the disposal of superior age, experience, knowledge. Neither process can be regarded as uncommon in the teaching relationship.

Seduction is certainly present in *The Lesson*. At first the Professor flatters and conciliates his Pupil:[62]

> *Pupil*   One and one make two.
> *Professor* (astonished by his pupil's erudition) But

that's very good indeed! You're extremely
advanced in your studies. You'll have very
little difficulty in passing all your Doctorate
examinations.

Later he displays his own prowess in the field of comparative
philology, in a long nonsensical declamation about the neo-
Spanish languages; the Pupil is at first delighted and fascinated.
However, as the Professor becomes more insistent and aggressive
in his self-display, refusing to permit any interruption, the Pupil
suddenly announces that she has toothache. From this point
onwards she defies the Professor by means of her toothache,
rejecting and even mocking his instruction; he only succeeds in
overcoming her defiance by an increasing, and increasingly
violent, pressure. The toothache may perhaps indicate loss of
the power of speech and so of language; the parody of the whole
learning process is an important element in the play. Just as,
positively speaking, language is seen as an instrument of power,
so negatively the communication of knowledge is mocked in the
nonsense games played by the pair in language and arithmetic:[63]

> *Pupil*   I can count up to . . . infinity.
> *Professor* That's impossible.
> *Pupil*   Up to sixteen, then.
> *Professor* That's quite far enough. We must all recognize
> our limitations.

It is worth noting here, in the context of the parody of learning, a
comic device by which Ionesco reinforces the 'progressive height-
ening and intensification' he is seeking: the Pupil can do complex
sums of addition with miraculous ease, but she cannot subtract,
arguing, for example, that three from four makes seven.

The toothache has perhaps an additional significance: the
persistent but feeble resistance to instruction offered by this
means is seen to act as provocation to the Professor, whose tone
and manner, already assertive, are transformed into open sadism:[64]

> *Professor* . . . And so on and so on. . . .
> *Pupil*   That's enough! That's enough! I've got . . .
> *Professor* The toothache! The toothache! . . . Teeth, teeth,
> teeth, teeth! . . . I'll have them all out for you in
> a minute. . . .

There is even a hint, in the obsessive nature of the Pupil's complaints of toothache, that to her teaching in itself is experienced as a violation, a painful penetration of her body by the voice of the Professor:[65]

> Pupil   That's enough! I've had enough! Besides, my teeth ache and my feet ache and my head aches.... You make my ears ache, too. What a voice you've got! How piercing it is!
>
> Professor Say Knife.... Kni ... Fff. ...

Her fantasies may be thought to play a part in the situation, operating in collusion with the Professor's fantasies to bring about the fatal conclusion; this is certainly in keeping with the general impression made on us by the play. Admittedly, at this point the Professor is already threatening her with sadistic violence; as we know from the opening stage direction, by now his voice has grown more powerful and piercing. However, the passage is reminiscent of one in *Amédée*, where Amédée's loving enthusiasm is experienced by Madeleine, his wife, as a sadistic attack: 'Your voice is so piercing! You are deafening me! Hurting me! Don't rend my darkness! S-a-dist! . . .'[66] As Martin Esslin comments: 'The situation is that of an ardent lover and a girl who regards all advances as acts of violence and rape.'[67]

I suggested earlier that Ionesco understands how ubiquitously a primitive, infantile sadism operates in normal adult human affairs in a concealed and displaced form. By a bold paradox, this point is made by a reversal – by the presentation of a normal activity, teaching, that develops rapidly into a grotesquely sadistic situation. A final touch reinforces our sense of the operation of a basic aggressive drive in a form unrecognized, and so socially and morally acceptable. We learn from the Maid – she is speaking of the Professor's crime – that 'it's the fortieth time today! And every day it's the same story! Every day! . . .'[68] Clearly she is used to it, just as people in general are used to the sight of the coffins of his victims. The extravagance, by being pushed so far, succeeds brilliantly since 'one can dare anything in the theatre',[69] in the author's words. *The Lesson* points the moral, in its own essentially comic terms, that sadism is not merely a psychopathic perversion but a universal, even commonplace, illness, affecting respectable professors and their bright pupils. Ionesco calls

The Lesson a comic drama; whatever the wider implications, it is certainly comic in its preoccupation with incongruity and also in a certain emotional detachment. There is none of the plangency of feeling or poetic suggestiveness to be found in *The Killer* or *The Chairs;* I suspect that for Ionesco there is little or no poetry in sadism. This is greatly to his credit – a refreshing contrast to writers whose only source of poetry seems to lie in the sado-masochistic areas of experience. If *The Lesson* has less depth for this reason, it has a compensating concentration of effect. More importantly, it displays, in common with the other plays of Ionesco I have discussed, the power and insight of a veritable master of the irrational, one who follows 'the true road into my own darkness, our darkness, which I try to bring to the light of day'.[70]

Notes

1 E. Ionesco, 'Expérience du Théâtre', *Nouvelle Revue Française*, (Paris, 1 February 1958), pp. 258–9. I owe this and other quotations from Ionesco's writings on the drama to Martin Esslin, *The Theatre of the Absurd* (New York, 1961), ch. 3.

2 Ionesco, 'The Playwright's Role', *Observer* (6 July 1958). Tynan's criticism appeared in the previous number of the paper.

3 Esslin, op. cit., ch. 3, p. 99.

4 Ionesco, 'The Point of Departure', *Cahiers des Quatre Saisons*, no. 1 (Paris).

5 Ionesco, 'La Tragédie du Langage', *Spectacles*, no. 2 (Paris, July 1958).

6 Ibid.

7 'Expérience du Théâtre', p. 258.

8 Ionesco, *Amédée*, trans. Donald Watson, *Plays II* (London, 1958), p. 226.

9 Ibid.

10 'Expérience du Théâtre', p. 268.

11 *Amédée*, ed. cit., p. 62.

12 Ionesco, 'Lorsque j'écris . . .', *Cahiers des Quatre Saisons*, no. 15.

13 *Amédée*, ed. cit., p. 227.

14 Ionesco, *The Killer*, trans. Donald Watson (London, 1958), p. 77.

15 Ibid., pp. 80–1.

16 Ibid.

17 Ibid., p. 82.

18 Ibid., p. 81.

19 Ibid.

20 See above.

21 *The Killer*, ed. cit., p. 82.

22 Ibid., p. 83.
23 The French title of the play.
24 *Evergreen Review*, March 1957 (trans. Stanley Reed).
25 Esslin, op. cit., pp. 122–3.
26 *The Killer*, ed. cit., pp. 68–9.
27 Ibid.
28 Ionesco, *Improvisation*, trans. Donald Watson, *Plays III* (London: Calder; New York: Grove Press, 1960), pp. 112–13.
29 Melanie Klein, *Our Adult World and its Roots in Infancy* (London, 1960), p.6.
30 See above, p. 104.
31 Ibid.
32 J. R. Sutherland, *A Preface to Eighteenth Century Poetry* (Oxford, 1948), p. 161.
33 *Improvisation*, pp. 112–13.
34 'Eugène Ionesco ouvre le feu', *World Theatre*, VIII, 3, Autumn 1959.
35 Letter from Ionesco to Sylvain Dhomme, quoted by F. Towarnicki, 'Des Chaises vides . . . à Broadway', *Spectacles*, no. 2 (Paris, July 1958).
36 Letter from Ionesco to Dhomme.
37 See above, p. 113.
38 Ionesco, *The Chairs*, trans. Donald Watson (London, 1968), p. 13.
39 Ibid., p. 13.
40 Ibid.
41 Ibid., p. 30.
42 Ibid., pp. 31–2.
43 Ibid., p. 50.
44 Ibid., p. 44.
45 Ibid., p. 53.
46 Ibid., final stage directions, pp. 59–60.
47 Letter from Ionesco to Dhomme.
48 *The Chairs*, final stage directions, ed. cit., pp. 59–60.
49 Ionesco, *The Lesson*, trans. Donald Watson (London, 1958), Penguin edition, pp. 182–3.
50 See above, p. 17.
51 Klein, op. cit., p. 8.
52 *The Lesson*, ed. cit., p. 214.
53 Ibid.
54 Ibid.
55 Ibid., p. 213.
56 Ibid., pp. 215–16.
57 Ibid., p. 198.
58 Ibid., p. 198.
59 Ibid., p. 211.
60 Ibid., pp. 216–17.
61 Ibid., p. 217. I discuss the point of the plurality of coffins later in this chapter (see p. 123).
62 Ibid., p. 189.
63 Ibid., pp. 190–1.
64 Ibid., p. 208.
65 Ibid., p. 212.

66 *Amédée*, ed. cit., p. 48.
67 Esslin, op. cit., p. 108.
68 *The Lesson*, ed. cit., p. 215.
69 See above, p. 113.
70 See above, p. 102.

Five

The *Marat Sade* Play: The Primitive in Action

There are two features of this remarkable play[1] of especial relevance to my theme. The first has to do with the form; the second, with the content, especially the role of the Marquis de Sade, as conceived and written by the author, Peter Weiss. In form, the play is an example of what has come to be known as 'total theatre'; it exploits a wide range of theatrical resources in order to make its peculiar, multifarious effect. The Aristotelian 'representation of an action' – the action here being the performance of a play about the murder of Marat, by the inmates of the asylum of Charenton – is supported by devices drawn from music-hall and cabaret, opera and ballet, and circus; especially important is the ancient theatrical art of mime and dumb-show. In constructing his play Weiss has put to remarkable use a detail of nineteenth-century history – that from 1801 to his death in 1814, Sade 'was interned in the asylum of Charenton, where over a period of years he had the chance of producing plays among the patients and appearing as an actor himself'. We thus have a play within a play; Sade's play of the murder of Marat, of which he is clearly the author, is performed by the inmates of the asylum before its Director, M. Coulmier, and under his surveillance and that of the asylum's male nurses and sisters. This device not only provides a double perspective, with a constant ironical movement between the acknowledged derangement of the actors and the actual, or supposed, sanity of the society that both confines them and provides the matter for their play – revolution, terror, murder. It also enables Weiss to combine the techniques of realism and expressionism under one roof. The activities of the inmates of Charenton are realistic enough in the context of the outer drama; this is how the deranged, and other outcasts from society – for Charenton embraced those regarded as socially incorrigible by the authorities as well as the mad – might be supposed to act a play, if directed by a man as peculiar as Sade. The theatrical joke by which Sade is acquainted with the style, and disposes of the resources, of the Royal Shakespeare Company and Peter Brook, is surely acceptable.[2] In contrast, the play itself offers no illusion of reality; in the first place, it is subject to constant interruption by Coulmier and his assistants – Coulmier often remonstrating with Sade over the latter's restoration of agreed cuts in the text. Second, it requires to be performed in an expressionistic style; Peter Brook's production utilized to the full the various theatrical devices of the epic theatre familiar to playgoers from the work of Brecht and Joan Littlewood (the analogy with *Oh what a Lovely War* is especially instructive). Mime is the most prominent of these devices; the four singers – described by Weiss as 'part crowd types, part comedians'[3] – mime acrobatic accompaniments to their doggerel songs, and the most dramatic events of the inner play, including the climax of the murder, are mimed by the participants. Charlotte Corday's arrival in Paris is celebrated by a dance of death as victims of the terror are dragged along in the tumbril to be guillotined; this scene is performed with appropriate enthusiasm by the actors, who themselves represent the guillotine, the horse pulling the tumbril, etc., and mime the actions of tormenting and executing the victims. Characterization is suitably summary and stylized; an important figure is the Herald, part chorus, part assistant producer, who gives us information about his fellow actors and the characters they play and assists them when they falter or go wrong. The absence of any illusion of reality in the inner play is paradoxically underlined by what is essentially a realistic aspect of the outer play: the supporting actors, though continuously on stage, only act intermittently, alternating between a passive withdrawal into their illness and an over-excited response to the violent events being portrayed which frequently leads to their forcible restraint.

This constant reminder that the actors are also mentally deranged patients has an important emotional effect; an analogy is established between the chaotic violence of the external world of revolution and that of the internal world of madness. Marat specifically points the analogy when, tormented by his painful skin disease, he cried out, 'My head's on fire I can't breathe.

There is a rioting mob inside me.'[4] Throughout the play the stage is crowded with extras of whom Weiss writes in the opening stage direction:[5]

> According to need they appear either in their white hospital uniforms or in primitive costumes. . . . Any not required in the play devote themselves to physical exercises. Their presence must set the atmosphere behind the acting area.

The dramatic method by which the open theatricality of the inner play is contained, like a picture in its frame, by the realism of the outer play is thus more than a clever device. Expressionism, which as a method exploits the freedom of dramatic illusion in order to give a plausible portrayal of the inner world, is intimately related to mental illness, a condition in which the social and cultural restraints on instinct are undermined. It is the method of the Freudian *Id* where, in the words of Strindberg's famous comment on his *Dream Play*, '. . . everything is possible and probable . . . there are no secrets, no scruples, and no law'.[6] Weiss shows how much expressionism gains in effectiveness, both as to form and meaning, by being set in the context of supposed social normality which in reality is deeply infected by the hidden dynamism of the presence of uninhibited instinct. We are thus prepared for the climax, in which the two plays effectively merge; the patients have been over-excited by the drama they have been acting, and the whole play ends in tumult and riot reminiscent of the mob activities earlier described and in fact presented by Sade. As the curtain falls, it is not clear whether the hospital authorities can re-establish control over their charges or not; Sade, triumphant at the course of events, has successfully carried through his own radical therapy, in defiance of the orthodox therapy of Coulmier. The *Id* of the patients' inner play has begun to penetrate the *Ego* and *Superego* of the outer play, a world where Coulmier, who models his pose on Napoleon's, exercises a benevolent dictatorship over his patients which is analogous to that of Napoleon over France.

Weiss strengthens the link between the two plays by a further subtle device whereby the producer, Sade, is seen to have clearly selected his actors with an eye to the roles they are to portray. The patient who plays Corday is described as suffering from sleeping-sickness and melancholia; she 'moves like a somnam-bulist',[7] a condition very appropriate to her haunted, hypnotized journey through blood-soaked Paris to Marat's door. There is no evidence that Corday approached her destiny in such a state of mind; Weiss has taken liberties with history in order to intensify his treatment. The patient who plays her lover, Duperret, a sentimental high-minded man of the Girondist persuasion, is held in the mental home as an erotomaniac; the irony here is almost too obvious, in the context of violence and murder. The contrast of flowery sentiments and furtive action – he makes constant sexual advances to Corday under cover of his role – is a microcosm of a similar contrast in society. Marat himself is acted, the Herald tells us, by a 'lucky paranoiac'[8] whose condition is improving under hydrotherapy; not only does this enable the actor to perfom without strain in the famous bath – with some historical warrant[9] Marat is shown, in the painful isolation imposed on him by his skin disease, as in truth suffering from a kind of paranoia.[10] By a brilliant paradox the whole device both underscores the element of obvious illusion and theatricality in the play, and reinforces the emotional effect on the audience of the mimed action of terror and violence. We respond simul-taneously to the cast as patients in the outer play and as actors in the inner play; indeed, we cannot always be sure which play we are witnessing. When Marat, desperate to finish his life's work before he is destroyed by illness or the enmity of his rivals, falls exhausted across the board of his bath, are we watching the reaction of the character or the actor? Either is appropriate; theatricality has surpassed itself by the very fact of its confine-ment within the realistic frame. We inhabit simultaneously one world and two.

As Peter Brook points out in his introduction,[11] this movement in and out of two worlds both distances the spectator and involves him more closely in the scene. It answers well to Weiss's purpose, which is to write at once a play of ideas and a drama of passion. The debate between the anarchic individualism of Sade and the purposeful socialism of Marat is ostensibly at the play's centre; whatever intellectual weaknesses there may be in the presentation of the debate, it certainly provokes reflection on a major con-temporary dilemma. Moreover, what it loses in clarity as a play of ideas it surely gains in force; reflection on the great issues involved, of the use and abuse of violence, is given an uncomfortably sharp edge by the extent of the emotional participation exacted from us. A debate on the primitive is staged as a display of the primitive, in a form that distinguishes it from the other plays I have discussed; the use of what is, basically, a popular dramatic tradition, and the continual shift of perspective between the illusory and the real, has the effect of undermining, in a limited but significant way, the barrier between stage and auditorium, actors and audience. The barrier is at its most strict in the naturalistic drama that, since Ibsen, has occupied by far the greater part of our stage; the *Marat Sade* play is one of a number of recent *avant garde* theatrical experiments that invite a kind of participation on the part of the audience. An older tradition is being revived here, examples of which would range from the ancient drama of ritual that survives in religious services, to music-hall; probably the most striking example of dramatic or semi-dramatic participation is the concert of pop music, where the devotees act out, within certain limits, the feelings aroused in them by the music. Significantly, perhaps, 'happenings' now occur sporadically in the theatre itself, occasions when the audience are invited to participate, individually or collectively, in some unheralded event. Dramatic tact on the part of the author of the *Marat Sade* – an awareness of the limits of what is possible in the contemporary metropolitan theatre – ensures that the invitation to participate is kept within the bounds of dramatic illusion, is in effect itself illusory. There is no actual breach of the convention by which one pays for one's seat and thereafter simply watches the performance; no attempt on the part of the company to have the audience join in the final tumult on the stage.[12] However, I suspect that such a breach is present to any responsive audience as an unrealized possibility, and thus contributes to the tensions aroused by the play in performance. An unresponsive audience would, I think, set special problems to a company performing this play; the high degree of involvement demanded would exaggerate by contrast the gap between auditorium and stage. It is not that the involvement is more profound, or even more exciting. I doubt if there is any passage in the *Marat Sade* as penetrating to a receptive audience, emotionally speaking, as the moment in *The Bacchae* when the messenger describes the murder of Pentheus by his demented mother; and this is a description merely, at second hand. But the involvement in the *Marat Sade* is a closer one, in terms of the external world of physical action; it is easier to envisage hypothetical circumstances in which we could join in such a collective display of primitive emotions without altering the effect – and this is not true of Euripides, Strindberg, or Pinter. At certain kinds of pop music concert, as I have mentioned, this kind of relatively primitive participation actually occurs; the congregation have been observed to sway, moan, and display hysterical reactions to the music, much as the inmates of Charenton react to the play Sade has them perform. It is worth noting that the technique of the double play presents us, the audience, with a stage audience who do as a matter of course participate in Sade's play about the murder of Marat; Coulmier, the director, supported by his family, watches the play as audience, while in his role as alienist and *censor morum* he interferes with actions he judges to be subversive or dangerous to his patients or to the ruling society of which he is the representative. By the end of the play the Coulmier family, enshrined as they have been hitherto in an unimpeachable authority and dignity, are in real danger of being submerged in the confused and violent world of the asylum inmates. This episode surely affects us, and is intended to affect us, as a mirror-image of our own hypothetical participation in that world, safely insulated although we remain – as spectators – within the walls of the theatre on whose stage the whole play is being performed.

The *Marat Sade* play thus exemplifies a new, or revived, dramatic tradition under which we, the audience, ourselves a collective though fragmented body of persons, are drawn closer to the collective action of the players. It is in the combination of this feature with the exploration of primitive instincts of violence and terror, through both action and reflection, that the originality of the play lies. Thus in *The Bacchae* the powerful impact made upon us by the death of Pentheus is achieved through an indirect and symbolic identification: by a realization, that is, of that aspect of the predicament of mother and son which is in essence our predicament too, however dissimilar the fictional situation and personalities concerned. Here, in contrast, although such indirect identification does occur, the appeal is also to our suppressed wish to act out, in a physical sense, our own primitive urges; the cast perform the enactment for us, through mime. A

question mark must clearly remain over any further development of this technique. Is an actual theatre of participation
conceivable without anarchy and even derangement, in a society
where the surviving social and religious rituals have lost the
power to contain and order the need for ceremonial participation? The question is not raised by the *Marat Sade* play, which
offers us an original kind of exploration of and participation in
the primitive in terms of a normal theatrical experience.

I turn now to the theme of the play, which takes the form of a
debate, by statement or implication, on the role of violence in
society. Few who know the play will disagree with the judgment
that Sade is the dominant figure; it is his view of life that, to
judge from this play, has made the greatest impact on the author,
and so on readers and audience also, despite Weiss's apparent
claim, referred to by Peter Brook in his introduction, that his
play is Marxist in sympathy.[13] The debate, though heavily
weighted in Sade's favour, and perhaps somewhat blurred by
the dazzling technique, gains greatly by being rooted in what we
know to have been its hero's actual opinions; Weiss has perceived
that these opinions are of great interest and relevance today,
bearing directly on the single most formidable problem facing
organized society.

Sade is attracted by the element of chaotic violence in the
French revolution, an event in which he sees a partial fulfilment
of his own most real wishes. Marat's extremism therefore appeals
to him, in that they share a belief in the inevitability of violence
and even in the need for change. However, he parts company
with Marat over two vital, and related, issues. First, Sade is an
uncompromising individualist, to whom the only ultimate reality
is the unplumbed depths of the self:[14]

> What we do is just a shadow of what we want to do
> and the only truths we can point to
> are the ever-changing truths of our own experience.

and later, in a direct address to Marat:[15]

> And why should you care about the world outside
> For me the only reality is imagination
> The world inside myself
> The Revolution
> no longer interests me. . . .

Second, what he discovers in the exploration of the self is, above all, pleasure in pain and destruction; the pleasure, to Sade, depends directly upon the pain (the historical Sade is known to have advocated compulsory sexual promiscuity as a way of neutralizing the most socially dangerous of all human instincts, that which finds an indirect sexual pleasure in destructiveness).[16] The clearest and most telling statement of this belief occurs in what is virtually a soliloquy by Sade just before the murder of Marat:[17]

> Marat
> as I sat there in the Bastille
> for thirteen long years
> I learned
> that this is a world of bodies
> each body pulsing with a terrible power. . . .
> Shut behind thirteen bolted doors
> my feet fettered
> I dreamed only
> of the orifices of the body
> put there
> so one may hook and twine oneself in them
> Continually I dreamed of this confrontation
> and it was a dream of the most savage jealous
> and cruellest imagining. . . . .

In his works, the historical Sade makes it clear that the supreme attraction of cruelty, as of crime, is that it is a milestone on the road to a self-realization which is in essence sexual. Believing that pleasure, basically of a sexual type, is the right true end of man, he also believed that pleasure could only be cultivated and extended by overcoming superficial reactions of repugnance and fear.[18] His view of the human personality thus appropriately embraces masochism as well as sadism, as the words Weiss writes for him make clear:[19]

> I do not know if I am hangman or victim
> for I imagine the most horrible tortures
> and as I describe them I suffer them myself
> There is nothing that I could not do and everything
> fills me with horror. . . .

That we have to do here with a pathological fantsy of omnipotence
of infantile origin seems clear; a fantasy that leads directly to
self-destructive wishes, through projective identification with real
or imaginary victims – a point made in the last line of the passage
quoted above, and more specifically later in the play.[20] Sade
was fascinated and haunted by the possibility of a life which,
'ruled entirely by instinct, would be a nightmare scramble of
insatiable desire'.[21] It is part of this infantile regression, to a time
when instinct is indeed king, and when only a combination of
external control and lack of effective opportunity preserve the
infant from the violence of his own instinctual wishes. For the
present, however, I wish rather to consider how Sade's personality
and experience, pathological though they clearly were, enabled
him to make a radical critique of the revolutionary idealist to
whom violence is *justifiable* as the necessary means to a socially
desirable end:[22]

> *Marat*   If I am extreme I am not extreme in the
> same way as you
> Against Nature's silence I use action
> In the vast indifference I invent a meaning
> I don't watch unmoved I intervene
> and say that this and this are wrong
> and I work to alter and improve them.

To the social revolutionary the notion that cruelty and extremism are justified because of the pleasure they bring is naturally
repugnant. Sade, however, turns the tables on his opponents.
His obsessive individualism, and his understanding of the hidden
connection between cruelty and sensuality, gives him a penetrating insight into that rationalized and legalized sadism that so
often walks abroad in respectable disguises. The revolutionary,
with his fanatical dedication to principle, is peculiarly blind to
this sinister phenomenon and so peculiarly vulnerable to the
individualist's attack; in defence and implementation of his
principles he is liable to give free rein and support to an unrecognized sadism which in the personal sphere he would recognize
and bring under some sort of control. Moreover, the dogmatic
principles of politics and religion, in their rigorous exclusiveness
and intolerance of opposition, have a repressive sadism built in
to the keystone of their arch; the history of organized religion

alone bears this out. Sade's dedication to cruelty as the source of ultimate pleasure may be felt to weaken his case; it is of course a condition of the whole debate in the play, for it is this dedication that gives him common ground with the reputed butcher, Marat.[23] Moreover, as a matter of history, Sade, who knew the revolution to be necessary, was imprisoned in 1793 by the revolutionary regime because of his moderation; opposed as he always was to the death penalty and to legal oppression in any form, he was genuinely shocked by the communal excesses of the Terror. Indeed he was sufficiently consistent, and humane, to extend a secret clemency to some of his worst enemies, during the brief period when he acted as a judge during the Terror.[24] His dislike of the Terror is in part, no doubt, because the cruelties were performed by others; Sade's individualism is rooted in a pathological egoism. Only where he himself is torturer or victim, or where, as with the execution of Damiens,[25] he can easily identify with a sado-masochistic situation, can he obtain pleasure from it; elsewhere he is repelled. Thus in Weiss's description he is forced to 'bend over in the courtyard and vomit'[26] at the sight of the official sacking of the Carmelite convent in Paris by the mob, an event that should in theory have appealed to him as being largely the product of instinctual passions. But whatever unresolved conflicts are suggested here – Sade clearly rationalizes his own sickness into a universal principle – it remains true that politically speaking he was a moderate and humanitarian, 'a black saint whose humanity must be set against the horrors of his imagination'.[27] (His personal moderation and humanity, in striking contrast to the vindictiveness and ruthlessness displayed by many of his respectable enemies, is subtly indicated by Weiss in the protective attitude he displays as producer towards his unfortunate cast.)

It is thus Sade's own intimate if distorted understanding of human sadistic and aggressive instincts, allied to an individualism implacably hostile to collective authority, that enables him to see how those in authority exploit these instincts in the pursuit of power:[28]

> I don't believe in idealists
> who charge down blind alleys
> I don't believe in any of the sacrifices
> that have been made for any cause.

Like Dostoevsky after him, Sade, as Weiss portrays him, sees the morality of the ant-hill in operation here:[29]

> as the tumbrils ran regularly to the scaffolds . . .
> all the meaning drained out of this revenge
> It had become mechanical
> It was inhuman it was dull. . . .
> now I see where
> this revolution is leading
> To the withering of the individual man
> and a slow merging into uniformity
> to the death of choice . . .
> in a state
> which has no contact with individuals
> but which is impregnable.

The new France will be a France where 'everything is controlled' by those who have transmuted their sadism into a repressive activity against others. Certainly we should allow today for a creative sublimation of the sadistic instinct into competition and necessary discipline, and for the presence of a benevolent protective instinct in those in authority to counteract the malevolence of a sadistic exercise of power. Sade's obsession blinds him to this possibility. But the obsessive distortions of Sade's outlook do not undermine the force of his insight into the largely unrecognized power of organized sadism. He sees, not only that it marches with flying banners under the progressive slogans of the revolution; it is even more potent, and far less obvious, in the 'fifteen glorious years' of Napoleon's rule (1808 is the year of the play's supposed performance in the asylum at Charenton). The director Coulmier's complacent reference to the enlightened times of the present are capped by the chorus's ironical praise of Napoleon; all this lends support to Sade's arguments, for since '[violent] death represents sadistic destruction at its most complete',[30] the domestic peace of the Napoleonic era achieved in its foreign wars greater triumphs of organized sadism than even the Terror. A particularly effective contribution of the chorus comes in Scene 31 of the play, *Interruptus*,[31] where like Raphael in *Paradise Lost* revealing to Adam the future course of human history the chorus in doggerel verse

. . . interrupt the climax so this man
Marat can hear and gasp with his last breath
at how the world will go after his death
With a musical history we'll bring him up to date. . . .

Fifteen glorious years . . .
Years of peace
years of war . . .
All the world
bends its knee
to Napoleon
and his family
Fight on land and sea
All men want to be free
If they don't
never mind
we'll abolish all mankind.

As the last line here suggests, Weiss takes anachronistic liberties
with the situation of Napoleonic France; much of what he writes
is more obviously applicable to our own times, whose pessimism,
in contrast to the comparative optimism of the former era,
seems to be the result both of the perpetration of atrocities on an
unprecedented scale and of greater awareness of what is involved.
The anachronism may be condoned on the grounds that Sade
was very much in advance of his own time; he makes a suitable
subject for a Brechtian confusion of past and present.

Brigid Brophy writes penetratingly of Sade that although[32]

> his egoism and destructiveness are . . . Napoleonic . . .
> he has not yet socialized his destructive wishes and
> created a machine for dealing death. This, of course, he
> cannot do because he is an essentially single adven-
> turer. . . .

Who can doubt today that organized and 'socialized' sadism,
something totally foreign to Sade's anarchic individualism, is
infinitely more dangerous and evil than the pathological sadism
of the individual? Elsewhere in her book[33] Miss Brophy points
out that in our culture

> We are still less humanitarian than he [Sade] in so far
> as we can contemplate a more or less naked Thanatos

without shock, and condemn it only when it is allied to so strong a force of Eros that we cannot avoid noticing its voluptuous character. Scenes where people are killed 'cleanly' though none the less agonizingly call forth no censorship; Sade's fictions we regard as obscene. . . .

Psychoanalysis would argue that that 'more or less naked Thanatos' still contains within itself a distorted Eros; but it is an important truth that, the more effectively the pleasure or sexual principle in cruelty and violence is concealed, the more dangerous, because more buried, the sadism becomes; dissociated from sexuality, it can be freely indulged, without guilt and inhibition. Gorer makes the point that 'the amount of sadistic satisfaction afforded by popular entertainment is as astounding as it is historically unparalleled'. He argues persuasively that the conditions of modern life have increased the need for vicarious sadistic satisfaction, whereas vicarious sexual satisfaction of a straightforward type is less sought after owing to the rapid growth of sexual permissiveness.[34] Sade, though he lacked the vital clue of unconscious motivation, had such a fanatical mistrust of organized authority that he enjoyed an understanding probably unique in his own time of the extent and depth to which that authority is liable to corruption. As Geoffrey Gorer writes, 'no European writer . . . has penetrated more deeply into the destructive motives of those who seek or hold power'.[35] It is not surprising that the dislike and distrust are returned with interest; Gorer recounts how since 1801, when Napoleon's ministers had all the copies of Sade's works that could be found destroyed, those works have been subject to continuous censorship and persecution. As Gorer convincingly argues, this is because Sade puts his finger on the true motives of the 'butchers and persecutors'; his psychological investigations[36]

> explain the horrible fact that whenever men get unrestrained power over their fellows, whether in revolution or counter-revolution, . . . they will practise on their victims the most revolting tortures, and tortures which receive a greater or lesser, and usually greater sexual tinge.

No wonder, then, that[37]

the authorities who still use the same excuses for the same brutalities have condemned and pursued his work with a vigour they have never applied to any other writer.

In Wilde's famous phrase, the reaction of authority to Sade is the rage of Caliban at seeing his face in the glass (it is evidence of Sade's disturbing originality that he was abominated by pornographers and libertines, for whom society has always kept a cherished place). It is thus appropriate that in Weiss's play Coulmier, the Director of the Asylum, angrily interrupts a sardonic attack on the church:[38]

> We agreed to make some cuts in this passage
> After all nobody now objects to the church
> since our emperor is surrounded by high-ranking clergy....

Napoleon had been crowned in Milan cathedral three years before.

It is a moot point whether Weiss's play is more effective in its development of Sade's undermining of Marat's revolutionary hopes by his understanding of the pathology of power, or simply in its powerfully disturbing rendering, again through the insights of a neurotic of genius, of the prevalence of an unacknowledged violence and cruelty in the life of civilized society. It has been argued that Weiss holds the balance between the two contestants, but it is hard to believe this is his intention. At best, his attitude to Marat is very ambivalent. Though he displays the kind of sympathy for him to be expected from one of Weiss's political affiliations, he allows his position to be damaged almost beyond repair not only by Sade's attacks and insinuations but by the whole ironic conclusion to the play, the celebration of the glorious years of Napoleon to which the revolution has led, years which have confirmed the continuing post-revolutionary misery and hopelessness of the poor. Immediately before Corday's third, fatal visit, Marat is made to acknowledge something like defeat:[39]

> Why is everything so confused now
> Everything I wrote or spoke
> was considered and true
> each argument was sound

> And now
> doubt
> Why does everything sound false.

The effect of this is hardly erased by a last-minute recovery that has the force of an ironical joke: his confidence regained, he calls for his ally, Bas, to write down at his dictation a call to the French people, but in his place comes Corday with the knife. In Sade's words, which have a double meaning[40]

> Marat
> what are all your pamphlets and speeches
> compared with her . . .
> an untouched virgin stands before you and offers
> herself to you. . . .

It may further be argued that Marat is never given an opportunity to develop those radical ideas which, if implemented, might have made all the difference to the future; his murder makes him a victim of the 'crass casualty' of history. He is certainly portrayed with some sympathetic understanding, a victim of chronic illness before he falls under Corday's knife. But the deeper truth of the matter is surely that he is portrayed even more as a victim of self-deception; in effect, if not wholly in intention, the play demonstrates that neither Marat's revolution, nor subsequent revolutions that have been even more thorough in their methods, bring the millennium any nearer. A half-awareness of this on the part of the chorus tinges their sympathy with something like contempt – 'Poor old Marat'.[41]

Weiss nowhere states, or even directly implies, this ideological pessimism. If Marat's hopes are illusory, Sade's obsession with cruelty blinds his vision too and brings him to a despair grimmer than Marat's self-deceptions. Sade's pathological sadism is recognizably sick; his destructive wishes, allied to his belief in self-exploration without limit or restraint, suggest to the student of psychoanalysis, as I have already suggested,[42] an omnipotent fantasy that in infantile terms is based on massive denial of dependence. (It may be worth noting that Geoffrey Gorer records that his mother 'seems to have had nothing to do with the Marquis de Sade after his earliest childhood'.)[43] The infantile envy that denies dependence also powers the sadism, which becomes a compensatory activity for the failure to achieve relationships of dependence and mutuality. One has the impression in reading his life not only of an obsession with ideal sadistic relationships but also of a crippling weakness in the capacity for love and affection, and even in sexuality – Gorer remarks that 'one gets the impression he was not particularly potent'. He adds that 'the aim of the sadist is to reach an intensity of sexual experience of which he has an inner imaginative picture';[44] in other words, it is a masturbatory activity. The ideal relationship, as Sade appears to have understood very well, is sado-masochistic, not merely sadistic; the numerous fantasy attacks on women in his books must be set against his sexual ideal, that of a cruel woman who takes pleasure in wounding and betraying those who love her. This alternation of roles between sadist and masochist, which also characterized Sade's actual sexual practices, is explicable in terms of infantile development; as I have tried to show elsewhere, the intimacy of the relationship of mother and infant may encourage projective identification on the infant's part. He may identify with the victim of his sadistic attacks, the mother, simultaneously projecting into her the bad parts of himself which are responsible for the original aggression. The infant may thus become identified with a mother who is not only damaged by his attacks but, as container of his bad parts, bad herself and thus deserving of the punishment inflicted upon her. (Gorer remarks that Sade was 'always trying to take his revenge on maternal figures',[45] relating this to his resentment against the mother who abandoned him.) Pain inflicted is thus pain experienced; analogously, if the impulse be pushed to its limits, destruction implies self-destruction. Sade in effect understood this; the Judge de Curval, one of the four debauchees of *Les 120 Journées de Sodome*, cries, 'How many times have I not wished that I could catch the sun and deprive the world of it, or use it to burn up the earth?'[46] In this work, written during his imprisonment in the Bastille, Sade's destructive wishes are extended and rationalized into an unparalleled misanthropy. It is interesting that Weiss attributes to Sade a wholly conscious impulse of self-destruction, whereas it seems more probable that it was unconscious; it is the moment in the play where he is denouncing the increasingly mechanical nature of the cruelty unleashed by the revolution:[47]

And now Marat
now I see where
this revolution is leading . . .
So I turn away
I am one of those who has to be defeated
and from this defeat I want to seize
all I can get with my own strength
I step out of my place
and watch what happens
without joining in
observing
noting down my observations . . .
And when I vanish
I want all trace of my existence
to be wiped out

Clearly, Weiss does not want us to miss this point; if Marat is a victim of false beliefs, Sade has nothing to offer but despair. (Weiss is surely correct that despair is the necessary outcome of Sade's emotional attitude; he has taken liberties here with the historical Sade, who with typical human irrationality did not draw the logical conclusion from his own beliefs.) The question is really one of levels of commitment; Weiss may show us Sade's vision as blinded by his obsession, but at a deeper level it is the controlling vision of the play.

Weiss's position, to judge from this play, is not an unusual one today; it could be paralleled among many Marxist sympathizers. Believing in the need for necessarily violent revolutionary change, he has perhaps been deeply impressed and disturbed by the overwhelming evidence of human propensity for savage irrational violence, a violence, as Sade knew from experience, only likely to be exacerbated by the opportunities provided by the licensed sadism of revolution. Weiss would perhaps prefer to retain his belief in change from without; but the play shows him to have lost faith in this belief, temporarily or permanently, although this is never clearly acknowledged. His position has been undermined by Sade, who in his understanding of instinctual violence is a true forerunner of Freud and Melanie Klein. Peter Brook, in his introduction to the play, while admitting that 'it is not polemical in the sense that it does not . . . draw a moral' argues that 'it is firmly on the side of revolutionary change';[48] and despite the disclaimer he quotes Marat as in effect embodying a kind of moral:[49]

> The important thing
> is to pull yourself up by your own hair
> to turn yourself inside out
> and see the whole world with fresh eyes.

Weiss, Brook continues, 'wisely refuses to tell [us] how'.[50] There seems to be an unconscious irony here, for the main burden of the play is to impress upon us the impossibility and indeed absurdity of the task. It is surely no mere accident of historical accuracy or theatrical convenience that Weiss has given both the writing and the production of the inner play to Sade, thus ensuring for him the dominant role. Nor is it surprising that the writer with Marxist sympathies, as he contemplates the violence and barbarism in the world around him, and the prevalent nihilism of many cultural attitudes, should find it difficult to adjust these impressions to a system of belief that embodies a nineteenth-century faith in secular progress. Weiss's attitude in the play is thus basically confused. As I have said, the confusion and conflict seem to me to be common; what is unusual is to find, in such an arena of conflict, an absorbing play of ideas. Such plays are rather inclined to a commitment to a single viewpoint, however complex, which the audience are tacitly invited to accept; to some extent this is true of Shaw, and much more true of Brecht. There is thus both profit and loss in *Marat Sade*'s account: on the one hand there is some uncertainty and inconsistency in the handling; on the other hand, we are not asked to make the usual Brechtian sacrifice of truth to propaganda. And it is I think a wrong judgment that 'the play does not sustain its own invention',[51] that in effect Weiss dazzles us with the brilliance of his technique in the hope of deflecting our attention from the poverty of the material; the plainness of the style is foreign to this sort of evasion. Moreover, the impact made by the technique is essentially the impact of confusion and violence; it succeeds in reflecting very powerfully both the central theme and a certain creative conflict in the author's mind as he contemplates his subject. The lack of intellectual coherence matters less than it might because of the depth of Weiss's commitment.

Marat remains an impressive and disturbing play, both debate about, and mimed enactment of, the force of primitive violence in action.

Notes

1 Peter Weiss, *The Persecution and Assassination of Marat as Performed by the Inmates of the Asylum of Charenton, under the Direction of the Marquis de Sade*, trans. G. Skelton and A. Mitchell (London, 1965), author's note, p. 110.
2 I refer throughout to the original English production of the play by the Royal Shakespeare Company, of which the first performance was 20 August 1964.
3 Weiss, ed. cit., p. 10.
4 Ibid., p. 24.
5 Ibid. (introductory stage directions), pp. 10–11.
6 Strindberg, *A Dream Play*, author's prefatory note.
7 Weiss, ed. cit., p. 10.
8 Ibid., p. 15.
9 Ibid., p. 113, author's note.
10 Ibid., p. 66.
11 Ibid., pp. 5–7.
12 Ibid., p. 107.
13 Ibid., p. 7.
14 Ibid., pp. 39–40.
15 Ibid., p. 42.
16 See Geoffrey Gorer, *The Life and Ideas of the Marquis de Sade* (London, 1934; revised 1962), ch. 7.
17 Weiss, ed. cit., pp. 98–9.
18 See Gorer, op. cit., ch. 9.
19 Weiss, ed. cit., p. 40.
20 Ibid., p. 58.
21 Philip Rieff, *Freud: The Mind of the Moralist* (London, 1960), ch. 2.
22 Weiss, ed. cit., p. 35.
23 Weiss argues that Marat 'on account of his violent and uncompromising character, was made the scapegoat for many acts of cruelty' (ibid., author's note, p. 113).
24 See Gorer, op. cit. ch. 1.
25 Weiss, ed. cit., pp. 33–4.
26 Ibid., p. 56.
27 Ibid., publisher's note (on back cover).
28 Ibid., p. 49.
29 Ibid., p. 57.
30 Gorer, op. cit.
31 Weiss, ed. cit., pp. 101–4.
32 Brigid Brophy, *Black Ship to Hell* (London, 1962), p. 321.
33 Ibid., p. 299.

34 Gorer, op. cit.
35 Ibid., p. 186.
36 Ibid., p. 172.
37 Ibid., p. 158.
38 Weiss, ed. cit., p. 37.
39 Ibid., p. 90.
40 Ibid., p. 96.
41 Ibid., p. 91.
42 See above, p. 135.
43 Gorer, op. cit., p. 23.
44 Ibid.
45 Ibid., p. 175.
46 Ibid., p. 74.
47 Weiss, ed. cit., pp. 57–8. Weiss may be adapting a sentence in Sade's will, where he gives instructions (subsequently ignored) to ensure that 'the traces of my tomb may disappear from the face of the earth' (Gorer, op. cit., p. 60).
48 Ibid., p. 7.
49 Ibid., p. 35.
50 Ibid., p. 7.
51 '*Marat/Sade* and the Theatre of Unrealism', *The Times Literary Supplement* (17 September 1964).

Part II

Orestes and Electra in Greek and Modern Drama

Six

Orestes in Greek Drama

At the most immediate level, Orestes appears before us as the son divided by the fatal discord of the parents; it is a fate he shares with Oedipus, and like Oedipus, if to a lesser degree, his history seems to embody the principle of psychic determinism, for both are enmeshed by events in the past over which they have no control and for which they bear no wilful responsibility. In his relationship to the parents, however, Orestes appears to be the exact reverse of Oedipus. Oedipus' hostility to the father is replaced, in Orestes, by loyalty to his memory, and love for the mother by murderous hatred. The reversal, however, is more apparent than real, for Oedipal and pre-Oedipal elements are actively present in Orestes. The basic situation, of the father's disappearance and the mother's guilty responsibility for it, is likely to reactivate those ambivalent feelings of the son towards the mother that are part of his earliest and most deeply buried experiences. The ambivalence is inherent in the relationship of mother and son, since in the first months of life she represents to him the whole of the external world, both good and bad. His attitude to her is formed both by feelings of love and dependence, and by contrary feelings of envy and frustrated greed, all such feelings, when projected into her, making her simultaneously a good and a bad object.[1] The appearance of the father, as successful competitor for her love, compounds envy with jealousy; thus in the love the adult son may feel for his mother there lies concealed a hostile and destructive component whose origins must be sought both in envy of her and in jealousy of his father. It is demanded of Orestes that he kill his mother as an act of retributive justice; but in terms of psychological reality the impulse to the act, which alone makes its performance possible, springs less from the external authority of moral principle or divine command than from the most deeply buried primitive impulses from the past, the rage and resentment of spoiled love.[2] The hostility is of course ratified by the guilt of the mother; in acting against her the son is identified with the destroyed father whose blood calls for vengeance. At the same time, his Oedipal hostility to the father, which is now denied all conscious expression, is displaced on to the justly hated substitute for the father whom the mother has taken into her bed; this figure – Aegisthus, Claudius in *Hamlet*, Brand in *Mourning Becomes Electra* – can be made the open object of the son's jealous resentment, both on the dead father's behalf and on his own. The Oedipal hostility to the father exacerbates the situation in an unexpected way, for both the mother and the surrogate father, we may suppose, are hated the more for having successfully enacted the son's own buried criminal wishes against the father. The conflict between conscious devotion and unconscious hostility to the father is expressed in terms of a process of simultaneous identification and rejection, itself enforced by the reality situation: an identification with the father's ghost, a rejection of the worthless creature who has taken his place. Mother and son are left face to face without the protective barrier the father once provided. The supplanter – significantly father's brother or cousin – clearly cannot protect the son against his dangerously ambivalent feelings towards the mother. In killing the mother, the son simultaneously responds to the dead father's call for vengeance and seeks to gratify his own buried impulses of envy and jealousy, impulses that seize upon and exploit the opportunity provided by the mother's responsibility for the father's death. At another level, the killing may even seem to resolve an unbearable conflict, for by removing the object of so much concentrated love and hatred it releases the son from the Oedipal tension. But freedom gained in this way is purchased at a terrible price; the consequences of the matricide are as terrible as the parricide and incest of Oedipus, perhaps more so, for Orestes is unprotected by ignorance of what he is doing.[3] The identification with the father that had been a spur to the act is replaced after the murder by an identification with the murdered mother. Intolerably burdened with both dead internal parents, the weight of the father's ghost and the corpse of the mother that corrodes him from within, the son is driven inexorably towards madness or suicide. The only way of escape is through the mysterious intervention of a higher power, as with Oedipus, to appease the injured parents' ghosts and bring the retributive cycle of blood guilt to an end. Such a solution, basically religious in its original implications, is adumbrated in several versions of the story, but perhaps with less confidence and persuasiveness than in the case of Oedipus; the significance it may retain for us will be examined later.

The fullest and richest version of the Orestes story is, paradoxically, one that appears to owe nothing to the original Greek legend: Shakespeare's *Hamlet*. All the elements are present, notably the hidden Oedipal pressures; though actual matricide is avoided, the impulse to it is unmistakably present, and the dead father is given a dynamic role unparalleled elsewhere. The crucial factor in the play, that of a crippling delay in avenging the father's murder on his supplanter, becomes explicable in terms of the buried Oedipal wishes of the hero, as Freud was the first to point out.[4] Only in *Hamlet* is this important aspect of the inner meaning of the Orestes story present, for in the other versions all the conflict is centred on the matricide, actual or intended, and the killing of the supplanter is a minor matter that creates no problems. Modern versions, written in conscious awareness of some of the story's implications, vary in emphasis according to the predisposition of their authors: in Eliot's *The Family Reunion* the emphasis is, in intention at least, religious; in Sartre's *The Flies*, existential; in O'Neill's *Mourning Becomes Electra*, Freudian. These three modern versions, especially the last, which with its remarkable attempt to articulate the deeper psychological implications of Orestes has the most relevance to my theme, will be considered later; first to claim attention are the Greek tragic dramatists, all three of whom treated the central event of the Orestes saga. The first of these in time, Aeschylus' trilogy of the *Oresteia*, much the fullest version of the story that we have, succeeds in penetrating the psychological essence of Orestes with unmatched power and understanding; a primitive, haunted piece that by a fine paradox leads the mind of the spectator up towards the light of civilization, it is the first in time, as it is much the most impressive, of the surviving Greek presentations of the theme. The range of the *Oresteia*, the only surviving trilogy in Greek drama, is proverbial; at its heart the tragedy, like that of Sophocles' *Oedipus*, is domestic and familial, the savage war of spoiled love between parents and children and the ruthless battle of sex. But the domestic tragedies – the successive murders of Agamemnon and Clytemnestra and her lover, the madness of Orestes – are seen in the context of wider issues of war, politics and religion. Political necessity, the sacrifice of Iphigeneia, is the spark that sets off the domestic conflagration, exacerbated by the frustrations and miseries of the war whose promotion depended on that sacrifice; subsequently, Aeschylus' moral theme emerges with ever greater urgency. Caught helpless in the net of fate, for there seems no means by which Agamemnon could have avoided the sacrifice of his daughter or Orestes the killing of his mother – are men simply predestined to crime and suffering without end? Is there justice, *dikē*, as well as sheer necessity, *anagkē*? Are the seemingly capricious, inscrutable ways of God capable of being understood and accepted by his creatures? It is through the vast choruses of the play, with their ornate and complex imagery, that these issues are presented. Action is simplified, stripped down in each of the three plays that comprise the trilogy to a single momentous event presented with ritualistic intensity: in *Agamemnon* and *The Choephori* the successive deaths of Agamemnon and Clytemnestra, in *The Eumenides* the acquittal of Orestes. But this simplicity of presentation is possible only because through the vehicle of the chorus Aeschylus can explore the deeper meaning of the action and its philosophical and moral implications; the whole play, especially the *Agamemnon*, in this way exploits to the full the resources of lyrical tragedy. The key method here is the use of imagery; its highly concrete, pictorial quality is immensely effective in conveying the primitive psychological reality of the action. Images already used by the chorus to express such an inner reality are extended further by the actors who like the chorus tend to express themselves in pictures at moments of intense crisis. Moreover, at two points in the play these images are enacted, so to speak, embodied not as metaphor but fact: the net in which Clytemnestra entangles Agamemnon at the moment of his death (this is later exhibited by Orestes, after the matricide, as proof of his mother's guilt)[5] and the snakes which appear on the heads of the mother's avenging Furies after the matricide. Metaphor as fact is no coincidence; for out of a great wealth of imagery, two, perhaps, stand out as central, that of the entangling object in the *Agamemnon*, and that of the

snake or viper in *The Choephori*.[6] Various metaphors of entangle-
ment – the bit used to gag Iphigeneia, the huntsman's snare in
which Troy is caught, the fisherman's net – reinforce powerfully
the key idea of creatures caught in a predestined doom, of their
own and God's making. But it is the image of the viper that is
central to Aeschylus' presentation of Orestes and the family
tragedy at the heart of which he stands, and it is to the analysis
of this image and its psychological meanings that I now turn.

The most familiar association of the viper or snake is, of course,
with poison; beyond this, there can be found both in modern
psychological theory and in early folk-lore and natural history
associations of striking relevance to Aeschylus' deployment of the
image in *The Choephori*. First, the phallic significance of the snake
is immediately of interest when considering the actual content of
early primitive impulses. Second, the fable of the viper reared or
revived in a person's bosom suggests the element of loving
nurture greeted with hate, which in general terms is central to
the Oresteian theme of the family feud[7] and more specifically
seems to symbolize early fantasies of the child's sadistic attack
on the mother's breast. Finally, there is the curious belief, referred
to by Pliny in his *Natural History*,[8] that the female viper is killed
by her young eating their way out of the womb at birth. The
eggs, according to Pliny, are hatched inside the uterus, but
delivery of the new-born vipers, usually about twenty in number,
only takes place at the rate of one per day. The frustration of
this process induces those who are being kept waiting to burst
through the mother's womb into the light of day. The symbolic
relevance of this curious belief to infantile fantasies of cannibalistic attacks on the mother seems very direct; mother-murder is
here enacted in a phase of life so early as to be, strictly speaking,
prenatal. Moreover, in other stories, certainly of early origin, we
find the two notions, both central to the *Oresteia*, of love in the
family turning to hate, and the child destroying the mother,
linked together. In Shakespeare's *Pericles* the riddle put to the
daughter's suitor by the incestuous father begins with these lines
(supposedly spoken by the daughter):

> I am no viper, yet I feed
> On mother's flesh which did me breed. . . .

The suitor, Pericles, guesses the riddle; the incestuous couple, he says, are like serpents breeding poison, the daughter in particular[9]

> . . . an eater of her mother's flesh
> By the defiling of her parent's bed. . . .

Incestuous wishes, and acts, are here assimilated in thought to murder; just such an assimilation as is found in the hidden motives of Orestes as he contemplates the act that lies before him.

The first character to be named as the viper is Clytemnestra. The children gather at Agamemnon's tomb for the eerie scene of invocation of their father's ghost, to incite him to anger against the murderous wife and mother, and to strengthen themselves for the test that lies ahead by enchanting power out of his spirit. First Orestes prays to god:[10]

> Zeus, Zeus! Behold us, and the deed we undertake.
> Behold the eagle's brood bereaved; the eagle killed,
> Caught in a net of death, in a cruel viper's coils.

Later he recalls his earlier words; standing over his mother's corpse, he exhibits to his judges the proof of her wickedness, the straitjacket in which she had enmeshed his father, and exclaims:[11]

> But she, who plotted this foul death against [a husband]
> . . . what does she seem to be? Some water snake, some
> viper whose touch is rot even to him who felt no fang. . . .

But long before this he has accepted the name of viper for himself, thus enacting a recognition that the act he is about to perform is an act 'not against an external enemy but against part of the self'.[12] In general, a fatal family likeness is insisted on throughout the play. First Electra, in the invocation scene, warns her mother that her children will not be deflected from their purpose by any attempt to placate them:[13]

> The savage cubs the she-wolf bred
> Are like their mother; fawn on them who dare!

But there is a deeper level of identification between the members of the family, simultaneously expressed both as a primitive belief in the existence of supernatural agencies – Agamemnon's ghost, prophetic dreams sent by the dead, Clytemnestra's Furies –

and as a remarkable awareness, familiar to psychoanalytical thinking, of the internal parent active in the child both in life and after death. Orestes appeals to the father's ghost not to let his children be blotted out, for[14]

You are dead – and yet not dead; still you can live in us.

When the terrified servant rushes to tell Clytemnestra of Aegisthus' murder, he utters his warning in these words:[15]

The dead, I tell you, come to life to kill the living!

There is a reference here to the false story of Orestes' death (part of the plot to allay suspicion) but Clytemnestra understands the deeper meaning, of the murdered father alive again in the son:[16]

You speak in riddles but I read the rhyme.

In the feverish exchange between mother and son before the murder, Clytemnestra abandons her desperate pleas with the recognition that it is useless:[17]

I feel like one who wastes live tears upon a tomb.

But it is chiefly through the dominant image of the viper that this ruinous identification of the family triangle, father, mother and son, is presented to the imagination. It may not be too fanciful to see, in the words Electra uses to urge her father's ghost to action, a hint of Agamemnon himself as the viper:[18]

Will you not rear up that beloved head?

For it is Agamemnon who sends the famous dream to his wife, more prediction than warning, of a snake she bears and gives the breast to: a dream whose meaning is at once seized upon by Orestes as due to come to fulfilment in him. The whole passage, crucial to an understanding of the play, must be quoted. Orestes asks why Clytemnestra has sent placatory libations to Agamemnon's tomb, and is told she has been shaken by dreams in the night:[19]

Orestes	Did you ask what the dream was? Can you describe it clearly?
Chorus	She told us herself. She dreamt that she gave birth to a snake.

155

Orestes	What followed? Or was that all? Tell me the point of it.
Chorus	She wrapped it in shawls and lulled it to rest like a little child.
Orestes	Surely this new-born monster needed food – what food?
Chorus	She herself, in her dream, gave it her breast to suck.
Orestes	Her nipple surely was wounded by its loathsome fang?
Chorus	Yes; with her milk the creature drew forth clots of blood.
Orestes	This dream was sent. It came from her husband Agamemnon. . . .
	I pray, then, to this earth that holds my father's bones,
	That the dream's meaning may be thus fulfilled in me.
	As I interpret, point by point it fits. Listen:
	First, if this snake came forth from the same place as I,
	And, as though human, was then wrapped in infant-clothes,
	Its gaping mouth clutching the breast that once fed me;
	If it then mingled the sweet milk with curds of blood,
	And made her shriek with terror – why, it means that she
	Who nursed this obscene beast must die by violence;
	I must transmute my nature, be viperous in heart and act!
	The dream commands it: I am her destined murderer.

In the words of Professor Lattimore's translation, 'I must make myself snake to kill her.' In submitting to the dream, his courage screwed up to the sticking point of action by its prophetic burden, Orestes is deliberately accepting for himself the viperous role of love-in-hate. Taken alone, this speech might seem to breathe a savage exultation; but this Orestes is a tormented creature, driven on by a complex skein of motives to an act he knows he cannot justify. Inner doubts and hesitations are rationalized as a mistrust of Apollo's oracles, which have threatened him with horrible punishments if he neglects his duty; devotion to his father's memory is powered by savage jealousy of 'the woman', Aegisthus, who has stolen his patrimony. But his quick, compulsive identification with the viper of his mother's dream betrays a deeper, buried, level of motivation; Aeschylus' intuitive understanding reveals to us a fundamental aspect of the inner meaning of Orestes. It is not too much to say that the external situation, at the heart of which lies the mother's responsibility for the father's death, has woken to feverish life early oral fantasies of greed and envy, enacted in sadistic and cannibalistic attacks on the breast. The soft mouth sucking in milk from the loving breast is transformed into the tearing fangs of the viper nurtured in the bosom. In this situation, the child experiences himself as a little monster who destroys the mother by devouring her; in the dream the fantasy appears in its earliest, purest state, without the projection that is more commonly found, as in *The Bacchae*, and that is to appear later here in the person of the Furies. As Orestes stands over Clytemnestra with his sword drawn, his mother displays her breast to him in a final plea, reminding him how often he had lain there and fed as a drowsy baby sucking in life-giving milk. The gesture makes him hesitate in an agony of indecision ('to kill a mother is terrible'), as the two contrasting aspects of the mother struggle for domination within him. Aeschylus understands that the situation gains immensely in tragic power if, despite all that has happened, love still fights with hate in both mother and son; Clytemnestra's earlier grief at the false news of Orestes' death is not a pretence and Orestes is appalled at the act he is about to commit. At the critical moment he is inclined to spare her until swayed by Pylades' intervention and, significantly, a jealous thought about the dead Aegisthus. Hatred wins, and he drags her in to kill her over the lover's body. The sexual associations of the dream look back to Clytemnestra's usurpation of the male role in the *Agamemnon* and prefigure this rankling sexual jealousy against his father's womanish cousin and supplanter, Aegisthus; father and son share the same resentment against the woman's sexual betrayal of them. Early pre-Oedipal fantasies are here blended with later Oedipal material. The husband and father had been killed and castrated by the wife; now he comes to life again in the son, an enemy armed both with his own infantile envy and the destroyed penis of the father. The sucking viper suggests the penis conceived in fantasy as greedy nipple or mouth, that feeds on the breast instead of from it, sucking out blood with milk; it seems a remarkably clear illustration of the earliest phase of life, where aggressive fantasy and impulse are dominated by oral sadism. In the scene of the murder, however, sexual jealousy is very prominent. Orestes coarsely enjoins his mother to sleep with her lover in death, since she had preferred him both to his father and to himself; he repeats Electra's bitter words earlier in the play, that Aegisthus had been the price she had obtained for selling her children. Having attacked the breast in fantasy, the penis-like viper now coils and strikes in actual fact, the son's sword penetrating the mother's breast.

It is interesting to note that Orestes is said to have bitten off a finger in order to appease the Furies. The consequence was that they changed in colour from black to white, so that his madness was healed.[20] This may suggest an act of self-castration basically reparative in nature. Moreover, according to one version Orestes, having surmounted the Furies' curse and resumed a normal life, died of a snake-bite at the age of seventy.[21]

Accompanying sexual jealousy is the deep sense of identification with his victim, already established by the dream of the viper. It is active in the words with which he justifies the killing; his reply to Clytemnestra's horrified realization that he actually means to kill her sounds like a meaningless sophism but has a deeper significance:[22]

> It will be your own hand that strikes you dead, not mine.

The act performed, Orestes in his public speech of self-justification tries to maintain a front of masculine confidence, insisting on the criminal guilt of his mother and his own blamelessness in the sight of Apollo; but there is a desperation in his tone – the viper's poison is working within him and, as he begins to utter a funeral speech for his dead father it rises into his mouth, choking him with disgust:[23]

> Her deed, her punishment – the whole business tortures
> me.

A moment later madness seizes him; he struggles with its on-coming surges in a final attempt to set the record straight. He will go for refuge to Apollo's shrine, he tells the chorus, carrying before him the suppliant's branch. They are puzzled and distressed by the inauspiciousness of his behaviour in the hour of triumph; has he not cleaned the house of snakes? As they speak, fresh snakes appear, coiling round the bodies of the mother's avenging Furies; it is the culmination, in this play, of the image of the viper, the poison of love turning to hatred, the self-destructiveness of the child who in attacking the mother, sole source of nourishment and life, is attacking part of the self. In the words of the Furies, it is blood which is self-spilt, against nature as Orestes himself had acknowledged earlier in the play. Presumably the newly hatched vipers who according to Pliny ate their way out of the womb[24] must have starved; it is the viperous nature recoiling on itself, symbol of the murder which is also a suicide.

The Erinyes, or Furies, in Aeschylus, though they later take on a ritual aspect of primitive barbarous goddesses of Ancient Night, appear first, here in *The Choephori*, as externalized expression of Orestes' guilty conscience; they are real only to him:[25]

> I know you do not see these beings; but I see them;
> I am lashed and driven! I can't bear it! I must escape!

Their other, objective, character is seen in *The Eumenides*, where their role becomes in essence a formal one, as prosecuting counsel in Orestes' trial and finally guardians of the Athenian heritage; but their inner aspect is never lost sight of entirely. It is this aspect which concerns me here, for in psychoanalytical thinking mythical figures, like the dream figures they closely resemble, are seen as 'thinly disguised representations of certain uncon-scious fantasies'.[26] They are perhaps an example of the kind of persecutory figures that appear both in normal dreams and in hallucinations of a persecutory type, and may be taken to repre-sent the bad parts of the child projected into one or both of the parents; it is noteworthy that Apollo calls them 'aged children'.[27] The description given by the priestess of Apollo in *The Eumenides* when she discovers this 'strange company of women – no, not women'[28] sleeping in her shrine, emphasizes both the destroyed and the persecutory aspect of the dead mother whose champions they are. With their foul breath and eyes dripping with pus or blood, they are themselves victims of their own repulsiveness; we are told, though admittedly by a prejudiced witness, Apollo, that neither God nor man nor beast will have anything to do with them.[29] The sadistic attack on the mother is accompanied by an act of projective identification, whereby the bad viperous part of the son is put out into her, a process powerfully reinforced when, as in this story, the mother's nature is in fact evil. The purpose is a cleansing, an evacuation of the bad parts of the self into the mother. But the act of self-cleansing is also the act of blood, a culmination in murder and subsequent pollution of the sadistic attacks. Through identification the son becomes the monstrous creature whom his own projections have called into existence, a viper fit only to be crushed in a process where destruction by the Furies, or ghost, of the mother is barely distinguished from self-destruction. Self-inflicted death is indeed the logical culmination for Orestes; the possibility is hinted at here ('when her life is ended, let mine end too');[30] it beckons insistently to Hamlet; in the purely secular context of *Mourning Becomes Electra* O'Neill's hero actually takes this way out. In Aeschylus, and indeed in all the versions of Greek legend, a different, less despairing solution is found. For the sake of the common good, and to preserve society from anarchy, an end must be found to the ruthless private justice that looks like sustaining the family feud indefinitely, and this means that Orestes must be allowed to purge his sin. In Aeschylus' *Eumenides*, after a period of submission to persecution by his mother's Furies, Orestes is brought to trial before the court of the Areopagus in Athens; Apollo acts as defence counsel, the Erinyes as prosecuting counsel. When the jury are divided equally between condemnation and acquittal, Athene gives her casting vote for acquittal and Orestes returns in triumph to Argos. The Erinyes are with difficulty reconciled to their defeat by Athene's placatory offer of a permanent sanctuary in Athens, where they will be honoured as Eumenides, well-favoured ones. Professor Lattimore argues that this famous conclusion shows the triumph of civilization over barbarism; Hellenic culture emerges out of the darkness of the past, not by denying but by absorbing the primitive childlike impulses symbolized by the Furies:[31]

> The new city cannot progress by exterminating its old order of life; it must absorb and use it. Man cannot obliterate, and should not repress, the unintelligible emotions.

It is a persuasive view, but a reading of Aeschylus' text goes to show that, though his intention was almost certainly to celebrate the emergence of civilization in this way, the civilization of Athens in particular, he was not altogether happy about the reconciliation at another, deeper level. Though this uncertainty weakens the argument in the *Eumenides*, so that the theme is not really satisfactorily presented in the culminating trial scene, it is consistent with those earlier insights into primitive realities that he displays in the *Agamemnon* and *The Choephori*. Part of the dissatisfaction the modern reader may feel about *The Eumenides* is of course of a different order. After the fundamental questions raised in the *Agamemnon*, about the reconciliation of human suffering with any kind of divine order, the solution, although impressive and moving in its way, is bound to seem somewhat parochial. There is a contraction in the scale of the argument, which in the *Agamemnon* and *The Choephori* had been concerned with deeper questions even than the establishment of civilized legality as a curb to unfettered human passions, vitally important though this is to human society. The power of great art to speak with the same persuasiveness to later ages as to its own time is less evident in *The Eumenides*; we can see that the play must have meant more to the Athenians of the fifth century than it can mean to us. There is no weakness or uncertainty of intention here, rather a limitation of appeal. It is in the handling of the trial scene that doubts of another kind arise, for Apollo's pleas in defence of Orestes are a tissue of casuistry and, when cornered, abuse of his opponent. The threat of naked force is deployed with what seems to be shameless openness; your oath, he tells the jury, cannot have the same force as the will of Zeus. In his final argument he denies the importance of motherhood, asserting that the woman merely receives and nurses the new-planted seed of

the true parent, the man. It is already disturbing that Orestes'
case should be presented in so unconvincing a way, but worse
is to follow. Though her tone is milder, Athene's stance is in
essentials the same in both these respects, the threat of force, and
the assertion of male superiority. She explains her casting vote
in favour of Orestes as the natural action of one who, lacking a
mother, supports the male cause with all her heart and is 'strongly
for the father'. Her partiality thus openly admitted, her offer to
the Furies of a secure home in Athens is really an ultimatum
masquerading as a compromise; for she, like Apollo, threatens
force in the same breath as speaking propitiation:[32]

> You are not dishonoured, you are goddesses; do not in
> your anger make the earth uninhabitable. I have Zeus
> on my side – what need is there to say more? I alone
> know where his thunderbolts are locked. But there
> is no need of that; let persuasion rule. . . .

The pulse of triumph and celebration that beats in the final
pages of the play cannot altogether efface the impression made
on us by the conduct of the trial; the Furies have been cajoled
into agreement, and this seems to call into question the soundness
of the basis of that civilized justice which is the fruit of the reconciliation. The paradox is that sounder arguments could have been
used in defence of Orestes, but are not; there seems to be a gap
between the establishment of the rule of law, which could have
prevented the blood feud originally and now brings it to an end,
and the actual conduct of the court, which places as much
reliance on naked force as the Furies wish to do, compounding
it with an unscrupulousness and dishonesty quite foreign to their
strict, if barbarous, integrity. Possibly Aeschylus is following
certain lost traditions here; but the bald statement of so unconvincing a case might suggest that he himself is dissatisfied with it.
In particular, it is hard to feel that a writer who in *The Choephori*
conveys with such power and persuasiveness the terrible love-
in-hate of mother and son can have been satisfied with the
unargued implication strongly present in *The Eumenides*, that
motherhood is less important than fatherhood. We may at least
divine the hint of a conflict in Aeschylus between a belief in
male domination and ascendancy characteristic of fifth-century
Athens, which emerges with a clarity, even crudeness, from the

rather stiff, naïve confrontation in *The Eumenides*, and a contrary
realization of the reality and depth of the world of feminine
values. It may be of significance that Orestes himself plays so
small a part in *The Eumenides*, becoming as Lattimore remarks
an issue or case, no longer important as a person.[33]

Sophocles' treatment in his *Electra* of the vengeance of Orestes
is in striking contrast. Sophoclean detachment is pushed to
extremes in this play, which presents with consummate skill
and dramatic irony the story of the wronged hero who triumphs
against his enemies; that one of them happens to be his mother
seems almost incidental. It is noteworthy that the Furies, implacable on behalf of the mother in Aeschylus, should here be invoked
by the chorus on behalf of the son. This Homeric Orestes experiences no inner conflict;[34] his only, momentary, doubt is practical;
all is well within the house, he tells Electra, 'if Apollo's oracle
spoke well'.[35] Hard and self-assured, he is troubled only by a
fear that the pretended story of his own death will prove ill-
omened, but reassures himself with the thought that 'no omen is
bad, that leads to glory and final advantage'.[36] His farewell,
after the savage climax of the murder, is typical:[37]

> If all who transgressed the law paid with their lives in
> this way, there would be less wickedness about.

No hint of future disaster mars the bland final chorus that
follows: in this triumphant end to their sufferings, the children
of Atreus have won back their freedom and patrimony. The only
strong emotion he displays is sympathy with his sister's grief, as
she cradles the urn falsely supposed to contain his own ashes. It
is on that sister, Electra, as the title implies, that the principal
focus of attention in the play falls; its bleakness is relieved by the
psychological insight and human sympathy displayed in the
portrait of its heroine, a figure conceived on a grand scale, as it
is in another way by the limpid beauty of the style and the
dazzling technical virtuosity of the set pieces. Even so, it remains
one of the harshest of all Greek tragedies, disconcerting in its
archaic reticence, its refusal to answer, or even directly to ask,
the insistent questions. Even with Electra we may feel cheated
of a true resolution, for her final triumph seems to be offered
as a permanent release from a hitherto desperate situation,
whereas on Sophocles' own showing it must clearly be the

seedbed of greater tragic suffering to come. When she declares
to her mother that to have killed her father was a monstrous act,
whether justified or not, and when she warns her that if she sets
up the law of vengeance, of blood for blood, she may live to
repent it, she is effectively condemning herself out of her own
mouth.[38] This remarkable character study only casts an incidental illumination on the inner history of the family tragedy;
the portrait of a passionate, loving nature thwarted and wasted
by the bitterness of suffering has a meaning independent of the
specific causes of that suffering, which Sophocles touches on but
does not explore in depth. She has been ill-treated until she has
come to resemble her tormentors, as she realizes herself – 'surrounded by evil, how can I be other than evil myself?';[39] it is
the source of her most bitter feelings, emerging even in the
violence of her quarrel with Clytemnestra:[40]

> If as you say I am wicked, violent, shameless, at least then
> I am like my mother . . . evil in one breeds evil in another.

Her present sufferings force her back, for comfort and sustenance,
to the memory of her adored father and of the brother whom she
had rescued as a child and smuggled into safety when his father
was murdered. This Electra, like the Athene of *The Eumenides*,
is all for the father. She acknowledges her own obession, but
justifies it, declaring that she will never cease to grieve for him or
dishonour his memory by forgetting him. The chorus, who are
sympathetic to her, point out that others who share her situation
are not wedded, like her, to their grief. Clytemnestra mocks her
devotion to 'that father of yours, whom you never stop weeping
for',[41] adding perhaps significantly, 'you take no notice of me,
when Aegisthus is away'.[42] In this identification with the father
there is the foundation of the later, more complex development
of the Electra figure, the unconscious envy of the father's power,
and the various attempts at masculinization that follow, from
Lady Macbeth to Hedda Gabler and the man-eating heroines
of Strindberg; some of these manifestations will be discussed in
a later chapter. An interesting aspect of this Electra is that her
emotional fixation on the father extends to his nearest replica,
her brother Orestes, where it consciously takes on the form of a
frustrated maternal devotion. When he finally reveals himself
she embraces him as 'my dearest father's own son'; earlier, like

a disappointed mother she has upbraided Orestes for not returning to one who in her own words 'has no husband and no other child'.[43]

When the disguised Orestes gives her the urn that supposedly contains his own ashes, she recalls how she alone had nursed him as a baby; he had been *her* child rather than their mother's. The lost father need no longer be mourned, for he is found again in the younger brother who is also a child. Electra notes this herself:[44]

> If my father were to come back now, alive I should not
> think him to be a ghost, but truly believe that I saw him.

In a telling touch, she even endows with fatherhood the older man who stands in a protective relationship to her (so real, we may suppose, is the father's presence to her); with passionate enthusiasm she greets the old tutor who once took Orestes from her hands and is now stage-managing the action on their behalf:[45]

> Welcome, father; for a father you seem to me to be.

When we come to Euripides' *Electra*, we find that it treats of substantially the same series of events as Sophocles' play of the same name and *The Choephori*, but again in a very different fashion. A new dimension of realism is added to the presentation, as Euripides fashions a dramatic answer to a question he often seems to ask himself – what do we find if we imagine actual people like ourselves performing such actions? The answer gives a clue, perhaps, to what lies at the centre of Euripides' sense of the tragic: man as the victim of irrational forces he cannot understand or control, compulsively driven into disastrous action by the marriage of external pressures with his ignorance of his own nature and motives. He shows a very modern awareness of the way in which the springs of action are buried in secret places, out of reach of reason and the calculations of rational advantage; Pentheus in *The Bacchae* is an outstanding example of this insight. In *The Bacchae* he resembles the Aeschylus of *The Choephori* in the psychological symbolism of his exploration of the dark places of the unconscious; elsewhere he is often content with a dramatic technique closer to modern realism, which contemplates the operation of such overmastering instinctual drives as sexual passion, jealousy, aggression, at the level at which their effects are observable in action. This is his method in the *Electra*; applied to an action unquestionably evil, as he clearly sees it to be, it results in an unflattering picture of human depravity and weakness. The tragedy, of the act of revenge in this instance, lies not as for Aeschylus in the oppressive mystery of God's law and the dark agony of the human beings who are compelled to fulfil it, nor, as for Sophocles, in the terror, splendour, and pathos of the spectacle of human life and character; it lies rather in the contemplation of the suffering human beings inflict on each other:[46]

> With what insensate fury I drove myself to take
> My grand revenge! How bitterly I regret it now!

Thus speaks Clytemnestra, to a daughter who, incapable of learning from her mother's experience, is to follow slavishly the same disastrous path. Remorse is an unexpected trait of this Clytemnestra, and is in keeping with Euripides' general plan, whereby everything we are shown in the play goes to emphasize the lack of justification in the killings and the moral weakness of all who take part in them. A Clytemnestra oppressed by guilt over the past, anxious to make peace with her daughter, and betrayed to death by a trick of peculiar repulsiveness, whereby she is lured into the grasp of her killers by the false news that her daughter has borne a child; a courteous, hospitable Aegisthus, struck down from behind in the act of sacrifice; a weak, irresolute Orestes, anxious if possible to avoid a task he knows to be 'blind and brutal',[47] his hesitations, as of some petty Macbeth, swept aside by his sister's ferocious pressure; above all, an Electra obsessed with envy and self-pity and so ignorant of her own nature that, like Stogumber in *St Joan*, her savagery gives way to an appalled recognition of what she has done as soon as the murder is committed; all go to form a consistent psychological and moral pattern whereby the act of vengeance is robbed of its mythological glamour and is seen for what it is, a sordid murder committed not by criminals on the grand scale nor from motives of righteous indignation, but by ordinary human beings whose weakness of character and vicious propensities blind them to reality. Earlier Electra had claimed the killing of her mother as her own prerogative[48] but we learn in the last scene that, when her mother hung round her neck, begging for mercy, the sword had fallen out of her hand and she had left the butchery to Orestes.[49] The chorus, speaking here for the author, only confirm what she and Orestes make clear in their own words – that 'no act could have been more dreadful'.[50] There is nothing heroic about this Electra; nothing of the sense, in Sophocles, of admirable qualities abused and perverted by suffering, strength and weakness equally blended in the character. We may feel some pity for her, but not, perhaps, a great deal, for she is portrayed in too unflattering a light, by an emphasis which shifts our attention away from the past crimes of Aegisthus and Clytemnestra to the sordid present. It is a vivid portrayal, entertaining in its typically ironical treatment both of the gods and of what was genuinely heroic in the myth, but somewhat undistinguished in comparison with Aeschylus and Sophocles. The story seems to have allowed only a limited scope for Euripides' poetic imagination or his sense of pity, its chief merit lying, perhaps, in its shrewd, penetrating understanding of the way human beings behave under pressure; he does not explore the deeper implications.

One further point may be made about the treatment of the Orestes story in Greek drama. Both Sophocles and Euripides stress the closeness of brother and sister. In Sophocles, Electra experiences passionate maternal feelings towards Orestes,[51] while in Euripides the painfulness of the finale is exacerbated by the knowledge that their mutual crime must part them for ever. At least, this is the implication in the *Electra*. Elsewhere, in *Iphigeneia in Tauris*, Euripides makes use of another story which unites the whole family in a happy conclusion through Orestes' discovery of another sister, long believed dead. The sacrifice of Iphigeneia by her father at Aulis had been the prime justification for Clytemnestra's hostility; in the *Iphigeneia in Tauris*, it is found that the goddess Artemis had rescued Iphigeneia from the knife and spirited her away to the Tauric Chersonese, where she was made priestess and guardian of the sacred image of Apollo, as he tells his sister after their reunion;[52] for the oracle has declared that he will be finally free from the curse of matricide only if he succeeds in the dangerous escapade of rescuing his sister, together with the sacred image, from the Taurians and presenting it to Athens. This oracle, and its successful fulfilment, suggests perhaps at one level a denial of the reality of matricide.

What is implied in a straightforward way in the intimate devotion of Orestes and Electra[53] is here given a symbolic statement; the dead mother, whose killing has been the most irremediable of all crimes, is found again in the person of another sister who has apparently been resurrected from the dead.[54]

Notes

1 See Introduction above.
2 Cf. R. Money-Kyrle, *Superstition and Society* (London, 1939), ch. 2, pp. 36–8.
3 R. Money-Kyrle suggests that matricide is 'the most ultimate . . . of all crimes, the destruction of the primary "good object", the mother on whom the child's life and happiness depend.' Money-Kyrle, op. cit., pp. 37–8.
4 S. Freud, *The Interpretation of Dreams*, trans. J. Strachey (London, 1954), ch. 5., pp. 264–6.
5 Aeschylus, *The Oresteian Trilogy* trans. P. Vellacott (Penguin, 1956), p. 140.
6 See Aeschylus, *I, Oresteia*, trans. R. Lattimore (Chicago, 1953), pp. 15–18. Professor Lattimore, whose discussion of the subject is of great interest, suggests that the viper may be seen as the prime symbol of the *Oresteia*.
7 Ibid., p. 17.
8 Pliny, *Natural History*, X, 82.
9 Shakespeare, *Pericles*, I.1.64–5.
10 Aeschylus, trans. P. Vellacott, p. 112.
11 Aeschylus, trans. R. Lattimore, pp. 128–9.
12 Ibid., p. 27.
13 Ibid., p. 118.
14 Ibid., p. 111.
15 Aeschylus, trans. P. Vellacott, p. 135.
16 Aeschylus, trans. R. Lattimore, p. 124.
17 Ibid., p. 126.
18 Ibid., p. 111.
19 Aeschylus, trans. P. Vellacott, p. 123.
20 Pausanias, *Description of Greece*, VIII, 34.
21 R. Graves, *The Greek Myths II* (London, 1955), p. 80.
22 Aeschylus, trans. P. Vellacott, p. 137.
23 Ibid., p. 141.
24 See above, p. 153.
25 Aeschylus, trans. P. Vellacott, p. 143.
26 Money-Kyrle, op. cit., p. 27.
27 Aeschylus, *The Eumenides*, l. 67.
28 Aeschylus, trans. P. Vellacott, pp. 148–9.
29 Ibid.
30 Ibid., p. 119.
31 Aeschylus, trans. Lattimore, pp. 30–1.

32 Aeschylus, *The Eumenides*, ll. 824–9.

33 Aeschylus, trans. Lattimore, p. 31.

34 Homer presents Orestes as a brave and dutiful son who gained great renown, among both Gods and men, by killing the traitor Aegisthus (Homer, *Odyssey*, I, 35, 298). The matricide, which is merely implied as though it does not deserve a separate mention, does not affect his reputation in the heroic world (*Odyssey*, III, 310). The contrast is marked with Oedipus, whose mother Jocasta is described as 'bringing him many sorrows, all that the Erinyes of a mother can inflict' (*Odyssey*, XI, 278–9).

35 Sophocles, *Electra*, ll. 1424–5.

36 Ibid., l. 61.

37 Ibid., ll. 1505–7.

38 Ibid., ll. 558–609.

39 Ibid., ll. 308–9.

40 Ibid., ll. 608–9.

41 Ibid., l. 530.

42 Ibid., ll. 519–20.

43 Ibid., ll. 164–5.

44 Ibid., ll. 1316–17.

45 Ibid., l. 1361.

46 Euripides, *Medea and Other Plays*, trans. P. Vellacott (Penguin, 1963), p. 142.

47 Ibid., p. 138.

48 Ibid., p. 127.

49 Ibid., p. 147.

50 Ibid.

51 See above, pp. 164–5.

52 Euripides, *Iphigeneia in Tauris*, ll. 77, 970 ff.

53 It is worth noting that Electra, as part of the final settlement of the curse of the House of Atreus, is married to Pylades. Total mutual loyalty between Orestes and Pylades is the one anchor of Orestes' sanity during the period after the matricide when, especially in Euripides' account in the *Orestes*, his behaviour is otherwise characterized by a frenzied violence and instability.

54 See Money-Kyrle, op. cit., p. 38.

Seven

Orestes in Modern Drama:
Mourning Becomes Electra

'The subconscious, the mother of all gods and heroes.'[1]

'A poet', writes George Steiner, 'borrows at his peril . . . today the context is so totally altered that the ancient myths appear in the modern playhouse either as a travesty or as an antiquarian charade.'[2] Of *The Family Reunion* he remarks that 'the Furies stand there either as pasteboard phantoms or as realities so intense that they bring the entire fabric of the play tumbling down around them';[3] this comment would be equally applicable to the generality of characters in such plays, in so far as they are versions of past originals. His recognition of the extent to which modern literary drama has turned to ancient Greek myth for its subject matter is only matched by his conviction of its failure to exploit the myth for any very worthwhile purpose; both the borrowed clothes, and the failure to wear them with the ancient conviction, being to him symptomatic of the decline of tragedy in the modern world. It may readily be admitted that Steiner makes out a powerful case; no single dramatic masterpiece of a quality to set beside not merely the great originals but the best work of Ibsen, Chekhov, or Strindberg, has been produced in the vein of a deliberate adaptation of the Greek. It is, of course, the mark of a sophisticated literary intelligence to become, in Steiner's striking phrase, a 'graverobber and conjurer of ghosts out of ancient glory';[4] the self-consciousness which to some readers is the bane of modern literature in general is a prominent feature of these experiments, in Cocteau, Sartre, Giraudoux, Eliot, O'Neill. Absolute conviction is, perhaps, always lacking, even where as in O'Neill or Sartre a powerful natural talent for the drama is in evidence. It may be significant that it is a novel,

Ulysses, which in its adaptation of Greek myth succeeds in transcending both parody and artifice to achieve the stature of greatness. The drama, always a more tender plant than fiction, has nothing comparable to show; but there is none the less a great deal of interest in the varying attempts to interpret traditional themes and motifs in the light of modern psychological, political, religious and aesthetic preoccupations. In all, or almost all, instances, psychoanalysis, like anthropology, plays its part in the reinterpretation of ancient myth; its role may be marginal, something of a fashionable trimming as perhaps in Cocteau, or the central informing spirit of the work, as in *Mourning Becomes Electra.*

This play, the first in time of the modern versions of Electra I want to consider (1931), is the most thoroughgoing and consistent attempt to date to interpret the myth in the light of Freudian psychoanalysis. It is constructed as a trilogy (*Homecoming, The Hunted, The Haunted*) on a very large scale; the model is Aeschylus, and the pattern of the first two plays follows very closely that of the *Oresteia.* Argos becomes the New England of 1865; in *Homecoming,* Brigadier-General Ezra Mannon returns from the American civil war to be murdered by his wife, Christine, and her lover. In *The Hunted,* the Mannon children, Orin and Lavinia, avenge their father; Brand, the lover, is killed, and Christine driven to suicide. The third play, *The Haunted,* which takes place after the interval of a year, departs from Aeschylus or any other model; it boldly develops ideas O'Neill sees as implicit in the inner relationships of the characters. The curse on the house of Atreus is translated into a peculiarly concrete form of psychological determinism; brother and sister, bound into the closest intimacy by their shared guilt and suffering, re-enact the double tragedy of the parents in a play whose true subject appears to be the effect of unconscious identification with the dead. In each case the consciously rejected and denied parent asserts himself to control the child from within: Orin, who had always disliked and felt himself to be different from Ezra, comes to resemble him, dominating the stronger Vinnie in a role that combines aspects of her once beloved father and a jealous, predatory lover; Vinnie, a true Electra in her passionate dedication to her father's memory, and like him hitherto in her repressed austerity, assumes the character of her sensual, pleasure-loving mother, finally driving Orin to suicide in order to escape from his neurotic destructiveness, an act which to Orin is just retribution for having driven his mother to her death, but which at another level is presented as a repetition of Christine's murder of Ezra. At the end only Lavinia is left alive. Her attempts to escape from the ghosts of the past have failed, and once more her father's daughter, she marches stiffly off the stage into the tomb-like Mannon house to live alone with her dead; for reasons that have to do with neither hope nor expiation, she dedicates herself to self-punishment:[5]

> There's no one left to punish me . . . I've got to punish myself! I'll live alone with the dead, and keep their secrets, and let them hound me, until the curse is paid out, and the last Mannon is let die!

This owes something, perhaps, to the end of *Rosmersholm*. Vinnie's farewell recalls Rosmer's: 'Since there is no God to judge us we must pass judgment on ourselves.'[6] Similarly, O'Neill's insistence on the power of the dead to impose their will on the living looks back to *Ghosts*. It is O'Neill's attempt to achieve a tragic conclusion of a kind whose power and relevance for a secular age had been first exemplified by Ibsen: that of a ruthlessly clear-sighted acceptance of guilt and responsibility. Does *Mourning Becomes Electra* 'achieve the tragic effect as few modern plays have done'?[7] Or does it remain at the level of an interesting melodrama, capable of stimulating reflection but without the power to move or disturb?

In the dedicatory note to his wife that prefaces *Long Day's Journey into Night*, a late work that is directly autobiographical in theme, O'Neill writes of[8]

> this play of old sorrow, written in tears and blood . . . I mean it as a tribute to your love and tenderness . . . that enabled me to face my dead at last and write this play. . . .

The emotional afflatus of the tone is very characteristic, as is the earnest, perhaps somewhat portentous concern, and the fondness for the rhetorical gesture. There is a large romanticism about O'Neill's work that sets him apart from his contemporaries, at any rate from those taken seriously in literary circles, and that gives him an old-fashioned air. Of recent dramatists only John Osborne comes near O'Neill in open, uninhibited emotionalism; he also shares O'Neill's fondness for rhetoric. O'Neill is Romantic, too, in his concentration on the self. Despite the range of his experiments, in his best plays he draws very closely on what we know to be compulsive autobiographical themes, the fierce tensions within the family circle whose members are bound to each other by an inextricable blend of love and hatred. For O'Neill the Oresteian theme must therefore have possessed a personal interest and significance; the play's strength lies partly in this personal commitment and partly in the opportunity the subject afforded for a large-scale psychological study of family relationships that would reflect adequately O'Neill's sense of the importance and relevance of Freudian ideas. There is certainly both originality and power in the working out of these ideas in the play; the handling of the characters shows both psychological understanding and a sympathetic human concern which is an appropriate consequence of that understanding, if one that is not found all that often in the literature of our times. None of the characters is judged; all are seen as victims of the disastrous personal compulsions that rule our lives:[9]

> Why can't all of us remain innocent and loving and trusting? But God won't leave us alone. He twists and . . . tortures our lives with others' lives until – we poison each other to death!

Though O'Neill has placed Vinnie at the centre and given her the final word, the fullest and most interesting character study is that of Orin. Described as tense and over-sensitive, with a 'gentle boyish charm which makes women immediately want to mother him',[10] he is very close to O'Neill, whose understanding of the Oedipal situation has a personal ring about it and is displayed in a number of his plays: one thinks elsewhere especially of Eben in *Desire under the Elms*. Here we find an Orestes who is openly motivated not by revenge for his father but by frantic jealousy of the father-substitute, Brand; though he is disturbed by the accusation of murder of his father that Vinnie brings against Christine, he is only aroused to action by the cold proof of the adultery with Brand. But O'Neill does not forget the relationship with the father, though he follows the Greek original in never having the two meet. He sets the relationship in the context of a common experience of the war that has just ended; it is the subtlest effect in the play. Orin has been scarred by the war; he excuses his indifference to his father's death to the reproachful Vinnie by the long, hateful experience of familiarity with killing provided by the war. But he is aware, immediately, of a greater complexity:[11]

> I hardened myself to expect my own death and everyone else's. . . . It was part of my training as a soldier under him. He taught it to me, you might say! . . . He was the war to me – the war that would never end until I died.

O'Neill's skill appears in the way he shows Orin struggling with the confused feelings he cannot understand himself as he tries to explain himself to Vinnie, while allowing the reader or audience to apprehend without difficulty a coherent pattern of inner meaning. Within the conscious hostility and half-conscious jealousy lies an involuntary but profound identification with the father, emphasized as this is, in a simpler way, through the physical resemblance that is later to become so marked, after the mother's death. His aggressive feelings towards his father associate him with the war – 'I can't grasp anything but war, in which he was so alive';[12] his inner feelings have found confirmation in the external circumstances, as often happens: Ezra Mannon's stiff, repressed personality, their respective roles as commander and subordinate, and his father's sudden death. He addresses his father's body laid out on its bier with 'a strange friendly mockery', as just another corpse among so many hundreds they two have seen together; a fellow-feeling emerges in the suggestion that 'you never cared to know me in life – but I really think we might be friends now you are dead!'[13] The motif of friends in death is developed and given a deeper meaning in Orin's account of how he killed two Reb soldiers on an expedition behind the enemy's lines, one on the way out and one returning:[14]

> It was like murdering the same man twice. I had a queer feeling that war meant murdering the same man over and over, and that in the end I would discover the man was myself! Their faces keep coming back in dreams – and they change to Father's face – or to mine. . . .

At the end of the same play, after he has shot Brand, he is fascinated by the resemblance between Brand and his father, and recalls his earlier dream; Brand, like Aegisthus, is a relative.[15]

> This is like my dream. I've killed him before – over and over. . . . He looks like me, too! Maybe I've committed suicide.

This is immediately followed by a fellow-feeling with his victim Brand:[16]

> If I had been he I would have done what he did! I would have loved her as he loved her – and killed Father, too – for her sake!

All three of the men over whom Christine exercises so disastrous a fascination merge in Orin's mind: the dead father whom she and Brand had murdered, Brand, the father's supplanter, whom he has just killed, and himself, the son. The self-destructive impulse in Orin which has been stimulated by the stress of war is shown to have deeper origins than guilt over his responsibility for his mother's death, and to spring from the over-indulgence of the twin Oedipal impulses of hostility to the father and possessive love of the mother. He has murderously attacked his father in fantasy, but he has attacked him for what he wishes to do himself; his jealousy masks an identification which in his mother's life-time is already, after the father's death, leading him towards suicide, and which is to culminate in the last play, *The Haunted*, when he 'becomes' his father. The reference to his mother, in the words spoken over Brand's body, shows the attack on the father to be Oedipal:[17] she is the true justification for hatred of the father, whether Brand's hatred or his own. The reference is extraordinarily, perhaps improbably, explicit; it must be supposed that the shock of Brand's murder has forced the real motive to the surface of Orin's mind. Earlier, O'Neill has been careful not to give too consciously an Oedipal motive to Orin for his hostility to the father; it is allowed to remain suppressed, in his confused thoughts as he stands by his father's bier. The crucial relationship of mother and son is thus set in the context of Orin's attitude to his father; the two passages quoted above[18] frame the duologue, in Act Two of *The Hunted*, that takes us to the heart of Orin's feelings about his mother and her reciprocal response to him.

It is a tragic relationship that O'Neill depicts here, with a convincingness and truth of detail that is not equalled elsewhere in the play. In the past they have shared a peculiar intimacy; for Christine, Orin was the compensation for a loveless marriage and mother and son have shared a secret world where 'no Mannons allowed was our password'.[19] But Orin is also a Mannon; he has come under Vinnie's influence as well as his mother's, and the war gave Vinnie her chance to separate them, as Christine bitterly complains:[20]

> I loved him until he let you and your father nag him into the war, in spite of my begging him not to leave me alone.

and later:[21]

> I'll never forgive her for that! It broke my heart, Orin.

Christine has now turned to Brand; when Orin comes home, his sensibilities screwed up to fever pitch by his war experiences, she is torn between love of, and fear for, her new lover and her agonized sense of what she has lost, of the son she has betrayed. The accusing presence of Vinnie, waiting outside the room to take Orin to pay his respects to his father's body, heightens the tension of their reunion. Christine fences nervously with him, trying to hold him at a distance in the role of responsible, loving parent, but hopelessly vulnerable to the alternating pressures of his quick suspiciousness and of a passionate devotion she had once encouraged but to which she is no longer free to respond. To protect herself and discredit Vinnie's accusation, she must draw Orin back into the old tender intimacy; but to do this is to assume a part which guilt and inclination alike will no longer permit her to play. She has found satisfaction with Brand, and to free herself for him she has murdered the father whom Orin in his jealousy is already beginning to resemble. Though he does not yet know it, to Orin she has now become the lost Paradisal place, the island from which both are permanently exiled: it is his tender, caressing evocation of this image, that sustained his dreams and fantasies during the harsh time of separation in

the war, that pierces her with the realization of all that she has
lost:[22]

> Orin   . . . I seemed really to be there. There was no
> one there but you and me. And yet I never
> saw you . . . I only felt you all around me. . . .
> The breaking of the waves was your voice. The
> sky was the same colour as your eyes. The
> warm sand was like your skin. The whole
> island was you. . . .
>
> Christine   Oh, if only you had never gone away! If you
> only hadn't let them take you from me!
>
> Orin   But I've come back. Everything is all right
> now, isn't it?

After Vinnie has convinced him of his mother's adultery with
Brand, in the immediately ensuing scene, he comes to the realization of the truth:[23]

> To think I hoped home would be an escape from death!
> I should never have come back to life – from my island
> of peace! But that's lost now! You're my lost island,
> aren't you, Mother?

Half unconsciously she confirms her betrayal of Orin in the
next scene, on board Brand's clipper, where he listens concealed, 'his face distorted with jealous fury',[24] as the lovers plan
desperately to get away:[25]

> You have me, Adam! . . . And we will be happy – once
> on your Blessed Islands! . . . It's strange. Orin was telling
> me of an island –

The final reference to the island image in *The Hunted* occurs
in the last scene, where Orin faces the terrified Christine with
his knowledge of the truth and tells her he has killed her lover.
In a state of 'morbid excitement', veering between savage
resentment and an appalled realization of what he has done to
her, he first reproaches her with her betrayal – 'our island – that
was you and I!' and then pleads with her to forget:[26]

> We'll leave Vinnie here and go away on a long voyage –
> to the South Seas –

It is an empty dream, as they both know, but the image survives.
It is Orin and Vinnie, not Christine, who after Christine's
suicide go on a voyage to discover the islands, Vinnie, by a
reversal of roles, discovering her mother's capacity for pleasure
while Orin sinks deeper into a wooden Mannon-like despair.
O'Neill has left on record, in a working note on the play, his
intention to [27]

> Develop South Sea Island motive – its appeal for them
> all . . . – release, peace, security, beauty, freedom of
> conscience, sinlessness, etc. – longing for the primitive –
> and mother symbol – yearning for pre-natal non-
> competitive freedom from fears – make this Island
> theme recurrent motive –

He does indeed make highly explicit, schematic use of this
motif; even Ezra, in a pathetic attempt on first returning home
to repair his marriage, speaks of 'a notion if we'd go off . . .
together . . . find some island where we could be alone for a
while'.[28] Immensely telling in *The Hunted*, as the image of a
primary good place still alive in the fantasies of mother and son,
it acquires through overuse a heavy artifice that is symptomatic
of a weakness found elsewhere in the trilogy. Even where the
idea seems dramatically apt and basically true, O'Neill's deliberate, self-conscious plotting of psychoanalytical effects can detract
from the tragic power; something external, superficial, even
somewhat mechanical takes over from the pity and terror of the
human conflict and leaves us unconvinced, intrigued merely by
the brilliant insights but not deeply moved. The last play, *The
Haunted*, suffers particularly in this way. The whole Island motif,
embedded as it is in the voyage taken by the brother and sister,
seems artificially imposed on the characters. More seriously,
the potentially fruitful idea of the guilty children re-enacting
the tragedy of the parents by taking over their personalities
loses its hold over us owing to an over-insistence on explicit
resemblances and echoes from the past; Lavinia 'now bears a
striking resemblance to her mother in every respect, even to
being dressed in the green her mother had affected'.[29] Later
Orin tells her that it is 'as if death had set you free – to become
her!';[30] and in their last agonized quarrel he insists, 'Can't you
see I'm now in Father's place and you're Mother?'[31] Orin's

death, and Vinnie's final lonely self-condemnation, are impressive, especially the former. Here O'Neill develops an idea implicit in *The Oresteia*. Orin experiences his overwhelming sense of guilt over his mother's death as poisonous vomit that crowds up in his throat; and at the climactic moment before his suicide 'his mouth grows convulsed, as though he were retching up poison'.[32] It is as though he can only rid himself of the dead chewed-up mother within him by a suicide that exactly parallels her own. It is an act of release and reparation:[33]

> I'll get on my knees and ask your forgiveness – and say
> . . . I'm glad you found love, Mother! . . . You're calling
> me! You're waiting to take me home!

The motif of the poisonous sickness also recalls the father, poisoned in *Homecoming* by the mother. Orestes, the tragically divided child, is identified in his death with both dead parents. This is absolutely right, and greatly reinforces the sense of tragic inevitability which O'Neill wished to recapture from the Greeks. A deterministic fate is experienced not as an abstract idea but as an inner psychological necessity of a relentlessly compulsive order. It is the relationship of mother and son, particularly in the last scene of the play, that gives *The Hunted* its peculiar power. Though it contains the powerful scene of Orin's suicide, *The Haunted* is primarily concerned with the relationship of brother and sister, and it is here that doubts arise. The pattern of their relationship has a willed, contrived air that lacks conviction and that contrasts with the reality and force of the earlier scenes between husband and wife in *Homecoming* and mother and son in *The Hunted*. In general, the explicit reference back to the Greek original, with a precise correspondence not only with the Greek character but with the blood-feud of the house of Atreus, comes to seem too much of a conscious contrivance. The circumstances of blood-feud are remote enough from the modern audience's experience, especially in the context of a totally different age and culture. Indeed, there seems to be a kind of unconscious irony in giving the play a pre-Freudian setting, when the characters behave, and talk, with so consistent a Freudian emphasis. The effect, in weaker passages, is to make them puppets of the author.

The problem is partly, and perhaps primarily, one of language.

A modern Orestes does not need to speak in Aeschylean verse –
it would indeed be inappropriate for him to do so. But a very
subtle, flexible, suggestive mode of speech will be required by a
dramatist who takes pains to keep the reader always mindful of
the heroic analogues from the past and who wishes to give his
characters a size and intensity transcending everyday reality.
That this was O'Neill's intention is clear from many recorded
comments, as when he asserts that the theatre 'should give me
what the church no longer gives me – a meaning'.[34] Elsewhere
he wrote that he was not interested in the relation between man
and man but only in that between man and God.[35] This spiritual
concern can be seen both in his technical experiments with
expressionism and in the recourse to ancient myth which, he says,
will enable drama to return to 'the spirit of Greek grandeur'.[36]
In his working notes for *Mourning Becomes Electra*, he urges
himself to 'use every means to get added depth and scope . . .
more sense of fate . . . more sense of the unreal behind what
we call reality. . . .'[37] To the reader in particular, the rhetoric
of educated speech that O'Neill employs throughout the play
is inadequate to the demands that this search for 'depth and
scope' imposes on it; as language it is flat and commonplace,
without undertone or implication, and lacking the vitality of
his inarticulate dialogue. O'Neill acknowledges its deficiency
himself:[38]

> [It] needed great language . . . I haven't got that. And,
> by way of self-consolation, I don't think . . . that great
> language is possible for anyone living in the discordant,
> broken faithless rhythm of our time. The best one can do
> is to be pathetically eloquent. . . .

His disclaimer suggests that he did not altogether realize his
own limitations; in literary drama the characters *are* the way
they talk, and O'Neill's failure to cut deeper into the texture of
human experience manifests itself directly in the relative failure
of his language. There is power and insight, but not quite the
power one might expect from the intensity of O'Neill's commitment to his theme and his undoubted theatrical skill. Indeed, the
play as a whole is a strange compound of strength and weakness.
Nowhere is this better illustrated than in the matter of its emotional effect. It is a grim and ruthless story worked out with

complete inexorability, but we are less moved to pity and terror than we have a right to expect to be, intrigued rather than disturbed. It all seems more enjoyable than it should be. There is a sentimentalism in O'Neill that leaves him closer to the surface than is compatible with true tragic power; at the same time, one source of our pleasure in the play is undoubtedly the active presence of a sympathetic understanding that feels for the characters' sufferings and never judges them from without, or simply exhibits them as interesting specimens. Similarly, *Mourning Becomes Electra* enacts some of the finest Freudian insights in modern drama, substantially adding to our under-standing of all that is implied in the story of Orestes. At the same time, the laboured closeness of the parallels with the original Greek and the painstaking explicitness with which the ideas are worked out suggests that the essential material of the play, in so far as it is not autobiographical, does not arise from the deepest strata of the author's psychic unconscious. J. I. M. Stewart remarks of the creative artist that 'the essence of his task is in exploring an inward abundance',[39] and that Shakespeare's characters in particular gain 'their haunting suggestion of reality and of a larger, latent being unexhausted in the action immediately before us'[40] precisely from the extent and depth of this abundance. O'Neill's characters and their concerns do not give the impression of such an 'inward abundance' in their creator; he has no access to the deepest springs, which is only to say, perhaps, that he is a writer of talent not genius. The reality and extent of that talent should not be underestimated, as it often is today when O'Neill's tone is unfashionable in what pass for sophisticated literary circles. If *Mourning Becomes Electra* is a failure by the highest standards it still merits our attention, especially in the theatre, and is a testament to the largeness of mind and penetrating insight of its author.

Notes

1 Eugene O'Neill, unpublished preface to *The Great God Brown.*
2 G. Steiner, *The Death of Tragedy* (London, 1951), pp. 328–30.
3 Ibid., p. 328.
4 Ibid., p. 304.
5 E. O'Neill, *Mourning Becomes Electra* (London, 1932), pp. 287–8.

6 Ibsen, *Rosmersholm*, Act IV.
7 C. Leech, *O'Neill* (Edinburgh, 1963), p. 84.
8 E. O'Neill, *Long Day's Journey into Night* (London, 1956).
9 *Mourning Becomes Electra*, p. 122.
10 Ibid., p. 123.
11 Ibid., p. 126.
12 Ibid., p. 126.
13 Ibid., p. 154.
14 Ibid., p. 156.
15 Ibid., p. 189.
16 Ibid., pp. 189–90.
17 See above.
18 *Mourning Becomes Electra*, pp. 126, 154.
19 Ibid., p. 141.
20 Ibid., p. 57.
21 Ibid., p. 144.
22 Ibid., p. 149.
23 Ibid., p. 166.
24 Ibid., p. 179.
25 Ibid., p. 183.
26 Ibid., p. 198.
27 Quoted by Leech, op. cit., p. 85.
28 *Mourning Becomes Electra*, p. 95.
29 Ibid., p. 222.
30 Ibid., p. 228.
31 Ibid., p. 252.
32 Ibid., p. 270.
33 Ibid.
34 O'Neill, unpublished preface to *The Great God Brown*.
35 See M. Cunliffe, *The Literature of the United States* (London, 1954), p. 302.
36 O'Neill, unpublished preface to *The Great God Brown*.
37 Leech, op. cit., p. 83.
38 Cunliffe, op. cit., p. 299.
39 J. I. M. Stewart, *Character and Motive in Shakespeare* (London, 1949), p. 122.
40 Ibid.

Eight

Orestes in Modern Drama:
The Family Reunion

In the last act of *The Cocktail Party* Sir Henry Harcourt-Reilly, attempting to explain to the assembled company the rationale behind Celia's apparently futile death as a martyr, calls Shelley in aid:

> For know there are two worlds of life and death
> One that which thou beholdest; but the other
> Is underneath the grave . . . where do inhabit
> The shadows of all forms that think and live
> Till death unite them and they part no more![1]

The theme of the relationship of the two worlds, material and spiritual, the natural and the transcendent, is ubiquitous in Eliot's drama; his efforts are always directed towards bringing them into creative interaction with each other, and his development as a dramatist is essentially a record of his attempts to bridge the gulf that, in his experience, opens between them. The structural pattern of the plays is as consistent as their theme. In each of the full-length plays there is a hero who enacts the spiritual process of dying into life. It is a way of self-discovery which is also a discovery of the full reality of the supernatural world, and involves the hero in a death which may be the literal death of the martyr or simply the dying to the old concerns and preoccupations of the material world and self. The other characters, set in sharp, almost schematic contrast to the dedicated or exceptional hero, are usually those of less spiritual capacity who are drawn irresistibly into his orbit and whose changing relationship to him throughout the plays is an index of the modifications in Eliot's attitude to the secular world in which it was his fate as a Christian to live. Increasingly in the later plays the less enlightened characters are permitted a significant if humble share in the spiritual banquet, until finally in the persons of the young lovers of *The Elder Statesman* they act as torch bearers for a hero whose acknowledged burden of guilt and failure no longer separates him from the rest of us. In the early plays the relationship is profoundly, if not perhaps always intentionally, ambivalent. The hero affects us simultaneously as being a saint-like figure whose office is the Christ-like one of the suffering servant and who mysteriously takes upon himself the burdens of those of less spiritual capacity, and a spiritual snob whose triumphant achievement merely serves to throw into a sharper relief the worldly darkness of his inferiors. *The Family Reunion* stands, perhaps, at the point of maximum tension between these two worlds. In his first full-length play, *Murder in the Cathedral*, Eliot had largely evaded the problem by remaining safely in the shadow of the church porch. Wisely, perhaps, in view of his inexperience in writing for the stage, he relied here on a historical Christian subject and approach and spoke to a religious audience in the tones of formal religious orthodoxy, even if spiced with a contemporary post-Prufrock seasoning. On the surface *Murder in the Cathedral* is a powerful and effective play, free of the unresolved conflicts and awkward changes of gear that mar all its successors except *The Elder Statesman*, but there is a hollowness about the power, like that of a man who wears the formal dress and assumes the formal manners of a bygone age because he does not want to come into too close a contact with his contemporaries; as Eliot himself saw, *Murder in the Cathedral* was 'a dead end'.[2] His judgments on the play in *Poetry and Drama* are modestly personal, as is appropriate to a work in which he is 'only tracing out the route of exploration of one writer';[3] but he makes it clear that, in his view, historical or mythological subject-matter is only tolerable today if the dramatist firmly grasps the nettle of contemporary relevance in style and characterization and avoids an archaizing or antiquarian approach:[4]

> What we have to do is to bring poetry into the world
> in which the audience lives and to which it returns when
> it leaves the theatre; not to transport the audience into
> some imaginary world totally unlike its own. . . .

This sentence occurs in the passage describing the genesis of

The Family Reunion, the first of his plays of contemporary life. If we look for an explanation of why Eliot had recourse for a subject to Aeschylus and Greek tragedy, the answer may be found in the need of his temperament to preserve some formal link with a meaningful tradition of the past while avoiding so open and dogmatic an assertion of Christian commitment as in *Murder in the Cathedral.* (The choice of the Orestes story seems to have been determined, as I shall hope to show, by a personal interest.) Aeschylus offered a religious and moral emphasis unusual among the writers of classical Greece; his salvation of Orestes is, however remotely, an analogue to the redemption of Eliot's hero. At the same time he may have hoped to reap the advantage of what he rightly assumed to be a profound ignorance, among his public, of the religious aspects of Greek mythology; the Eumenides were in no danger of bringing to mind the Established Church, with its undesirable associations for a secular audience. The religious theme could thus perhaps be slipped past the audience's guard, without their attention being drawn too overtly to its presence. Until his last play, where he adopts a notably less defensive position, Eliot seems to have acted upon the assumption that an audience used to secular prose drama would only be receptive to poetic drama on a religious subject if he could affect them without their being made directly aware of what it was they were getting. In the two plays that were to follow *The Family Reunion,* Eliot was to go a long way to meet his audience, the irony and humour of the presentation and the plainness and clarity of the verse misleading some critics into believing that he had abandoned both his poetry and his subject-matter. He has rather subdued them, with admittedly doubtful success, to what he sees as 'strict dramatic utility'.[5] In doing so he has rediscovered the familiar truth, exemplified from Aristophanes to Shaw, that comedy is particularly well suited to the presentation of ideas. In contrast, *The Family Reunion* is a transitional play, occupying a place between the religious tragedy of *Murder in the Cathedral* and the serious comedy of *The Cocktail Party* and *The Confidential Clerk.* The spiritual crisis of its hero is expressed with an intense concentration and complexity of style that casts doubt on the feasibility of it being rendered in comprehensible dramatic terms at all, while the familiar guide-lines of history and tradition that sustained *Murder in the Cathedral* have

been abandoned without the compensating advantages of a
contemporary comedy of manners. The result is an interesting
confusion, with many fine and moving passages but an absence
of control over the material which is manifest in various unresolved
tensions and unintended effects. Eliot himself remarked that 'I
had given my attention to versification, at the expense of plot
and character.'[6] This observation, like all Eliot's self-criticism
in the field of drama, is very shrewd; indeed, his inattention to
character, to call it that, has surprising and revealing consequences, in that what might be called Oresteian preoccupations
with self-defence against the dominating, predatory woman get
past *his* guard and are allowed to undermine the central theme
of the hero's discovery of spiritual vocation. Eliot himself has,
again, in his appraisal of the play, put his finger on the central
problem:[7]

> we are left in a divided frame of mind, not knowing
> whether to consider the play the tragedy of the mother or
> the salvation of the son. The two situations are not recon-
> ciled . . . my hero now strikes me as an insufferable prig.

But he does not go into reasons for this, beyond a suggestion
that it has to do with 'a failure of adjustment between the Greek
story and the modern situation'.[8] The problem seems to have
more to do with conflict of intention than 'failure of adjustment'. The central situation of the play shows Harry, Lord
Monchensey, discovering the truth about the loveless marriage
of his parents and so freeing himself from the burden of
neurotic guilt over the wife he has failed to love and has
possibly murdered. In the central scene of the play he learns
that his father, with whom he has become strongly identified,
attempted to get rid of his mother when he himself was an unborn
child in the womb. Both father and son have been faced with the
woman's ruthless will to dominate and control. Harry describes
how he 'felt the trap close' the night his father died, an occasion
for the 'low conversation of triumphant aunts'.[9] We hear on
unimpeachable authority – that of Agatha – that his father had
yielded to his mother's power, who in the end simply took his
place at Wishwood, just as Harry, the son, has been compelled
in his turn to play a part imposed on him by his mother:[10]

Everything has always been referred back to mother . . .
The rule of conduct was simply pleasing mother; . . .
What was wrong was whatever made her suffer,
And whatever made her happy was what was virtuous . . .

We learn, too, that the wife whose death at sea has plunged
Harry into his present state of hallucinatory terror had attempted,
like his mother, to strangle him with her possessiveness; he
remarks bitterly to Agatha that his mother's training had been
the right preparation for his marriage, expressly comparing the
'stifling of his decision' by his wife's 'apparent strength'[11] to his
father's similar predicament in his own marriage. He sees his
wife as a succubus whose imperviousness he had come to take for
granted; in describing his surprise at her death, which he believes
himself to have contrived, he says[12]

> I had always supposed, wherever I went
> That she would be with me; whatever I did
> That she was unkillable.

This aspect of their relationship is strongly reminiscent of that
between the husband and wife, Edward and Lavinia, in *The
Cocktail Party*. Edward refers to his wife as 'the python. The
octopus'[13] and describes what his wife 'had made him into':[14]

> I felt . . .
> The whole oppression, the unreality
> Of the role she had always imposed upon me
> With the obstinate, unconscious, sub-human strength
> That some women have.

Edward, it will be remembered, believes himself to be incapable
of loving, a condition that is explicitly compared to the fear
of impotence; Lavinia believes herself to be unlovable. There
is the strong implication that, not only for Edward but also for
Harry and his father, a significant though unstated aspect of the
woman's predatory possessiveness lies in the sexual demands the
men are unable to satisfy. Amy in *The Family Reunion* speaks of
'the humiliation' of the sexual relation between her husband
and herself:[15]

> . . . the chilly pretences in the silent bedroom,
> Forcing sons upon an unwilling father.

Downing, the chauffeur, confirms of Harry's wife that 'she wouldn't leave him alone';[16] but the most striking passage occurs during the quarrel between Amy, the mother, and Agatha, the sister whom Amy's husband had loved and whom she now accuses of having taken her son away from her also. Amy recalls bitterly how after she had lost her husband's love she was left with nothing 'but what I could breed for myself':[17]

> Seven years I kept him,
> For the sake of the future, a discontented ghost,
> In his own house. What of the humiliation . . .
> Forcing sons upon an unwilling father? . . .
> I *would* have sons, if I could not have a husband:

The picture emerges of a woman whose voraciousness is experienced at a primitive level; her insatiable demands suck the man dry and like the octopus threaten him with total absorption. His only useful function is to provide the woman with children, after which he can be cast aside. He becomes at best, in Edward's words in *The Cocktail Party*, incapable of any existence of his own,[18] a ghost living in a world of unreality. Seen in this light, Orestes' matricidal act becomes a desperate piece of self-defence; it is a role that any man might find himself forced into, as Charles, Harry's uncle, remarks:[19]

> In any case, I shouldn't blame Harry.
> I might have done the same thing myself, once.
> Nobody knows what he's likely to do
> Until there's somebody he wants to get rid of.

This passage recalls the sinister Sweeney of *Sweeney Agonistes*, who also speaks, with comic frankness, on behalf of the rest of us:[20]

> I knew a man once did a girl in . . .
> Any man has to, needs to, wants to
> Once in a lifetime, do a girl in.

Thus a curious new twist is given to the myth of Orestes; the hidden or part-hidden Oedipal jealousy of the father, and the hatred against the mother which stems from the bitter medicine of spoiled love, seems to be replaced or reinforced by a basically more primitive terror of the threat posed to the child's very existence by the mother's greed, that 'fury for possession' of which the sisters in *The Family Reunion* accuse each other, so that he is forced to strike at her to preserve his freedom. The dominating role of Amy, the mother, in the play, and the absence of the wife, already dead before the play begins, confirms that Eliot sees the crucial relationship in the play as being that of mother and son, not wife and husband; the threat posed to her husband by Amy's possessiveness is repeated in the second generation by Harry's wife, as though the family, like the house of Atreus, are always caught in the same fate; but as the play develops, and Harry seeks relief from his suffering in the discovery of the truth about his father, the wife's role pales into obscure insignificance compared with the reality of the relationship with the dead father and living mother. Mother and wife are anyhow merged in the persecutory fantasy about the woman. Moreover, if the attempts of Harry's father to get rid of his wife in 'a dozen foolish ways' are paralleled in Harry's probably delusional belief that he has murdered his own wife, the actual death of Amy, Harry's mother, as a direct consequence of his action in leaving home at the end of the play, carries far more weight. The latter we witness for ourselves, while the truth of the former belief is never confirmed.

The central action of the play, a duologue in the second scene of the second act between Harry and Agatha, sees Harry, like Orestes in *The Eumenides*, released from the overwhelming burden of past guilt and sin into a life of meaningful freedom. Release comes about through the discovery of the truth about that past, through the agency of Agatha, the spiritual intercessor and guide whose role as inhabitant of 'the neutral territory between two worlds'[21] is to form a link between them and so reveal to the hero the way of true vocation. The implications of this scene, whose language is complex enough to make it at times difficult to follow, are worth examining. For Harry it is a kind of spiritual birth, this time from the right mother, a woman who once loved his father and who had saved Harry, an unborn child, from his father's murderous designs on his mother. Spiritual maternity and sonship is explicitly acknowledged by both Harry and Agatha:[22]

> *Agatha*   I wanted you! . . .
>   I felt that you were in some way mine!

> And that in any case I should have no other
> child.
> *Harry*   And have me. That is the way things happen.

Agatha can give Harry the love and understanding denied him
by his real mother. Harry's father had been starved of love in a
loveless marriage; his son, denied his father in childhood, had
repeated that pattern of lovelessness in his own marriage, but
he now rediscovers his father in a different way, becoming
momentarily the lover his father might have been:[23]

> What did not happen is as true as what did happen
> O my dear, and you walked through the little door
> And I ran to meet you in the rose-garden.

Agatha reminds him at this point that the ecstasy, as well as
the nightmare, of the past must be left behind; she has given
him the glimpse of a vision of happiness but[24]

> We do not pass twice through the same door
> Or return to the door through which we did not pass . . .
> You have a long journey.

It is the decisive moment of the play, a shift from the secular
to the sacred, from the worldly concept of crime and the psychological concept of illness to the religious concept of sin and
expiation. Harry has[25]

> crossed the frontier
> Beyond which safety and danger have a different meaning.

He is mysteriously chosen to be 'the consciousness of your unhappy family', to bear their burdens and atone for their sins,
and so purge the lovelessness that has plagued them. It is the
passage, in Harry, from the role of Orestes to that of the saint;
but whereas in Aeschylus release and expiation follow, as they
must, the crime to which they refer and which is central to the
story of Orestes, here the Oresteian matricide is still to come.
Harry leaves Wishwood on his dedicated journey in the clear
knowledge that his act will be death to his mother; his silence,
in answer to her quiet[26]

> If you go now, I shall never see you again

is a tacit admission of the truth. It is this uncomfortable fact, whose force Eliot seems to recognize, that casts doubt on the validity of the whole spiritual pilgrimage, and suggests irresistibly the presence of unresolved elements in the author's material. We can accept, perhaps, the religious mystery of Harry's discovery of 'election';[27] in the central scene, his, and Agatha's, spiritual struggle is sensitively and movingly presented, although the core of the experience is hard to express in dramatic terms, and perhaps in words at all:[28]

> In this world
> It is inexplicable, the resolution is in another.

But historical and psychological truth is altogether too summarily dismissed in the central scene. Eliot's attitude to analytical psychology has always been equivocal; he has recognized its especial relevance to the artist's experience of the modern consciousness, but his posture towards it has been, most characteristically, one of ironic defence: in his famous *Dial* review of *Ulysses* he writes of the aesthetic possibilities which psychology, with other studies, has opened up to the writer, but the parenthetical reservation is typical: 'Psychology (such as it is, and whether our reaction be comic or serious) . . .'.[29]

The whole characterization in *The Cocktail Party* of Reilly, the spiritual guide, concealed as a psychiatrist, is very revealing; the cloven hoof of the moralist and spiritual teacher emerges very quickly from behind the healer's mask. In *The Family Reunion* Harry, at first appearance, strikes us as mentally ill and this impression is partially correct. The therapy Agatha provides is, rightly, powered by her love and understanding, but its essential content is the revelation of the true facts of his parents' relationship. In the first place, such a revelation is simply not enough. It is unconvincing that so radical a cure, changing Harry's whole attitude to the present and the past, should be effected by such information, however important. Human beings, as any experienced analyst will confirm, change very slowly, and we cannot believe that Harry can so easily undo the past simply by hearing what it was. It may be argued that the moment of psychological release is subsumed in a religious conversion which, by definition, is no longer explicable in psychological terms alone; but as the issue has been raised partly in psychological and historical terms, the solution strikes one as evasive.

There is a still more serious, because more specific, objection to what we are offered in this scene. Harry's spiritual discovery is based upon a clear initiative of his own, which breaks through the hallucinations and delusions of his mental illness; a determination to discover his lost father. In the moment of release there is a powerful sense of identification with the dead father. Might he not, then, find his own murderous wishes confirmed, rather than disposed of, by the news that his father has tried, with good reason, to get rid of his mother? On the face of it this is an obviously absurd conclusion; yet when we recall that Eliot has himself identified Harry as Orestes by his introduction of the Eumenides, and further that the play ends with the death of the mother as a direct result of Harry's actions, the conclusion is not all that easy to resist. I return here to the significant material, in this play and elsewhere in Eliot, about the predatory woman who threatens the child's existence by her greed. There is a disturbing suggestion of projection here, of the buried Oedipal wishes forcing themselves out and finding a scapegoat in the woman. In psychoanalytical terms the infant's greed is put out into the mother, turning her into the python or octopus whose insatiable mouth or womb passively but relentlessly absorbs her victim. It is interesting to find that Sweeney, the most primitive of Eliot's dramatic heroes, who, it will be recalled,[30] speaks for all of us in our need to get rid of the oppressive woman, reaches back beyond projection to the original wish. He tells Doris[31]

> I'll gobble you up. I'll be the cannibal . . . Yes, I'd eat you!
> In a nice little, white little . . . missionary stew.

I have suggested that frustrated Oedipal wishes directed towards the mother are implicit in the original Orestes; but it is hard to see that they have any place in the story of Eliot's Christ-like hero, the more so because their existence is unacknowledged, except indirectly and, as it were, involuntarily. As Eliot saw, it is the mother, Amy, 'the only complete human being in the play',[32] who draws our sympathy, and this is true of her defeat by Agatha as well as her more important rejection by Harry. It is not simply that, as Eliot himself puts it, sympathy for the mother is liable to make Harry seem an 'insufferable prig';[33] it also casts some doubt on the accusations of predatory possessiveness brought against her by both Harry and Agatha. Like Harry's, Agatha's role and personality are essentially ambiguous; a frustrated possessiveness shows disconcertingly through the selflessness of her spiritual midwifery. This is partly, no doubt, a technical problem; Eliot is aware of the danger that the role of spiritual guide will deprive Agatha of human qualities, including human weaknesses, and has done his best to redress the balance. We are no doubt meant to feel that Amy when she accuses Agatha of stealing Harry from her, is blaming her for her own faults, but the repressed vehemence of Agatha's personality, and her admitted years of frustration since the death of Harry's father,[34]

> thirty years of solitude . . . in a woman's college,
> Trying not to dislike women,

lend plausibility to Amy's twice-repeated charge:[35]

> Your fury for possession
> Is only the stronger for all these years of abstinence.
> Thirty-five years ago you took my husband from me
> And now you take my son.

At best, Amy's tenacity is matched by Agatha's; their whole relationship, especially their likeness and unlikeness as sisters, is one of the unexpected successes of the play. If Agatha is possessive, may not Harry be possessive too, in a much more obscure, buried manner? Can we accept his obsessive fear of female possessiveness without *arrière-pensée*, as wholly warranted by the behaviour of his mother and his wife? It is noticeable that Harry's role is only made possible by the suppression of almost all the real feelings, of whatever kind, a son might be expected to show towards a mother. Though Eliot tries to give the words with which Harry consoles her for his departure some loving concern, and even warmth, his attitude to her after his conversion is chillingly impersonal, a blend of superior contempt for her lack of enlightenment and a hardly less patronizing pity. The original Orestes became a religious hero by expiating his crime of matricide; this Orestes, by a seemingly absurd paradox, is to become a religious hero in its performance. It is essential, if the play is not to break down, that this truth be concealed, or at any rate given minimal stress; this I take to be the reason for the impersonal remoteness of Harry's attitude to his mother in the last Act. Her death is necessary in order that he may proceed on the road of spiritual salvation; otherwise it seems to be experienced by him as a sort of irrelevance, for which in his self-absorption he feels no responsibility. It may be concluded that Eliot tries to evade the central problem of Oresteian guilt by suppressing a great deal of what must really be there in the relationship of mother and son. It is plainly an impossible task; Eliot's interest in Orestes forces indirectly into the open deeply felt material about the predatory woman which is never successfully absorbed into the central theme of the play, the hero's 'dying into life'.

A third heroic figure from the cultural past plays his part in the make-up of Eliot's composite hero; like Harry, he suppresses his true feelings towards a mother, and also like Harry, he is weighed down by the presence of an injured father's ghost. Orestes and the Christian saint are joined by Hamlet, whose shadowy influence is in some ways the most marked of all. Harry resembles Hamlet in that he is surrounded by inferior persons who do not understand him; his tone towards them recalls the mordant superiority and contempt Hamlet displays towards the courtiers. We identify with the tone, which brings us close to Harry in his Hamlet-like difference from common men. In instances like the following we share his sense of conscious superiority, though in a very different and less comfortable context:[36]

> . . . how can I explain, how can I explain to *you*?
> You will understand less after I have explained it.
> . . . people to whom nothing has ever happened
> Cannot understand the unimportance of events . . .
> You are all people
> To whom nothing has happened . . .

or[37]

> A brief vacation from the kind of consciousness
> That John enjoys, can't make very much difference
> To him or anyone else.

The difference, of course, is that Hamlet, unlike Harry, is not a religious hero in the Christian tradition. He has no mysterious responsibility for those around him, and so avoids the spiritual snobbery and arrogance that embarrass us in Harry. A second point of likeness is that Harry, like Hamlet, is mad, even if only north-north-west; and in his distress he shows, like Hamlet, suspicious resentment of the wrong kind of interference. Speaking of the Eumenides, Harry comments that if they were inside him, symptoms merely of his mental illness, [38]

> I could cheat them perhaps with the aid of Dr Warburton –
> Or any other doctor, who would be another Warburton,
> If you decided to set another doctor on me.

Warburton plays Polonius to Harry's Hamlet, spying on him, as he believes, and trying to entangle him in the inessential; Harry's dismissal of him is very much in Hamlet's manner: [39]

> What you have to tell me
> Is either something that I know already
> Or unimportant, or else untrue.

If Warburton is Polonius, Mary, Harry's cousin, is Ophelia. She offers Harry release from his suffering through sexual love, but this is a mere illusion; there is no escaping the demands of the supernatural world. Mary cannot see the Eumenides, and is dismissed: [40]

> . . . have you such dull senses
> That you could not see them? . . . Can't you help me?
> You're of no use to me. I must face them.
> I must fight them.

The reminiscence of Ophelia does not have to be close to be unmistakable; one has only to recall how much closer Mary's role is to Ophelia's than to Electra's. Finally, the Eumenides, those incongruous ghosts, take the place of Hamlet's father's ghost as messengers from the other world, pursuing the hero with their seemingly impossible demands. There is an obvious debt to Aeschylus here, in that Harry, in Part I, is tormented like the Aeschylean Orestes by what appears, in his case, to be a paranoid delusion; but the echo of old Hamlet is equally striking. Hamlet's ambivalent feelings towards the ghost are paralleled in Harry's attitude towards the Eumenides; he knows that he must listen to them, and even in Part I of the play, before they have become the Bright Angels who guide him in his sacred mission, their sinister aspect – sleepless hunters with distended claws – seems factitious and superimposed. It is true that they represent the unredeemed past, the part of himself that Harry cannot face until Agatha shows him the way. Even here there is a curious parallel to Hamlet, for it is the unresolved elements in Hamlet's relationship to his father that are a major cause of his suffering. The consistently benevolent aspect of the Eumenides, as of a parent who chastises where he loves, is emphasized by their surrender of their role to Agatha, the one character who never fails to support Harry; this really occurs as early as the end of Part I, when, alone on the stage, she utters a runic prayer for the future:[41]

> The eye is on this house
> The eye covers it
> There are three together
> May the three be separated
> May the knot that was tied
> Become unknotted . . .

The substitution is formalized after Harry has been released from his imprisonment; we are told in a stage-direction that 'Agatha goes to the window, in a somnambular fashion . . . disclosing the empty embrasure. She steps into the place which the Eumenides had occupied.'[42] It is perhaps significant, when weighing the influence of Shakespeare against that of the Greeks, that the one specific example of Greek influence, the Eumenides, become an embarrassment who rate a facetious reference from the chauffeur in the last act ('You mean them Ghosts, Miss!'),[43] and who should be omitted from the cast of future productions if Eliot's advice is followed.[44]

The appropriateness of the many echoes of Hamlet in the play cannot be disputed; for an English dramatist, especially a verse dramatist, it would be hard if not impossible to avoid the influence of the most impressive of all Orestes figures in our language. But Eliot's use of Hamlet in the making of his hero is curiously equivocal, and gives the impression of being partly involuntary. It is as though Shakespeare, consciously rejected by Eliot as a model for poetic drama because his achievement was too great to be capable of successful absorption, has entered by the back door and asserted himself in a manner that confirms our sense of a divided intention in the author. The likeness to Hamlet is indirect but powerful confirmation of the presence of Oedipal feelings in Harry; it suggests that we are right to see his fear of being possessed and dominated by his mother as in part projection of his own frustrated Oedipal wish to possess and dominate her. I have suggested that material about the child's fear of the predatory mother is both very important in *The Family Reunion* and not brought into a proper relationship with the central religious theme of the play; it seems to be significant that Eliot's famous comment on Hamlet could be applied with so much more appropriateness to his own play: [45]

> Hamlet . . . is full of some stuff that the writer
> could not drag to the light, contemplate, or
> manipulate into art.

Eliot quotes with approval J. M. Robertson's view that the essential emotion of the play is the feeling of a son towards a guilty mother, and that 'the guilt of a mother is an almost intolerable motive for drama';[46] he goes on to ask why Shakespeare 'tackled a problem that proved too much for him . . . under compulsion of what experience he attempted to express the inexpressibly horrible, we cannot know'.[47] It is a reasonable inference that Eliot's dislike of *Hamlet* – 'the play is most certainly an artistic failure' – springs from a recognition, unacknowledged in this essay except in the odd revealing aside,[48] that it deals centrally with psychological material which was to continue to press disturbingly on his own consciousness and so prove something very difficult to 'manipulate into art'. Gertrude is, of course, guilty in a much more specifically criminal sense than Amy in *The Family Reunion*; she has betrayed her son as well as her husband and is forced to acknowledge the black and grained spots in her own soul. In contrast, Amy believes herself always to have acted out of love for Harry; the most she comes to see, at the end, is that she is punished because she 'always wanted too much for my children'.[49] But Hamlet, though he is tempted, like Orestes, to matricide, as a punishment for his mother's treachery and, at a less conscious level, perhaps, as a solution to his Oedipal conflict, speaks daggers but uses none; Harry, with far less apparent reason, effectively kills his mother by abandoning her at her moment of greatest need. The equivocation that plays round the relationship of mother and son in *The Family Reunion* is evidence that Eliot could not yet deal directly with the material from Orestes and Hamlet within the context of his chosen theme of the interaction of the seen and the unseen worlds. It is not that the expression of this material lacks force and reality; the facts and emotions associated with it – man's neurotic fear of woman, woman's frightening tenacity, the bitterness of family tensions – are much more adequately expressed than the more rarefied religious emotions at the heart of the play. In the same way, the mother, Amy, is better realized as a character, and partly for this reason a much more sympathetic figure, as Eliot came to see, than the son. The Orestes and Hamlet material thus exists independently of, and at the expense of, the play's central theme. In the central episode – the moment of illumination that comes to Harry through Agatha – Orestes and Hamlet, as I have suggested, are dismissed from the scene with indecent haste, only to prove unkillable, as Harry had believed his wife to be. The divided intention remains to the very end. By a curious paradox, it endows the play with abundant life, though at the expense of consistency and control, and means that *The Family Reunion* is at once the least successful and in many ways the most interesting of all Eliot's full-length plays.

Notes

1 Shelley, *Prometheus Unbound*, ll. 195–9.
2 T. S. Eliot, *Poetry and Drama* (London, 1951), p. 23.
3 Ibid., p. 26.
4 Ibid., p. 27.
5 Ibid., p. 32.
6 Ibid., pp. 27–8.
7 Ibid., p. 31.
8 Ibid., p. 30.
9 T. S. Eliot, *The Family Reunion* (London, 1939), p. 77.
10 Ibid., p. 74.
11 Ibid., p. 106.
12 Ibid., p. 30.
13 T. S. Eliot, *The Cocktail Party* (London, 1950), p. 89.
14 Ibid., p. 99.
15 *The Family Reunion*, p. 117.
16 Ibid., p. 41.
17 Ibid., p. 117.

18 *The Cocktail Party*, p. 99.
19 *The Family Reunion*, p. 35.
20 T. S. Eliot, *Collected Poems 1909–1925* (London, 1936), p. 130.
21 *The Family Reunion*, p.121.
22 Ibid., p. 104.
23 Ibid., p. 108.
24 Ibid.
25 Ibid., pp. 120–1.
26 Ibid., p. 123.
27 Harry's own word, ibid., p. 115.
28 Ibid., p. 120.
29 T. S. Eliot, 'Ulysses, Order and Myth', *Dial*, LXXV, November 1923, p. 483.
30 See above, p. 188.
31 Eliot, *Collected Poems*, p. 126.
32 *Poetry and Drama*, p. 31.
33 Ibid.
34 *The Family Reunion*, p. 116.
35 Ibid., p. 118.
36 Ibid., p. 28.
37 Ibid., p. 87.
38 Ibid., p. 93.
39 Ibid., p. 76.
40 Ibid., p. 63.
41 Ibid., p. 70.
42 Ibid., p. 109.
43 Ibid., p. 130.
44 *Poetry and Drama*, p. 30.
45 T. S. Eliot, *Selected Essays* (London, 1922), p. 144.
46 Ibid., p. 144.
47 Ibid., p. 146.
48 'The play is puzzling, and disquieting, as is none of the others', ibid., p. 143.
49 *The Family Reunion*, p. 126.

Nine

Orestes in Modern Drama: *The Flies*

If *The Family Reunion* takes its point of origin from Aeschylus, and *Mourning Becomes Electra* looks both to Aeschylus and, in its realism, to Euripides, Sartre's *The Flies* (*Les Mouches*) is Sophoclean in its unequivocal endorsement of the hero who triumphs against overwhelming odds and who will have nothing to do with guilt:[1]

> Aegisthus   [after Orestes has struck him down] Is it true you feel no remorse?
>
> Orestes   Remorse? Why should I feel remorse? I am only doing what is right.

Electra is disturbed by the murder of their mother that follows; but Orestes reassures her:[2]

> Electra   Can you prevent us being the murderers of our mother . . . for all time?
>
> Orestes   Do you think I'd wish to prevent it? I have done *my* deed, Electra, and that deed was good.

Here, however, the resemblance ends. In Sophocles, a Homeric hero successfully reclaims his patrimony; the spirit of the play is conservative, and the author adopts an attitude of enigmatic detachment to the questions that for other writers on this theme insistently demand an answer. Insight and sympathy, in Sophocles, is concentrated on Electra, whose tragedy forms the centrepiece of what would otherwise be a superb melodrama. In contrast, Sartre presents the matricide as a revolutionary act, by virtue of which Orestes defies the tyranny of both God and man and wins his spiritual freedom. Zeus, brought in person on the stage as the 'God of flies and death',[3] is defeated by Orestes, for traditional religion is simply a device for enslaving those who lack the courage to assert their lonely existential freedom. Aegisthus appeals to Zeus to fell Orestes with a thunderbolt, but Zeus admits his own powerlessness:[4]

> the gods have another secret. . . . Once freedom lights its beacon in a man's heart, the gods are powerless against him.

Orestes' assertion of freedom is an atheist's religious faith. The act of matricide is presented as, in a sense, motiveless, and the gift of freedom that it brings is equally mysterious; the burden of the act itself, Orestes tells Electra, is his freedom.[5] It is his passport to self-discovery:[6]

> We will go . . . towards ourselves. Beyond the rivers and mountains are an Orestes and Electra waiting for us. . . .

The rhetorical gesture is very effective, but is it anything more than rhetoric? From the point of view of this study, the interest of *The Flies* lies in its occasional exploitation of Freudian psychoanalysis followed by a rejection of it more decisive, perhaps, than can be found in any other treatment of the story. It is part of a general exploitation, hostile or parodistic, of the ideas of the past, preparatory to the presentation of what seems to be claimed as a new religion of the present; religion, psychoanalysis and the myth itself are all, in effect, parodied. Mordant, witty, and coldly depersonalized, the play is a marginal commentary on the myth which totally transforms its nature. Orestes as a successful tyrannicide may be thought to be a natural development from the Greek, topical of course in the France of 1945, but even this has little to do with the original Orestes; he is barely a political figure. That Sartre has chosen to preserve the Greek names and events is a typically bold paradox that underscores the arrogant originality of his approach; the past must be rejected, and thus the central idea of this philosophical melodrama is reflected inversely in its form.

The question of guilt, which is at the centre of Sartre's ironical treatment of psychology, is first raised in the first scene of Act Two, the rites of the dead. In a mock-imposing tableau of mass auto-hypnosis the spirits of the dead are invoked in order to wreak their hatred on the living; at their head is Agamemnon, but the whole population is included by virtue of the harm that every living being has done to his or her dead: the wife who betrayed her husband, the child who treated a parent cruelly, the money-lender who drove debtors to despair. The dead are the 'dear departed [who] have laid waste our lives',[7] whose resentment is unappeasable if for no other reason than because they are dead and the living are living. A child tells his mother he is frightened, and she replies:[8]

> And so you should be, darling. . . . That's how one grows
> up into a decent, god-fearing man.

The fear is partly pleasurable, a masochistic submission to the lustful embraces of the dead; the rite itself is simply the annual culmination of the process of exploiting their hidden fears and desires by which Zeus and his henchman Aegisthus keep the people in servitude. The conformity that Zeus depends on for his power and indeed for his very existence is an example of bad faith, in existential terms; the evasion of personal responsibility by a slavish reliance on some external authority. Orestes is free as soon as he refuses to play this game. This external authority, which draws its strength from human cowardice, may take the form of a traditional morality, which teaches us it is right to obey our elders and rulers, or, apparently, Freudian psychology, which teaches us that our lives are determined by the power of the past and the dead. In this way Sartre constructs his tableau of the rite of the dead out of Freudian insights, but only to discredit them; once his hero has seen the light, the psychological 'fact' becomes simply part of what Orestes must reject in order to become a hero. This is made very clear in the duologue between Orestes and Electra that closes the same scene, after the miracle of Orestes' self-discovery. Orestes tells his sister that, in the name of 'guilt-stealer', he will take over the crimes of 'all those people quaking with fear in their dark rooms'.[9]

Electra	So you wish to atone for us?
Orestes	To atone? No, I said I'd house your penitence, but I did not say what I'd do with all those cackling fowls; maybe I'll wring their necks.
Electra	And how can you take over our sense of guilt?
Orestes	Why, all of you ask nothing better than to be rid of it.[10]

Orestes, it will be recalled, is to feel no remorse over the matricide, for 'the most cowardly of murderers is he who feels remorse'.[11] To 'wring the neck' of guilt and penitence is precisely how Orestes sees his own actions as a hero; in the last act he defies his mother's Furies, the Flies, and once again proclaims that, like the Pied Piper, he will free his people of the plague of guilt and crime by acting, alone, as scapegoat:[12]

> As for your sins and your remorse . . . and the crime
> Aegisthus committed – all are mine, I take them upon
> me. Fear your Dead no longer; they are my Dead.

It is now the turn of religious insights to be handled in the same spirit of derogatory parody as, earlier, religious ritual and psychological insights; as Electra notes, Orestes sounds as though, like Harry in *The Family Reunion*, he is undertaking in his own person the burden of his people in the spirit of the Christian saint. But it is clear that he is only shouldering this burden – 'a load of guilt so heavy as to drag me down . . . into the abyss' – in order that, as a free man, he may deny its reality; the 'precious load' that he is to carry with him into the future is the load of his own lonely destiny. Guilt is not something to be endured for the sake of others, but rejected as contemptible, the morbid self-indulgence of the slaves of bad faith. We may surmise that in order to end this play with the requisite flourish Sartre imposes on his hero a scapegoat role at variance with his lonely existential destiny, but unavoidable, perhaps, if he was to use the name of Orestes; for an Orestes to withdraw altogether from society would be impossible. It also seems to symbolize a contradiction at the heart of Sartre's attitude as expounded in the play. Among the many agile balancing feats performed in our time by left-wing intellectuals, Sartre's fusion of existentialism with Marxism is a noteworthy example; the first an anti-historical and anti-social doctrine, that sees man as in essence a solitary being, his true destiny the aloneness of the outsider; the second the most comprehensive of all attempts to see man collectively, as a social and historical phenomenon. This contradiction, or paradox, is reflected in the role of Orestes in *The Flies*. In his final dialogue with Zeus, in which he stands firm against the threats of established authority, he glories in his aloneness: it is the direct consequence of the matricidal act that established his 'freedom':[13]

> I *am* my freedom. . . . Suddenly, out of the blue, freedom
> crashed down on me . . . my youth went with the wind,
> and I knew myself alone, utterly alone in the midst of this
> well-meaning little universe of yours.

At the same time Orestes is given a central social role to
play as scapegoat and saviour of his people; in his final speech,
when he defies the crowd who are calling for his blood, he
claims their loyalty and undertakes their burdens:[14]

> Men of Argos, you understand that my crime is wholly
> mine. . . . And yet, my people, I love you, and it was for
> your sake that I killed. Now . . . there is a bond of blood
> between us, and I have earned my kingship over you.

An uneasy awareness of the contradiction is barely concealed
in the flamboyant rhetoric of this last speech. His crime was
entirely for the sake of the people; he proclaims the day as his
coronation day as rightful king of Argos, yet he refuses to sit
on the throne and prefers an obscure exile:[15]

> I wish to be king without a kingdom, without subjects.

Those subjects might well ask how he is to take on their burden,
let alone govern them, *in absentia*; his parting advice seems a
feeble evasion:[16]

> Farewell, my people. Try to reshape your lives. All here
> is new, all must begin anew.

Sartre's intellectual absolutism has denied all virtue to authority,
and leaves him with an insoluble dilemma: how do we distinguish
the just from the unjust ruler, the free man from the slave of
bad faith? In the same way, Sartre attempts here a rejection of all
traditional values while simultaneously exploiting the audience's
sense of their continuing reality – the nobleness of tyrannicide,
the cowardice and morbid fear associated with the life-hating
rituals of the old, unregenerate Argos. His purpose seems to be
partly dramatic, to retain some sympathy for his Orestes, and
partly ideological, to avoid the moral nihilism which, as Dostoevsky had pointed out long before, is the only logical consequence
of the belief that every man must be the creator of his own values.
Whatever the purpose, the effect is to open up a yawning intel-

lectual chasm in the fabric of the play's thought. Sartre cannot explain, except on the basis of values he himself must reject, what makes the act of matricide a free and good act for his Orestes; why it releases him from bondage, instead of thrusting him into the prison whose nature and extent has been delineated by Aeschylus, Euripides and O'Neill. It remains on the level of pure assertion, flavoured with a strong whiff of omnipotent fantasy. Similarly, one does not need to be a committed Freudian to feel uneasy over the mere assertion of Orestes' claim to dismiss the past and the dead. It is as though the commitment to action is held to be enough in itself to dispose of the whole of the psychological implications of the central act of matricide. *The Flies* is perhaps most effective as a political melodrama, a mordant tract for the times tricked out with mythical and philosophical overtones. As a version of the Orestes story it has the merit of originality, but the substitution of theatrical and intellectual sleight of hand for psychological and dramatic insight does not provide a very nourishing diet. The play's rhetoric, though stimulating, has a hollowness at its centre, as does indeed its central character, who is, intentionally, a walking abstraction. Both are enlivened by Sartre's gifts for tense rhetorical confrontation, and the mordant wit which seasons all his theatrical work.

Notes

1 J. P. Sartre, *The Flies*, trans. S. Gilbert (London, 1964), p. 75.
2 Ibid., p. 79.
3 Ibid., p. 7.
4 Ibid., p. 74.
5 Ibid., p. 79.
6 Ibid., p. 99.
7 Ibid., p. 44.
8 Ibid., p. 37.
9 Ibid., p. 60.
10 Ibid., p. 61.
11 Ibid., p. 93.
12 Ibid., p. 102.
13 Ibid., pp. 95–6.
14 Ibid., p. 102.
15 Ibid.
16 Ibid.

Ten

Electra in Later Drama: Shakespeare and Ibsen

In discussing Sophocles' Electra, I suggested that her strong identification with the father stops short of that destructive envy that, in children of either sex, characterizes the Oedipal relationship in its negative aspect. Her hatred is reserved for Clytemnestra, the parent of the same sex, whose actions provide ample support for her positive Oedipal wishes and needs; this leaves her free to adopt, in relation to lost father and brother, the maternal role that the real mother has abjured. The successful rivalry with the hatred and denigrated mother makes possible an idealization of her own maternal role which preserves her femininity intact. In contrast to this simple but effective portrayal of the Oedipal daughter, later dramatists have explored the conflicting emotions that are inherent in the father/daughter relationship, often at the unconscious level, analogous as these are to the Oresteian tensions in the relationship of mother and son that I discussed in chapter three. I wish to examine in particular Shakespeare's representation of Lady Macbeth and Ibsen's portrayal of Hedda Gabler; Strindberg's Miss Julie, already discussed in Part I, is also relevant here. The common theme is a denial of femininity that seems to be directly associated with an Oedipal relationship with the father. An aggressive masculinization suggests, in all instances, the presence of envy as well as love of the father. Hostility towards him may be expressed consciously, or it may manifest itself in a displaced form in attacks on other men. Thus there is no actual murder of the parent, as with Orestes; either the murderous attacks are made obliquely and in fantasy, as in *Hedda Gabler* and *Miss Julie*, or a substitute parent, not the real father, is chosen as victim, as in *Macbeth*. There may be conscious feelings of guilt over the whole relationship with the father, as with Miss Julie, or Rebecca West in *Rosmersholm*: or a repressed guilt may force itself uncontrollably to the surface in sympto- matic acts, as with Hedda Gabler and Lady Macbeth. Retribu- tion takes the form of a sterility that blights human relationships and projects alike; it may be experienced as appropriate punish- ment for the necessary barrenness of a sexual relationship with the father, or there may be an identification with a father destroyed or damaged through envy. There are interesting parallels not only to the Oedipal conflicts of mother and son, but to the par- ricidal son motivated by direct Oedipal rivalry of the father – Brutus, Hamlet, Macbeth himself. In *Macbeth* we find, uniquely, an example of a shared, simultaneous conspiracy by a parricidal son and daughter, the guilty couple so acting that 'together they exhaust the possibilities of reaction to the crime'.[1] It is to this instance that I turn first.

In *Collected Papers*, volume 4, Freud writes:[2]

> It would be a perfect example of poetic justice . . . if the childishness of Macbeth and the barrenness of his Lady were the punishment for their crimes against the sanctity of *geniture* – if Macbeth could not become a father because he had robbed children of their father and a father of his children, and if Lady Macbeth had suffered the unsexing she had demanded of the spirits of murder.

There is a wealth of suggestion in this passage, as in most of Freud's rare comments on Shakespeare; for my present purpose, I want to concentrate on the implications of Lady Macbeth's 'unsexing', seen in the context of her crime against geniture, which in her case, unlike that of her husband, has a single aspect only – that of the child's parricidal attack on the father. Two points should be mentioned by way of preliminary. In two earlier tragedies of Shakespeare, *Julius Caesar* and *Hamlet*, the theme is found of the parricidal wishes of the child, but the treatment is different from that in *Macbeth* in two important respects relevant to my subject. Brutus kills a man who is his putative father and who anyhow treats him as a son; on any interpretation of the play, Hamlet's relationship to his father and his father's brother is of central importance. But Macbeth is merely cousin to his victim, Duncan, and neither he nor his wife are shown as in any sort of intimate relation to him. The

second difference is the awareness, in *Macbeth*, of the wholly
forbidden nature of the act. Whereas Hamlet is shown as devoted
to his father's memory at a conscious level, and Brutus justifies
the killing of Caesar on public and impersonal grounds, the
criminality of the act in *Macbeth*, aggravated as it is by numerous
circumstances, is fully recognized and acknowledged. Guilt about
the crime is immediately experienced at a level so primitively
deep that in fantasy Macbeth sees his guilty hands as tearing
out his own eyes; a comparable guilt is later to unhinge his
wife's mind. Though outwardly successful, they are left in a
world emptied of meaning. Macbeth's later actions of ever-
increasing savagery are partly explicable in terms of his sense
of his own utter damnation, for the original act is felt to be
so wicked as to rule out the possibility of reparation; with Lady
Macbeth we experience an accumulating sense of her withdrawal
and despair, leading to suicide. Motive, in *Macbeth*, has always
puzzled commentators, in both Macbeth himself and his wife;
there is so much to be said against the murder of Duncan, and the
act inspires so much horror and resistance in its perpetrators. To
see Macbeth and his wife as, in essence, parricidal children,
may throw some light on the matter; and there is here, I think,
a significant connection between the relatively distant relationship to Duncan, and the conscious criminality of the murder.
Envious parricidal wishes are displaced from the father to a
substitute father; for this very reason they are free to exercise a
more compulsive grasp on their victims, so compulsive, indeed,
as to drive them, against all reason, into a totally forbidden
act. Duncan as king stands in the relation of father to his subjects,
especially perhaps to those whom he has honoured for services
rendered; Ernest Jones, in *Hamlet and Oedipus*, writes:[3]

> Psychoanalytical work has shown that a ruler, king,
> president etc. is in the unconscious mind a typical father
> symbol, and in actual life tends to draw on to himself
> the ambivalent attitudes characteristic of the son's feeling
> towards the father.

Jones is referring here to Julius Caesar, a more immediately
obvious example of the ruler as father than Duncan; in *Macbeth*,
the father-figure himself, and his living relationship with the
children, play a much smaller part. However, the relationship is

essentially of the same kind; the point, in *Macbeth*, is a highly significant shift of emphasis away from the relationship to the father to the parricidal wishes of the children, on which all the concentration falls.

Duncan's murder is seen to hold in prospect a terrible independent fascination for Macbeth, as though he is in the power of some more powerful unknown self. However, it is the vehement promptings of his wife that, notoriously, bring him to the sticking place of action, and if all she does is done to get him the throne it is also true that he is in some sense her tool. Thus it is that we see more clearly articulated in her the operation of that parricidal envy of the father that also instigates him; the inner meaning of his act is only made clear later, in his reactions to what he has done. In her speeches in the two crucial scenes (Act I scene 5, Act II scene 2) this envy is manifested at a pressure so intense as to drive her to attempt a total denial of her own femininity in order to acquire the coveted phallic power. Significantly, in this woman who has been a mother and yet is mysteriously childless, the denial takes the form of a ferocious attack on the child. Like her husband, she has experience of the power of good impulses of dependence and love:[4]

> I . . . know
> How tender 'tis to love the babe that milks me;

but she can see herself as deliberately strangling that maternal protectiveness within her:[5]

> I would while it was smiling in my face
> Have plucked my nipple from his boneless gums
> And dashed the brains out. . . .

so destroying the naked new-born babe whom her husband has just visualized as Pity itself. She has previously invoked the spirit of murder to substitute the bitterness of gall for milk in her breasts; it is as though she is so dominated by the child's consuming envy of the parent that, as mother, she can only offer poison to the children who depend on her for maternal food and love. The sterility of the crime, as Freud pointed out, is ironical confirmation that her prayer to the spirits of murder has indeed been heard. She has unsexed herself, and consequently all her works are barren; in analytical terms, she has substituted the barren destructiveness of envy for the loving dependence, of child on father or subject on king, which is the foundation of good relationships. The child's way of looking is significantly dismissed in her words after the murder, when she refers contemptuously to her husband's horror at the sight of what he has done:[6]

> 'Tis the eye of childhood
> That fears a painted devil.

With a superb insight Shakespeare shows her coming closest to the buried source of her impulses at the moment of greatest tension, when she is waiting for Macbeth to return from the king's bedchamber:[7]

> Had he not resembled
> My father as he slept, I had done't.

The recognition here takes the familiar form of a screen that serves to mask the deeper motives while simultaneously revealing them. We see here why for all her ruthless violence of will she cannot act herself but must act through her husband. That she sees herself as performing, not simply instigating, the murder is confirmed by the use of the personal pronoun in[8]

> That my keen knife see not the wound it makes . . .

but the resemblance to the father is an unconsciously inhibiting force, as is also, perhaps, that residual femininity that later is to exact its revenge, in her guilt-laden reaction to the crime and final collapse. She is ruled by powers that she does not understand, and her strength has a hollow, illusory quality about it. Macbeth, whom she has employed as a tool in her phallic fantasies, becomes a Frankenstein's monster in her hands, 'a tool run wild' in Schneider's telling phrase;[9] she has released in him a destructive, sado-masochistic power that she cannot influence or control. In herself she suffers the savage recoil of reality as her injured femininity reasserts itself through guilt:[10]

> Fie, my lord, fie! A soldier and afeard? – What need we
> fear who knows it, when none can call our power to
> accompt? – Yet who would have thought the old man
> had so much blood in him?

It is as though she has believed that by contriving the death of the old king who resembled her father she had acquired so much power that no one could call her to account; but there was more blood than her omnipotent fantasies had reckoned with, and she drowns in it. Her blood-haunted somnambulism recalls of course Macbeth's agonized vision after the murder, of hands that great Neptune's ocean cannot wash clean of blood, and her own literal-minded dismissal of the stain that she cannot get rid of now with endless washing of her hands:[11]

> A little water clears us of this deed.

The 'rooted sorrow' of her madness, like the self-inflicted death that follows, is an enacted acknowledgment of guilt, an over-whelming protest by the femininity she has tried, but failed, to destroy. The failure is not only exactly appropriate to the original wish, but gives her a tragic status. Feminine tenderness and sensitivity are a reality to her and will not be denied; it is what we had suspected from her first ferocious invocation to the spirits of murder, for if she had never known such tenderness, there would be no need for the hysterical rejection of that speech, the unsexing, the stopping up of the access to remorse, the trans-formation of her milk to gall. The impression is quickly confirmed in the temptation scene, where protective and destructive impulses are polarized, the tender love of the babe and the dashing out of its brains. By her death she is identified, like Brutus, with the father whom she had destroyed; it is, perhaps, the only reparation open to her, and, as with Macbeth's awareness of all that he has lost through his actions, serves to keep her within the range of our sympathies, as a tragic, not a Satanic or merely patho-logical figure. *Macbeth* is indeed one of the supreme expressions in dramatic poetry of the tragedy wrought by parricidal envy.

Hedda Gabler, as Ibsen makes clear by his title, is above all her father's daughter; his portrait looks down on us in the drawing-room of the new villa bought for her by the husband she holds in such contempt. It is in this room that the whole action of the play takes place. General Gabler, unlike Hamlet's father's ghost, plays no part in *Hedda Gabler*, and is indeed only referred to twice; but he dominates the action and the fate of his unhappy daughter. In a mood seemingly of cold ironical detachment, Ibsen here carries further his rigorous analysis of the pathology of emancipation that stretches back through *Rosmersholm* and Gregers Werle in *The Wild Duck* to *Ghosts*. The immense force of the analysis, at its formidable best in *Hedda Gabler*, derives as perhaps it must from the banked fires that burn concealed, revealing themselves only in the sheer concentration and tension of what is offered to us, the hint of a pity and terror underlying the ironical bleakness of the treatment. In a lesser dramatist, *Hedda Gabler* would emerge as black comedy, with all the limitations of human feeling implied in that phrase; Ibsen gives us something richer and more ambiguous. There is in an obvious sense an element of self-criticism in Ibsen's ruthless analysis of the pitfalls of emancipation; but at a deeper level he is personally implicated in the fate of his hero-victim, offering us a kind of symbolic self-portraiture of his own inner fears, aspirations and guilt. No creative writer ever put the act of self-judgment to more effective use than Ibsen; it is in many ways the central preoccupation of the plays, and it is of course one of the signs of his greatness that he can so universalize a personal predicament – the sacrifices demanded of self and others in the free choice of a vocation – that he becomes the representative dramatist of a whole age. In the last plays, from *The Master Builder* onwards, the presence of a radical self-judgment is unmistakable; here, in Miss Bradbrook's striking phrase, he has returned home to Norway to face 'the accusing ghosts'.[12] *Hedda Gabler* is the last of the plays written abroad before his return; self-judgment here masks itself as judgment of the other, the cold dissection of a pathological heroine, but its felt presence gives a deeper dimension to the play. It could be said that Ibsen could not have penetrated so deeply into the life-denial of Hedda had he not feared it, and experienced it, in himself. The obsessive theme of child-sacrifice in Ibsen seems to be related to his increasing fears that he had sacrificed a uniquely valuable part of himself to the exacting demands of a successful literary vocation. Brand's child, Oswald in *Ghosts*, Hedvig, Aline's and Solness's dead children in *The Master Builder*, little Eyolf, Hedda's unborn child denied life by her mother's suicide: all these child-murders and child sacrifices offer eloquent testimony to the strength of Ibsen's feeling on the subject, his unappeasable fears that vocation had been bought at the price of the child's capacity for happiness and love. The plays suggest that Ibsen's intuitive identification with his destructive heroes and heroines enables him to extend his understanding of them into areas which, though more remote from, and indeed unconnected with, his external experience, none the less reflect a major psychic preoccupation of his inner life. The son of an unsuccessful man who in external terms denied his own inheritance by cutting himself off from his family, he was well placed to examine the whole question of the inherited burden children receive from their parents. For Hedda it is the burden of a Oedipal relationship with her dead father that imprisons her within its shadows and denies her the possibility of a meaningful life without him; this, I would suggest, is the inner meaning Ibsen conveys to us both in the general pattern of the play and in the majority of its detailed effects.

Hedda Gabler has grown up with great expectations, as Ibsen characterizes her in his preliminary notes for the play: 'The pale, apparently cold beauty. Great demands on life and happiness.'[13] Her father's death has left her poor, without the means to maintain herself in that aristocratic station of life to which she had become accustomed (Ibsen's multi-level craftsmanship invariably roots his psychological studies in social reality). Her only inheritance from him is the pistols, and a temperament marked indelibly by the nature of the relationship between them. We hear nothing of the mother. It becomes clear that Hedda has taken in her father's habits and attitudes though now wholly divorced from the values that, for him, gave them life. Thus the military man's respect for conventions becomes, in her own words, cowardice; his correctness, a horror of scandal; his authoritarianism, a kind of neurotic sadism. She insists vehemently on the importance of correctness while making clear that she does not believe in it. To Lövborg, her former admirer, she admits her contempt for her husband, but insists that[14]

> There isn't going to be any kind of disloyalty, anyhow. I won't have that sort of thing.

When earlier, before her marriage, Lövborg had taken their intimacy to its natural conclusion and attempted to make love to her, she had threatened him with her father's pistol. Her reaction is recalled in a scene between them in Act Two; Lövborg is in a mood of theatrical self-pity induced by her absurd marriage:[15]

> *Lövborg*   Why didn't you shoot me down when you
>   threatened me!
> *Hedda*   Yes . . . I'm as terrified of scandal as all that.
> *Lövborg*   Yes, Hedda, you are a coward at bottom.
> *Hedda*   An awful coward.

The same 'cowardice' plays an important part in her final act of suicide. Brack, another admirer, who wishes to ensure he has no rivals, other than the complaisant Tesman, blackmails her with the scandal of a revelation of her part in Lövborg's sordid death; she had given him the pistol. He warns her that, unless he keeps silent,[16]

> What happens then is a scandal. . . . The thing you
> have such a deadly fear of.

Rather than submit to being in his power, she kills herself. Her unquestioning enactment of her father's values without any continuing respect for them seems crucial; like her frantic boredom and the marked sexual coldness that gives her a horror of every sort of creativity, it is a classical statement of the fruits of the daughter's Oedipal relationship to the father. 'Cowardice' is an unthinking instinct in her that, supported by the sexual coldness of which it seems in part a rationalization, has prevented her from plucking the fruits of emancipation. Significantly, she has in the past enjoyed vicarious sexual experience, as a young girl eagerly questioning the older Lövborg about his sexual adventures while they sit side by side on the sofa 'always with the same illustrated paper in front of us'. The picture emerges of two children engaged in secret sexual games under the parental eye:[17]

> . . . The General used to sit right over by the window
> reading the papers, with his back to us. . . .

Simultaneously Hedda appears as voyeuristic child prying into male sexuality, in this 'hidden intimacy' marked by an 'absolute frankness' on Lövborg's side; her object not, as he naïvely believes, to cleanse his soul by receiving his confession, but to indulge her fantasies of sexual knowledge and therefore power. When a real sexual relationship, based on mutual response, becomes a possibility, she threatens to shoot him, for to be meaningful for her such a relationship must involve a sadistic control of the man. Here, again, we see the father's shadow; the General's authoritarianism, like his conformity, are traditional and socially acceptable ways for men of power and influence to compel submission in others. In Ibsen's world – still the world, socially, of *The Doll's House* – such impulses, acceptable in a man, are likely in a woman to take a neurotic form. The only sphere in which Hedda could dictate conformity to others is the domestic sphere, from which she is barred by the selfsame Oedipal complex that only allows her a power relationship with the men in her life. It is, incidentally, no accident that all the three male admirers Ibsen surrounds her with are poor creatures, tame cocks in the hen roost; none can be allowed to rival the beloved father. At his death she felt herself to be Electra abandoned, 'on the way towards becoming an old maid'.[18] Explaining to Brack why she married the 'undistinguished . . . but honourable' Jorgan Tesman, she remarks, 'I had simply danced myself out. . . . My time was up.'[19] Pressed further, she makes it clear that she has married him as an unloved father. Such a man at once repeats the relationship to the father and avoids any sort of comparison with it:[20]

> And since he insisted . . . on being allowed to support me, I don't know why I shouldn't have accepted the offer.

To Brack's solicitous 'You're not really happy' she replies with a kind of bitter blankness, 'looking straight in front of her'[21]

> And can you tell me why I should be happy?

It is her tragedy that, since her father's death, everything seems empty and sterile; as Ibsen puts it in his preliminary notes for the play, 'It is the want of a goal in life that torments her.'[22] Surrounded, as it seems to her, by the stifling admiration and affection of dull, worthy, people, she is frantic with boredom:[23]

> *Hedda* It often seems to me that I've only got a gift for one thing in the world.
> *Brack* And what is that, if I may ask?
> *Hedda* For boring myself to death.

Her only relief from boredom lies in envious sadistic attacks on others, which are finally turned upon herself; to manipulate others in the service of her fantasies is to gratify that frustrated urge to power that can find no other satisfying outlet. Ibsen offers us a masterly analysis of this pathological urge, accurate, powerful, and totally subdued to the expressive needs of the dramatic situation; there is no 'explanation' outside the drama, no authorial nudges or hints to the audience. Sadistic attacks, of varying degrees of seriousness, characterize Hedda's relationship with all the other characters, but most importantly with Thea and Lövborg. First, however, a small episode that effortlessly carries a great deal of weight of meaning must be noted; no one who sees or reads the play is likely to forget it. Tesman's Aunt Julle has called early on the happy pair to welcome them back from their honeymoon. Hedda, who has been showing signs of impatience and irritation at the cosy domestic rapport between aunt and nephew, complains to Tesman that Berte, the family maid, has left her old hat behind her on the sitting-room chair; the hat is Aunt Julle's new hat, bought for the occasion, and Hedda's mistake, as it seems at the time, leads to an embarrassing scene.[24] Later in the play she explains to Brack that she had only pretended to think it was the servant's; when he remonstrates with her, she replies:[25]

> Well, you know that kind of thing comes over me – just like that. And then I can't stop myself. I don't know, myself, how to explain it.

Hedda is right. This trivial act has the force of compulsion about it, and so illuminates other, more important actions which are less obviously the result of 'nerves'. There is an element of panic in Hedda,[26] a blind destructiveness running out of control and only partially in touch with reality; she cannot assess the consequences of what she does, to Lövborg especially. To see this is to see her to a certain extent as a pathological study driven by neurotic compulsion; at the risk of diminishing her stature, it brings her within the orbit of our sympathy, pitiful as well as terrible.

In her relationship with Thea, Hedda's envy is stimulated by jealousy. This timid, shrinking woman, whom Hedda had terrorized at school, has succeeded where Hedda herself was precluded by her neurotic needs from even making the attempt.

She has reclaimed Lövborg from dissipation and by her faith in what is still untainted in him has inspired him to write a masterpiece. Moreover, with a kind of desperate courage, equally beyond Hedda's capacity, she has left her husband and her home to mother him and guard him against any relapse. Her insecurity is grounded on a particular fear:[27]

> There's the shadow of a woman standing between
> Eilert Lövborg and me. . . . Someone from his past.
> Someone he's never really forgotten.

This admission gives Hedda her opportunity. She regains her old power over Lövborg by the simple device of getting Thea's confidence and then betraying it to him. The scene with Thea is a kind of seduction, the word Ibsen himself uses to describe it in his preliminary notes; the sexual element is unmistakable, and entirely appropriate to the Oedipal daughter who is thus sadistically attracted to the feminine sexuality she must deny in herself. At their first meeting Thea reminds Hedda of their schoolgirl relationship:[28]

> . . . Dreadfully frightened of you. Because when we met
> on the stairs you always used to pull my hair . . . and once
> you said you would cut it off.

Act Two ends with Hedda's triumphant recapture of Lövborg, symbolized by his departure for a drinking party in defiance of Thea's distress. The triumph allows a momentary impulse of frankness and generosity towards Thea whose true nature is immediately revealed:[29]

> Ah, if you could only realize how poor I am. And here
> are you, offered such riches! (Throwing her arms
> passionately round her.) I think I shall burn your hair
> off, after all.

Her last gesture to Thea, in the finale, is to 'let her hands stray gently through Mrs Elvsted's hair', as Thea and Tesman, ignoring her, settle down to work on the notes of Lövborg's lost masterpiece. There is a hint of a need for love in this last human contact before her suicide; it reminds us that Ibsen never loses touch with what is pitiable in Hedda. There is pity as well as, more obviously, irony in Hedda's final defeat at the hands of the frail,

clinging, Thea; she affects to despise the maternal devotion that
has allowed Thea to reclaim Lövborg, but she is bitterly envious
of the priceless 'gift' that has been denied to her. In her words to
Brack,[30]

> I have no gift for . . . things that make claims on me.

Brack is here referring, indiscreetly, to the probability of a
new meaning coming into her life through the birth of a child.
There are clear hints throughout the play that Hedda is pregnant
by the husband she despises; the impatient frenzy with which
she greets well-meaning references to her condition is a simple
but effective testimony to her compulsive sterility, a horror that
extends to the whole process of generation, the 'creative mess'.
When Tesman pleads with her to visit his dying Aunt Rina, she
replies, 'dismissing the matter wearily',[31]

> Don't ask me to do things like that. I don't want to
> think of illness or death.

The crude fact of pregnancy, so distasteful to Hedda, is merged
by Ibsen with characteristic subtlety with the great theme of
child sacrifice and child murder. We see this illustrated with
incomparable power in the final development of her relationship
with Lövborg. The tension of the hated pregnancy underlies
Hedda's behaviour throughout the play, and lends a plausible
colour to neurotically destructive actions which she cannot
herself explain; the most dramatic and unbalanced of these
actions, the burning of the manuscript of Lövborg's masterpiece,
is correctly seen by her as the destruction of a child:[32]

> Now I am burning your child, Thea. You, with your
> curly hair. Your child and Eilert Lövborg's. I'm burning
> it – burning your child.

It is a moment of pathological triumph comparable to Lady
Macbeth's success in driving her husband to the murder of
Duncan; the flash of insight into her own motives that accompanies the act is not sustained, though we feel that with Hedda
it is less a matter of failing to understand herself than of an absolute
refusal to submit herself to any kind of scrutiny or self-examination.
Certainly we sense both conscious and unconscious irony in the
excuse she gives to the appalled Tesman for destroying the

manuscript, that her pregnancy has unbalanced her emotionally and that by attacking Lövborg, his academic rival, she is expressing her love for her husband.[33] The innocent envy for his friend's superior abilities casually expressed by Tesman is made cover and excuse for Hedda's deeply destructive envy of the 'child' of Lövborg and Thea. The metaphorical child is to be sacrificed to the real child, a situation ironically reversed in the finale, when Thea and Tesman set about reconstructing the manuscript at the exact moment when Hedda destroys the unborn child by shooting herself with her father's pistol. Hedda strikes at Thea with snake-like force and cunning, simultaneously destroying Lövborg and the 'child' – the manuscript – fathered by Lövborg on Thea's devotion. But it is Thea who has the last word, for her maternal instinct and devotion to her lover's memory is strong enough to enable her to survive his loss and dedicate herself to the remaking of the 'child' out of the remaining notes. Her triumph is sealed by the acquisition of Hedda's husband to help her in her task. The sense that child murder is involved in the loss of the manuscript is reinforced by the choice, by all three characters, of the same metaphor. Thea declares to Lövborg that[34]

> what you have done to the book – all my life, it will seem to me as if you had killed a little child. . . .

Lövborg agrees; he tells Hedda that he is worse than a murderer, and later Brack, describing the brawl that has led to his death, informs her that Lövborg

> . . . talked wildly about a child that had been lost.[35]

Immediately before the burning of the manuscript, Hedda has sent Lövborg out to his death; in despair at having betrayed Thea, and, so he supposed, lost the manuscript in a drunken orgy, he tells Hedda that he intends to[36]

> make an end of the whole business. The sooner the better.

Hedda, with the supposedly lost manuscript in her possession – in Ingmar Bergman's National Theatre production in 1970 she clasped it to her breast as though it were a child – urges Lövborg to 'see to it – that it is done beautifully',[37] and gives him as a souvenir for his last journey General Gabler's pistol, the same pistol she had once aimed at him when he tried to make love to her:[38]

> There it is. Use it yourself now. . . . And beautifully, Eilert Lövborg. Promise me that.

The burning of the manuscript follows as soon as he has left the house. It is Hedda's moment of supreme sadistic triumph, a two-handed expression of power over Lövborg, who is reduced to an object for the satisfaction of her fantasies. First there is the sport of deception, in which he is reduced to despair by a trick; second, the gift of the pistol with the accompanying injunction. Finally the sterility of the contact is ensured by the rapturous destruction of the 'child'. The ultimate expression of power at his expense is, of course, this act, the burning of the 'child' he has fathered on another woman, an act which at another level seals the sterility of the sexual bond between herself and him.

The nature of this bond is expressed through the phallic pistol which is her last gift to Löbvorg; the masculinized woman seizes the father's penis to strike down her inferior lover in a sadistic act of love. That for Hedda it is an act of love as well as destruction is made clear by the romanticism of her plea, its lyrical urgency; the fantasies by which she is now increasingly dominated require Lövborg as a willing victim:[39]

> Could you not see to it that – that it is done beautifully?

The importance to Hedda of a 'beautiful' death for Lövborg is eloquent testimony to that sterile aestheticism already evinced in her over-valuation of elegance, her hatred of ugliness and pain, and her love of sport – both sport with the pistols, 'shooting into the blue'[40] to relieve her excruciating boredom, and sport with other human beings, who are to be manipulated, like pieces on a board, in the service of her fantasy of power. The human material, however, proves recalcitrant. The rapture with which she greets the account of Lövborg's death as 'something irradiated with spontaneous beauty'[41] is dissipated by Brack's news that the death was not a romantic suicide but a sordid accident; at the same time her attitude has of course betrayed her to Brack, and confirms what he has already guessed by the discovery that the fatal weapon had been Hedda's. She who must have others in her power cannot bear to be in the power of another; suicide is thus her only means of defeating Brack and saving herself. But behind this obvious motive, operating on a woman whose sanity is clearly shown to be in question,[42] there lies another. The whole complex richness of Ibsen's representation, as I have tried to show, brings before our eyes the intolerable burden of the unresolved Oedipal relationship to the father. We may suppose that her choice of inferior men as admirers is not simply that they must not be allowed to rival the father, but also so that an unconscious hostility to the father can be expressed in their defeat. The unswervingly aggressive nature of her sexuality expresses the extent of this hostility which the no less powerful identification with the father is bound to turn into self-aggression and self-destruction; Ibsen shows convincingly how the whole process is stimulated by her apparent triple triumph over Tesman, Thea, and Lövborg. The self-penetration by a bullet from her father's pistol is in fantasy an act of sexual union with him which also acknowledges the irreparable damage done to him by those hostile projections of envy and jealousy whose conscious and outward manifestations have been directed not against the father but against father substitutes (and perhaps in Thea, a mother substitute). It is worth noting that, of the three men, the one who most resembles her father is also the one who, after appearing to have her under his control, alone suffers complete defeat at her hands: Brack. Both Lövborg and Tesman escape her influence, Lövborg by dying in the wrong way and Tesman by turning to Thea and consigning his adored Hedda to the margin of his attention. In a kind of desperate pique at the failure of her power games Hedda withdraws into the original Oedipal situation, in which identification with a father figure both vengeful and damaged leads her, as it leads Strindberg's Miss Julie, to death. It is the culmination, in the play, of the great theme of infanticide: Hedda is both the child destroyed by the Oedipal conflict with the father, and the murderer who denies life to the unborn child in her womb; fact and fantasy, as so often in Ibsen, come together.

The reference to *Miss Julie* may serve to remind the reader how much less explicit Ibsen is than Strindberg. In *Hedda Gabler* especially, where soliloquy and self-analysis are alike absent, everything is subsumed to the needs of drama. At the same time every piece of evidence needed to build up the complete picture is provided; no clue is missed. The ironic understatement is in keeping with the mood of the play, bleak and curiously neutral in feeling. There is a striking absence of the happiness so important to Ibsen and his characters, who usually know its value even if they are denied it by the wrong choices they have made. Of the characters here who seem capable of it, both Tesman and Lövborg are portrayed by Ibsen as absurd figures in their different ways (ironic self-parody, familiar to readers of Ibsen, appears in the picture of the Bohemian artist). Even Thea is viewed with a certain sardonic detachment. There is a bleak polarization of qualities – good-heartedness is only vestigially present, weak, in-effectual, and largely made ridiculous; in contrast bad-heartedness is embodied in a fascinating and effectually destructive personality. There is something of the detachment of black comedy about the play, but to read it in this light is ultimately to read it super-ficially. The formidable tension tells another tale. The mood is certainly bleak, but Ibsen's Shakespearean humanity shows itself in his understanding of what is pitiable and tragic as well as what is pathological and ugly in the deep Oedipal crisis of the daughter. Elizabeth Robins, the American actress who was the first English Hedda, saw into the heart of the matter. After remarking on Hedda's 'corrosive' qualities 'that made her the great acting opportunity she was', she writes:[43]

> . . . though in those days I accepted, and even myself used, the description of Hedda as a 'bloodless egoist', I was under no temptation to play her like that. Here I was in debt to Ibsen's supreme faculty for giving his actors the . . . master-key. Ibsen's unwritten clue brought me close enough to the 'cold-blooded egoist' to feel her warm to my touch; to see Hedda Gabler as piti-able in her hungry loneliness – to see her as tragic [as well as] insolent and evil. . . .

Notes

1 S. Freud, *Collected Papers IV* (London, 1949–50), p. 333.
2 Ibid., p. 329.
3 E. Jones, *Hamlet and Oedipus* (New York, 1949), p. 137.
4 *Macbeth*, I.7.54–5.

5 Ibid., 56–8.
6 Ibid., II.2.54–5.
7 Ibid., II.2.12–13.
8 Ibid., I.5.53.
9 D. E. Schneider, *The Psychoanalyst and the Artist* (New York, 1950), p. 221. His 'Analysis of Shakespeare's *Macbeth*', to which I owe the suggestion that self-destructive parricidal envy is central to Macbeth, is of great interest.
10 *Macbeth*, V.1.35–39.
11 Ibid., II.2.67.
12 M. C. Bradbrook, *Ibsen the Norwegian* (London, 1946), p. 122.
13 H. Ibsen, 'Some Preliminary Notes for *Hedda Gabler*' (1889–90), trans. J. Arup. Quoted by J. McFarlane, *Henrik Ibsen, A Critical Anthology* (Penguin, 1970), p. 120.
14 H. Ibsen, *Hedda Gabler* (1890); trans. U. Ellis-Fermor, *Hedda Gabler and Other Plays* (Penguin, 1950), p. 315.
15 Ibid., p. 317.
16 Ibid., p. 361.
17 Ibid., p. 316.
18 Ibid., p. 120.
19 Ibid., p. 299.
20 Ibid., p. 300.
21 Ibid., pp. 303–4.
22 'Some Preliminary Notes for Hedda Gabler', p. 121.
23 *Hedda Gabler*, ed. cit., p. 307.
24 Ibid., p. 274.
25 Ibid., p. 303.
26 Cf. 'Some Preliminary Notes for *Hedda Gabler*', p. 122. 'Hedda . . . is seized almost by panic when she sees the landscape so autumnal '(on her first entrance).
27 *Hedda Gabler*, ed. cit., p. 288.
28 Ibid., p. 283.
29 Ibid., p. 324.
30 Ibid., p. 306.
31 Ibid., p. 333.
32 Ibid., p. 345.
33 Ibid., p. 350.
34 Ibid., p. 312.
35 Ibid., p. 358.
36 Ibid., p. 344.
37 Ibid.
38 Ibid.
39 Ibid., p. 344.
40 Ibid., p. 296.
41 Ibid., p. 357.
42 The manner with which she receives the news of Lövborg's death indicates that her control is beginning to break down.
43 Elizabeth Robins, *Ibsen and the Actress* (1928); quoted by McFarlane, op. cit., p. 416.

Conclusion

'For its power, art depends on an appeal that is hidden from the artist as well as the audience . . . all psychic texts lie out of reach of the mind that produced them.'[1] This view of Freud's will be widely shared even by those sympathetic to psychoanalytical interpretations of literature; they would echo Heraclitus: 'The unseen harmony is stronger than the seen.' As noted earlier,[2] Freud paid the poets the tribute of ascribing to them the discovery of the unconscious, but he believed their knowledge to be intuitive. The poet's grasp of such matters as the role of the unconscious and the psychopathology of everyday life is achieved 'through intuition – really from a delicate self-observation', in contrast to the 'laborious work' which the scientific investigator must perform in order to 'uncover' them.[3] It seems pertinent to enquire, at the end of this study of some of the themes and material of tragic drama of different periods, what has been the effect on modern dramatists of the wide dissemination of Freudian ideas. It is at least a strong presumption that writers who in this century have presented what is clearly recognizable as enacted fantasies of the inner life (Pinter, Ionesco), or offered versions of ancient myth which reflect to a greater or less degree analytical interpretations of their latent meaning (O'Neill, Eliot) have been aware of their debt to Freud and have planned their effects in full if sometimes grudging awareness of this debt. Intuitive understanding, as hitherto found, is modified by an intellectual awareness of the issues involved. Has it been enriched or undermined? Has awareness meant a loss of power, as seems to be the implication of Freud's view? Or have writers been liberated to tap what have previously been more completely hidden sources of creativity with a greater freedom, insight and confidence?

Consciousness, in this context, implies self-consciousness. The writer's self is implicated in the symbolic presentation of the fantasy life, and no less obviously if less immediately in the sophisticated reworking of ancient myth, where he assumes the self-conscious mantle of the critic in revealing hidden meanings behind the narrative façade, and in drawing the audience's attention to contemporary psychological significances. Such psychological awareness on the writer's part is an aspect of a much wider awareness of self and others which is one of the distinguishing features of this century, with 'its innumerable attempts to describe what is happening while it is still happening'.[4] It is obviously too early to estimate the impact of this historical process on the quality of literature in general; but it does not seem to have inhibited the development and achievement of major writers, for self-consciousness is as much part of the mental furniture of a Joyce, a Mann, or an Eliot as of those of lesser stature. Inevitably, it has led to an elevation of criticism and critical interpretation, which by infiltrating creativity has profoundly modified it. Creativity has itself become, in varying degrees, interpretative and self-critical. What has been the effect of that especial kind of interpretation of the human personality we know as psychoanalysis?

Alfred Kazin, in 'The Language of the Pundits', deplores what he believes to be the bad influence of psychoanalysis on creative writing, arguing that it has encouraged self-absorption and self-centredness, a failure to confront the object 'with entire directness, with entire humility, and with concentrated passion.... It is not possible to write well with one's own wishes as the only material.'[5] Yet this weakness, in so far as it exists, is not peculiar to psychoanalytical influences but is, again, characteristic of modern self-awareness in general. The Alexandrianism that is content with surface cleverness of a narcissistic order, or substitutes the application of fashionable theories not proved on the pulses for creative penetration, is certainly recognizable as a contemporary aesthetic phenomenon, but it is not one that can be attributed specifically to psychoanalytical influence. Indeed, if the modern plays reviewed in previous chapters are considered in the light of such criticism as Kazin's, it is striking how often the impact of Freudian theory seems to have been absorbed into the life of the drama. Pinter and Ionesco in particular seem to have achieved an extraordinary freedom in their exploration of primitive themes which, as I have tried to show, carry a significant burden of psychoanalytical meaning. Weiss is clearly indebted to psychoanalysis for his grasp of the true significance of Sade; it is this understanding that lends such force and vitality to what is explicitly presented as a play of ideas, even at the price of some intellectual confusion. The case of Eliot is a peculiar one. His avowedly religious aims in *The Family Reunion*, and his curious ambivalence towards psychology, seem to direct our attention elsewhere; but the play gains abundant life from a compulsive presentation of Oresteian guilt that seems to admit a Freudian influence in the very act of turning its back on it. Of the dramatists considered, O'Neill is the most vulnerable to the charge of a too explicitly self-conscious application of Freudian theory. I have however argued that the weaknesses of *Mourning Becomes Electra* cannot properly be attributed to O'Neill's Freudian allegiances; they are rather evidence for a lack of access in him to the deeper springs of creativity. Indeed the strength of the play – its commitment to its theme, and its sympathetic understanding of human suffering – is reinforced by the illumination O'Neill obtained from Freudian theory into what were fundamentally his own problems. His understanding of Freud is responsible for some of the play's most telling effects.

With Ibsen and Strindberg we face a paradox. Undoubtedly they are the two modern dramatists whose exploration of character in depth seems most profound and compelling, who in their deepest interests can be described as psychoanalytically orientated. Strindberg is the mad genius of Romanticism armed now with an insight into the self comparable to Freud's own. He perfectly illustrates the psychoanalytical principle enunciated by Thomas Mann, that 'there is no deeper knowledge [of the human psyche] without the experience of disease. . . .'[6] Ibsen as aptly exemplifies Freud's claim that 'the greatest dramatists', of whom he cites Ibsen as one, 'have pursued the problem of psychological responsibility with unrelenting vigour'. As Freud himself demonstrated in his study of Rebecca West in *Rosmersholm*,[7] Ibsen showed a masterly accuracy and subtlety in his rendering of pathological states. Like the analyst, he always relates the present to the past, and frequently explores the fundamental psychoanalytical theme of the burden passed on by parents to their children. His early poetical statement, relevant to all his later work, that 'to be a poet is to sit in judgment on oneself',[8] is a profoundly psycho-analytical belief. He even resembles Freud in his passion for seeing the truth whatever the cost – according to Ernest Jones 'the deepest and strongest motive in [Freud's] nature',[9] and probably the deepest in Ibsen's. Yet both Strindberg and Ibsen come too early in time to be influenced by psychoanalytical ideas. Their achievements run parallel to those of Freud and must be held to represent the near-simultaneous emergence of a new revolutionary understanding of the human psyche. It may of course be concluded that there is a relationship between the superior power of Ibsen and Strindberg and their lack of knowl-edge of Freudian ideas. The historical moment at which they appear may not be irrelevant to the power they display, but when the accident of genius appearing when it does is taken into account the question remains, at best, obscure and hypothetical. Who can even begin to imagine what they might have written had they lived fifty years later? Such evidence as there is from later dramatists suggests a different conclusion. As with the absorp-tion of other formative ideas, much seems to depend on the creative power and stamina of the individual writer. Freud remarks in his study of Jensen's *Gradiva* that the author 'directs his attention to the unconscious in his own psyche, is alive to its possibilities of development and grants them artistic expres-sion'.[10] As Norman Brown remarks in his comment on this passage, the implication of Freud's view is that art, like psycho-analysis itself, has as one of its functions the bringing into con-sciousness of the unconscious.[11] The better access the artist has to his own unconscious, the more 'alive to [the] possibilities of development' he is, the more likely it is that he can absorb without indigestion or loss of balance the whole complex of ideas and insights which serve to teach him useful lessons about his own creative powers. If art is play in the most serious sense, if, in the words of Nietzsche, the artist must seek to recover the seriousness of the child at play, then psychoanalytical awareness may be thought likely to afford a valuable knowledge of the game and its rules. Given a living wellspring of contact with the deeper self, such awareness may be beneficial, channelling more effectively into the consciously composed and ordered artefact the hidden sources of creative power. Those of us who believe in the profound kinship of literature and psychoanalysis may take modest encouragement from our experience so far.

Notes

1 P. Rieff, *Freud: The Mind of the Moralist* (London, 1960), pp. 126–35. Rieff is here summarizing Freud's known views.
2 Cf. Chapter One.
3 S. Freud, Letter to Arthur Schnitzler, 14 May 1922, 'Sigmund Freud, Briefe an Arthur Schnitzler', *Die neue Rundschau*, LXVI (1955), pp. 96–7.
4 J. Isaacs, *An Assessment of Twentieth-Century Literature* (London, 1951), p. 15.
5 A. Kazin, 'The Language of the Pundits', *Contemporaries*, 1961. Quoted by L. and E. Mannheim, *Hidden Patterns: Studies in Psychoanalytic Literary Criticism* (New York, 1966), pp. 41–9.
6 T. Mann, *Essays of Three Decades*, trans. H. Lowe-Porter (New York, 1947), 'Freud and the Future', p. 414.
7 See Freud, 'Some Character Types Met with in Psychoanalytical Work' (standard edition, trans. J. Strachey and others, vol. 14, 1952).
8 Ibsen, 'Et Vers'; quoted by M. C. Bradbrook, *Ibsen the Norwegian* (London, 1946), p. 16.
9 E. Jones, *The Life and Work of Sigmund Freud* (New York, 1953–7), vol. II, p. 433.
10 S. Freud, *Delusion and Dream and Other Essays*, ed. P. Rieff (Boston, 1956).
11 N. Brown, *Life Against Death* (London, 1959), p. 63.

Select Bibliography

(a) Main texts discussed, with translations

AESCHYLUS, *The Oresteia*, trans. P. Vellacott (Penguin, 1956); R. Lattimore (Chicago, 1953).

ELIOT, T. S., *The Family Reunion* (London, 1939).

EURIPIDES, *The Bacchae*, ed. E. R. Dodds (Oxford, 1944); trans. P. Vellacott (Penguin, 1954). *Electra*, trans. P. Vellacott in *Medea and Other Plays* (Penguin, 1963).

IBSEN, HENRIK, *Hedda Gabler* (1890); trans. U. Ellis-Fermor in *Hedda Gabler and Other Plays* (Penguin, 1950). 'Some Preliminary Notes for Hedda Gabler' (1889/90), trans. J. Arup. See J. McFarlane, *Henrik Ibsen, A Critical Anthology* (Penguin, 1970).

IONESCO, EUGENE, *La Leçon* (1950), *Les Chaises* (1951), *Amédée* (1953), *Tueur sans Gages* (1957); trans. Donald Watson (*The Lesson, The Chairs, Amédée, The Killer*) (London, 1958).

O'NEILL, EUGENE, *Mourning Becomes Electra* (London, 1932).

PINTER, HAROLD, *The Birthday Party* (London, 1960), *The Caretaker* (London, 1960), *The Homecoming* (London, 1965).

SARTRE, J.-P., *Les Mouches* (Paris, 1942); trans. S. Gilbert (*The Flies*) (London, 1946).

SHAKESPEARE, WILLIAM, *Macbeth*.

SOPHOCLES, *Electra*, trans. E. F. Watling in *Electra and Other Plays* (Penguin, 1953).

STRINDBERG, AUGUST, *The Father* (1887), *Miss Julie* (1888), *A Dream Play* (1902), *The Ghost Sonata* (1907); trans. E. Sprigge, *Six Plays of Strindberg* (New York, 1955).

WEISS, PETER, *The Persecution and Assassination of Marat as Performed by the Inmates of the Asylum of Charenton under the Direction of the Marquis de Sade* (Frankfurt, 1964); trans. Geoffrey Skelton with verse adaptation by Adrian Mitchell (London, 1965).

(b) Literary and general criticism

BENTLEY, ERIC, *The Modern Theatre* (London, 1948).

BRADBROOK, M. C., *Ibsen the Norwegian* (London, 1946).

DODDS, E. R., *The Greeks and the Irrational* (Berkeley, 1951).

ELIOT, T. S., *Poetry and Drama* (London, 1951).

ESSLIN, MARTIN, *The Theatre of the Absurd* (New York, 1961).

ISAACS, J., *An Assessment of Twentieth Century Literature* (London, 1951).

LEECH, CLIFFORD, *O'Neill* (Edinburgh, 1963).

STEINER, G., *The Death of Tragedy* (London, 1961).

STEWART, J. I. M., *Character and Motive in Shakespeare* (London, 1949).

TRILLING, L., 'Art and Neurosis' (1945), 'Freud and Literature' (1947): both essays included in *The Liberal Imagination* (London, 1951).

(c) Psychoanalytical works, both original treatises and works of exposition and interpretation

BROWN, J. A. C., *Freud and the Post-Freudians* (London, 1961).

FREUD, SIGMUND, *The Complete Psychological Works of Sigmund Freud* (standard edition, 1953–). Individual works as follows: *Delusions and Dreams in Jensen's 'Gradiva'*, trans. J. Strachey (Boston, 1970). *The Interpretation of Dreams* (1900), trans. J. Strachey (London, 1954). *Introductory Lectures on Psychoanalysis* (1916/17), trans. J. Rivière (1922). *Leonardo da Vinci and a Memory of his Childhood* (1910), trans. A. Tyson (1957); (Penguin, 1963). *Collected Papers IV* (1924/5; Hogarth Press 1949/50).

GORER, GEOFFREY, *The Life and Ideas of the Marquis de Sade* (London, 1934, revised 1962).

KLEIN, MELANIE, *Our Adult World and its Roots in Infancy* (London, 1960).

MONEY-KYRLE, R., *Superstition and Society* (London, 1939).

RUITENBEEK, H. (ed.), *Psychoanalysis and Literature* (New York, 1964).

SCHNEIDER, D. E., *The Psychoanalyst and the Artist* (New York, 1950).

SEGAL, HANNA, *Introduction to the Work of Melanie Klein* (London, 1964).

Index

Index